Queer Chimerica

The Global Queer Asias series provides an interdisciplinary platform for conceptual, archival, and ethnographic research that pushes academic discussions of Asia in new directions. The series publishes groundbreaking books from both established academics and rising scholars with innovative rubrics, frameworks, and agendas. Works in this series should engage with inclusively defined "queer" issues, that is, the social and cultural dynamics of gender and sexual diversity. Though situated in geographic sites typically associated with the label "Asia," this series pushes for comparative and global perspectives and calls for rigorous attention to themes, approaches, and social-cultural patterns that either emerge from cross-border movements or transcend regional and national boundaries. Studies in which diaspora and migration experiences come to the fore are especially welcome, as is research that brings critical race/ethnic theory, disability studies, and other intersectional approaches to bear on inter-regional studies outside the modern West.

SERIES EDITORS

Howard Chiang is the Lai Ho and Wu Cho-liu Endowed Chair in Taiwan Studies and Professor of East Asian Languages and Cultural Studies at the University of California, Santa Barbara.

James Welker is a Professor in the Department of Cross-Cultural Studies at Kanagawa University.

Queer Chimerica
A Speculative Auto/Ethnography of the Cool Child
Shana Leodar Ye

Queer Chimerica

A SPECULATIVE AUTO/ETHNOGRAPHY
OF THE COOL CHILD

Shana Leodar Ye

University of Michigan Press

Ann Arbor

Copyright © 2024 by Shana Leodar Ye
Some rights reserved

This work is licensed under a Creative Commons Attribution-NonCommercial 4.0 International License. *Note to users:* A Creative Commons license is only valid when it is applied by the person or entity that holds rights to the licensed work. Works may contain components (e.g., photographs, illustrations, or quotations) to which the rightsholder in the work cannot apply the license. It is ultimately your responsibility to independently evaluate the copyright status of any work or component part of a work you use, in light of your intended use. To view a copy of this license, visit http://creativecommons.org/licenses/by-nc/4.0/

For questions or permissions, please contact um.press.perms@umich.edu

Published in the United States of America by the
University of Michigan Press
Manufactured in the United States of America
Printed on acid-free paper
First published September 2024

A CIP catalog record for this book is available from the British Library.

Library of Congress Cataloging-in-Publication data has been applied for.

ISBN 978-0-472-07700-7 (hardcover : alk. paper)
ISBN 978-0-472-05700-9 (paper : alk. paper)
ISBN 978-0-472-90464-8 (open access ebook)

DOI: https://doi.org/10.3998/mpub.12531948

The University of Michigan Press's open access publishing program is made possible thanks to additional funding from the University of Michigan Office of the Provost and the generous support of contributing libraries.

For
Welly

Contents

Preface		ix
Introduction: "Queer Chimerica" and the (Un)Cool Child		1

Part I Chimerica

Chapter 1.	Here Comes the Cool Child	25
Chapter 2.	Zhang Shanping the Hooligan I	29
Chapter 3.	History Is What Hurts	37

Part II Life Beets

Chapter 4.	Red Father, Pink Son	45
Chapter 5.	The Noise	55
Chapter 6.	Guang Hui's Box	62

Part III One Is Not Enough

Chapter 7.	The Genital Squad	85
Chapter 8.	Zhang Shanping the Hooligan II	100
Chapter 9.	Beijing Comrades I	107

Part IV The Best Moment of Love

Chapter 10.	Your China Will Not Work	129
Chapter 11.	Ex-Queer	135
Chapter 12.	Queer-Ex	142

viii   *Contents*

Part V The Transporters

Chapter 13.	Inequality Must be Created	159
Chapter 14.	Zhang Shanping the Hooligan III	166
Chapter 15.	Battle for the Queer	175
Chapter 16.	The Love That Dares Not to Speak Its Name	184
Chapter 17.	Till Death Do Us Part	190
Chapter 18.	Beijing Comrades II	197
Chapter 19.	Unqueer the Cool Child	201

Part VI Beijing Dome

Chapter 20.	Homecoming No More	209
Chapter 21.	Here Comes the Cool Child	212

Coda	215
Appendix: The Missing Pages	219
Acknowledgments	223
References	229
Index	245

Digital materials related to this title can be found on the Fulcrum platform via the following citable URL: https://doi.org/10.3998/mpub.12531948

Preface

This book is about the messiness of queer world-making. It is a coming-of-age story told in a midlife; an invitation from a future self to visit many pasts through others; it is a tale of holding on and letting go.

As an academic inquiry, the book's form is a bit unorthodox. It is a speculative auto/ethnography that interweaves fieldwork, history, memoir, cultural critique, and science fiction. The content of the book is grounded in my doctoral fieldwork from 2012–2015 in the People's Republic of China (PRC) and the United States (US), where I conducted eighty-two in-depth interviews and collected thirteen oral history stories of LGBT, queer, *tongzhi* (homosexual 同志)[1] and *lala* (lesbian 拉拉)–identified individuals across gender and age groups; and my follow-up research conducted through 2017–2019. The archival sources the book draws on span from the mid-twentieth century (the 1950s–1970s) to the present day (the 1980s–2020s). These scholarly works are nested within the narrative framework, presented in the form of dialogues, internal voices, research notes, and a fictional plotting device—the "Immersive Synchronization" of memory. The stories of people I interviewed and studied are laced with the self-discovery journey of the protagonist, resonating with the complexities of identity, social relations, cultural transformation, hope, and destiny.

Experimenting with form stems from my curiosity to embody a queer method rather than simply discussing it. By adopting this approach, I hope to challenge the established ways in which stories of Chinese queerness have been told. Through speculation, I want to engage the *performativity, fictional-*

---

1. *Tongzhi* is a euphemism for homosexuals, especially gay men. It is also homophonic with the socialist term "comrade."

ity, and *theatricality* of the layered representations of Chinese queer life on a global stage and to see what storytelling as both politics and activism can tell us beyond the familiar genealogy of queer theorization, as being originated from French poststructuralist critiques of gender and sexual identity and the US LGBT social movement that got disseminated to different parts of the world.

A prevailing narrative curve of the rise and fall of Chinese queer culture goes like this: In the early 1980s, after the post-Mao market reform and under the influence of Western liberalism, Chinese homosexuals finally walked out of their dim "closets" of the patriarchal familial and communist oppression. With newfound LGBT identities, queer liberation marched into a new era of glory starting in the 2000s, where increasing representation of gender and sexual variances in media and popular culture was accompanied by the flourishing business of LGBT organizations, international collaboration, and the pink economy of cinema, TV, dating apps, transnational adoption, and surrogacy. But sadly, in the second decade of the new millennium, LGBT activism and culture circled back to a new "dark age" as the Chinese state tightened its authoritarian control and regulation of the "deviants."

In this "queer drama," the protagonist is the Cool Child. Cool Child, or *ku'er* (酷儿), is the Mandarin translation of "queer." Vernalized by Taiwanese queer theorists, the word was first brought to the PRC in the late 1990s and gained immense popularity starting from the 2010s with the rise of social media platforms.[2] In contrast to Western queers whose historical structure of feeling revolved around the reverse discourse of backwardness,[3] the collective affect that the Chinese *ku'er* embodied was a mixture of juvenile and chic vibes, coupled with a revolutionary future-looking energy that resonated particularly

---

2. Although being introduced in the 1990s, *ku'er* did not gain much velocity till twenty years later. In its early years, *ku'er* or *ku'er lilun* (queer theory 酷儿理论) was largely confined to the scholarly and activist circles for those who were interested in postmodernism and Michel Foucault. Despite the scarcity, the affect that *ku'er* embodies is nevertheless not unfamiliar to Chinese society and people writ large. In modern China, the figure of the rebellious son or daughter is frequently used as a cultural metaphor to challenge the old political power and bring out radical changes in history (Zhu 2020). During the New Culture Movement (1915–1924), radical intellectuals were the symbolic patricidal children who waged war against traditional Chinese culture. In fact, the PRC's founding father Mao Zedong himself could be regarded as a Cool Child whose vision of a new China was predicated on the revolt against the established values and authority. Likewise, the postsocialist period was jump-started by the avant-garde who bid goodbye to their socialist "fathers" in the *xungen yundong* (searching for the roots literature movement 寻根文学运动). Although *tongzhi* and *lala* artists, activists, and scholars tend to see themselves as emerging out *against* communist oppression and Chinese traditions, their shared ethos with the *ku'er* forebears could signal a unqique path of queer awakening apart from their Western counterparts.

3. Heather Love, *Feeling Backward: Loss and the Politics of Queer History* (Cambridge, MA: Harvard University Press, 2007), 1–4.

well with urban cosmopolitan elites and the *zhichan jieji* (the intellectual class 知产阶级) during the early stage of the PRC's ascent as a global power.

The Cool Child's rise to "stardom," however, is intricately linked with its inherent counterpart, the Uncool. As the convenient antagonist, the Uncool is the subjugated sodomite haunting the cultural memory of repressive socialism; the promiscuous Men Who Have Sex with Men (MSM) bringing forth the HIV/AIDS epidemic; and the low *sushi* (quality 素质) rural cock-sucker lingering outside the glittering world of night clubs, "pink traveling," and transnational surrogacy. It could also be ill-fitted activists with agendas that no longer match the mainstream rhetoric of LGBT organizing; "politically incorrect" scholars with works and claims obsoleted for academic theorizing; and cultural producers who fail to participate in the global economy of commodifying local artifacts. The Uncool resembles what Neferti X. M. Tadiar calls "life as waste";[4] yet as "remaindered forms of sociality"[5] whose modes of noise[6] are seemingly unabsorbable but not completely disposable, they exemplify a kind of fluidity substantially different from yet indispensably central to the Cool Child's fluid expression of gender and sexuality. Their histories are extrapolated from archives, standardized to satisfy academic desires for rescue; their experiences are rolled into stock figures to catch the fleeting attention of the media economy; their personhood is denied to fulfill the promise of queer triumph; and their bodies are forced to press against one another to survive increasing precarity . . . . . . it is precisely the malleability and squeezability of the Uncool that foregrounds the transformative fluidity of the Cool Child, producing measurements of valorizable social values, novel venues of capital accumulation and profitable "queer business," such as the NGO industry, the pharmaceutical intervention, and the transnational institutionalization of queer and feminist studies. Thus, the question arises: how is it that "queer," whose political relevance depends so heavily on fluidity, antinormativity, and radical energy, ends up perpetuating the very norms of "stuckness" in its supposedly borderless circulation?

Queer's reliance on racial, cultural, and classed others is no big news for those who study homonormativity, homonationalism, and homocapitalism.[7] Building upon these works, *Queer Chimerica* takes up the question of queer's

---

4. Neferti X. M. Tadiar, "Life-Times in Fate Playing," *South Atlantic Quarterly* 111, no. 4 (2012): 787–88, https://doi.org/10.1215/00382876-1724183
5. Neferti X. M. Tadiar, "Remaindered Life of Citizen-Man, Medium of Democracy," *Japanese Journal of Southeast Asian Studies* 49, no. 3: 482, https://doi.org/10.20495/tak.49.3_464
6. Tadiar, "Remaindered Life of Citizen-Man," 489.
7. See Duggan, *The Twilight of Equality?*, for homonormativity; Puar, *Terrorist Assemblages*, for homonationalism; Rao, "Global Homocapitalism," for homocapitalism.

stuckness from the perspectives of political economy and postsocialist conditions. Emphasizing postsocialism as transnational and global,[8] the book moves beyond the analytics of the nation-state and toward relationality to unpack the intricacies of "homopostsocialism" and to trace how queerness as social, economic, and affective relations is organized in the planetary restructuring of geopolitics, labor, and culture since the late Cold War.

More specifically, I want to reckon again the question that has been frequently asked and answered in the fields of transnational queer Sinophone and global queer Asias studies, namely, "Why queer theory needs China."[9] I do not mean, however, why Queer Studies needs China to decenter or decolonize the prevalence of Western centrism, nor how queer China as both a method and an empirical site can enrich transnational theorization of sexualities. Rather, I am interested in how the production of the very queerness as we know it today is predicated on the reduction and abstraction of "China," as a *symbolic other* that evokes both fear and excitement and as a *material infrastructure* that produces social relations, affect, and labor in the service of racialized capitalism, neoliberalism, and transnational surveillance. Let's consider the following "coincidences": the conceptualization of queer as infinitely mobile occurred at a time when capital's demand for flexibility was amplified by "China on the rise"; the dissemination of Queer Studies and NGOization of LGBT rights-based advocacy coincided with the reconfiguration of the Chinese population as a worldwide labor force, consumer base, and buffer zone for economic and financial crises; and the mainstreaming of queer visibility and homonationalism in the West intensified as the PRC became a major player in the military-industrial complex, joining the global War on Terror and overseas expansion.

To pursue these questions, the book is organized around three theoretical frameworks: queer Chimerica, social reproduction, and the politics of (in)visibility. I use "Queer Chimerica" to describe the antagonistic amalgamation of the PRC and the US and its racialized deployment of sexuality and gender in shaping identity, subjectivity, and methods of activism. In a time when Sino-US relations are often viewed through the lens of rivalry and delinking, turning to the interdependence and the intertwined histories of the two allows me to unpack how authoritarian and democratic neoliberalisms work hand in hand

---

8. Neda Atanasoski, *Humanitarian Violence: The U.S. Deployment of Diversity* (Minneapolis: University of Minnesota Press, 2016), 23.

9. Petrus Liu, "Why Does Queer Theory Need China?" *positions: East Asia Cultures Critique* 18, no. 2 (2010): 291–320. https://doi.org/10.1215/10679847-2010-002; see also Bao, *Queer Comrades: Gay Identity and Tongzhi Activism in Postsocialist China* (Copenhagen: Nordic Institute of Asian Studies), 2018.

in molding the ways in which political agency and pleasure are conceptualized, experienced, and constrained.

As the recent field of queer studies in North America has made a "left" (re)turn and sought to rematerialize queer through engaging questions of precarity and dispossession, I enter the "queer Marxist" debates from a less explored perspective—feminist and queer social reproduction—to make visible how queer life is abstracted in the service of its economization.[10] By examining the material conditions of the postsocialist postcolonial changes through which the Cool Child and the Uncool are differentiated and become fungible, I seek to call out the romanticization of queer fluidity, rootlessness, and radical resistance that is too often taken for granted by scholars, activists, and cultural producers of queer studies.

Furthermore, I privilege a "politics of living" over a "politics of representation" in accounting for the life experiences of the book's characters and the individuals on whom the characters are based. While the politics of visibility has been a torch, a beacon of hope for those who have historically been erased and disproportionately dispossessed, this same torch can also ignite a blaze of neoliberal appropriation and fan the flames of violence perpetrated by self-identified radicals, particularly in the heated arena of today's mass and social media culture and industry. Therefore, the book is less about celebrating representation, diversity, and marginalized voices than foregrounding the experience of the *improper* and the "dark matter" whose ways of being have already profoundly transformed what queer means.

On Method

A politics of living requires us taking stories as both theory and practice. Thus, this book urges the readers to explore what has been overlooked in normative knowledge production and history under the names of objectivity, professionalism, and serious research—the vulnerability and unreliability of experience, the promiscuous creativity of memory and trauma, the unapologetic rawness of intimacy, the love for knowledge, the pleasure of labor, the myriad disappointments and unfulfillments of life . . . . . .

---

10. Michelle Murphy, *Economization of Life* (Durham: Duke University Press, 2017), 5–14. Here Murphy distinguishes the economization of life from the capitalization of life, such as biowealth, biovalue, biocapital. Economization emphasizes the macrological management of national economy; it is a practice that differentially values and governs life in terms of their ability to foster the macroeconomy of the nation-state. It is not a mode of generating surplus value through labor but instead designates and manages surplus aggregate life.

xiv *Preface*

Being queer often means being out of sync with the ordinarily linear temporality and living with multiple temporal dimensions.[11] In envisioning Chimerica's queer future-histories, I owe a great deal to the visionists—queer and feminist writers, artists, filmmakers, and theorists whose innovative works boldly bend genders and genres, and beautifully break the boundary between the real and the imaginative. These works include, to name a few, Todd Haynes's *Velvet Goldmine* (1998), Cheryl Dunye's *The Watermelon Woman* (1996), and Trinh T. Minh-ha's *Surname Viet Given Name Nam* (1989).

Among many, I am most indebted to Saidiya Hartman's praxis of "critical fabulation."[12] In writing at the limit of the unspeakable and the unknown, Hartman weaves scattered information from constrained sources into full narratives of what lives of Black individuals could have been, to address the archive's violence and to honor the lost and ignored souls throughout history. I have been seduced by this method of "both to tell an impossible story and to amplify the impossibility of its telling"[13] since I was a graduate student, and I am grateful for trying this method in converting my dissertation into the book. It bestows me the power to make visible erased lives while reflecting on the meanings of "voice," "agency," and "representation," especially when these concepts are often used in self-explanatory and uncritically celebratory ways.

"Critical fabulation" also gives me a chance to engage the performativity of history and archive as a "reiterated act"[14] beyond gender. To trouble the dominant "history-makers" who are regarded as natural in a "heterosexual matrix" (let me add white, global North, and colonial here), ethnographic speculation allows me to play with Dipesh Chakrabarty's idea of "history I" and "history II,"[15] that simultaneously confirms and disrupts the logic of capital and its implications on sexuality, identity, injury, and desire.

There has been a plethora of work recently regarding queer and feminist autoethnography and autotheory, especially after the publication of Paul B. Preciado's "body-essay" *Testo Junkie* (2013). Both Lauren Fournier's *Autotheory as Feminist Practice in Art, Writing, and Criticism* (2021) and a recent

---

11. Carolyn Dinshaw, *How Soon is Now? Medieval Texts, Amateur Readers, and the Queerness of Time* (Durham: Duke University Press, 2012), 4.

12. Saidiya Hartman, "Venus in Two Acts," *Small Axe* 12, no. 2 (2008): 11.

13. Hartman, "Venus in Two Acts."

14. Judith Butler, "Performative Acts and Gender Constitution: An Essay in Phenomenology and Feminist Theory," *Theatre Journal* 40, no. 4 (1988): 519, https://doi.org/10.2307/3207893

15. Dipesh Chakrabarty, *Provincializing Europe: Postcolonial Thought and Historical Difference* (Princeton: Princeton University Press, 2000), 71. Chakrabarty considers History I as purely analytical whereas History II is narratives that create room for incorporating subjective experiences into the history of capital.

call for papers by the journal *Feminist Studies* on autotheory/autoethnography in 2022 stress the promises of autoethnography to innovatively address questions of "power and authority, access and legibility, embodiment and affect," and to investigate "the resurgence of standpoint theory, decolonization efforts, and efforts to dismantle structural racism" from interdisciplinary and multimodal dimensions. Aligning with this praxis, the book slashes the word "auto/ethnography" to further explore the uneasy relationship between the self and the other in autoetheorization. Although grounded in experiences of the self and told through first-person narrative, the narrator "I" shouldn't be taken as the author "I," except for in the "Preface," "Introduction," and "Coda." The author "I" appears as one of the characters whose voices take the forms of noises, whispers, and murmuring reminiscent of fading memory, resembling what Avery Gordon defines as "ghostly matters."[16] The "death of the author" method gives me an opportunity to step back and look at myself from some distance. Through a third-person point of view, I learn to reflect on the violence of research and the privilege of the researcher, as well as the vulnerability, trauma, and injury entangled with knowledge, activism, and writing. To further deconstruct the righteousness of the "authentic" and "autonomous" speaking subject, I use composite characters as a feminist and queer method to engage the interconnectedness of subjectivity and bodies. The mutual contamination of body, personages, time, ideologies, political investments, and affect that spill over one another allows me to show the "complex personhood"[17] of those I met in my fieldwork and daily life of queer worlding.

Stepping away from the unfulfilled career of "utopian alternatives" that too easily slips into scholarly elitism, I also want to smudge the neat boundaries between history and memory, archive and imagination, and arts and politics while attending to the limitations and constraints that material relations of gender, race, capital, geopolitics, language, and narration place on present political engagements with queer liberation and emancipation. It is my hope that this journey to Chimerica will give shape to the messiness of queer lives that unsettles the teleology of oppression/liberation; to disrupt the dehumanizing technology of reproducing coherent self-centered subjects without cheapening agency and pleasure; and to attend to the tenderness of love and connections among friends and foes in the postsocialist postcolonial queer worldmaking.

---

16. Avery Gordon, *Ghostly Matters: Haunting and the Sociological Imagination* (Minneapolis: University of Minnesota Press, 2008).

17. Avery Gordon, *Keeping Good Time: Reflections on Knowledge, Power, and People* (New York: Routledge, 2004), 102.

Introduction

"QUEER CHIMERICA" AND THE (UN)COOL CHILD

The Queer Crossroads

In September 1995, nearly 180 government delegations and 2,500 nongovernmental organizations (NGOs) met in Beijing to attend the United Nations Fourth World Conference on Women. At the governmental forum, Hillary Clinton, the then First Lady of the United States, famously claimed "Human rights are women's rights and women's rights are human rights," marking the advent of global gender mainstreaming.[1] Despite the NGO forum being moved to Huairou, a remote location outside the city, feminist activists managed to organize a parade that drew 500 women from thirty countries and successfully secured a "lesbian tent" for panel discussions, strategy planning, and cultural events. International Lesbian and Gay Human Right Commission (ILGHRC) obtained 6,000 signatures from more than two hundred organizations to petition for the recognition of sexual rights, campaigning to write lesbian rights into the *Beijing Declaration and Platform for Action*.

Bringing Chinese women closer to their global sisters, the conference was and has been regarded as the most important landmark event for the advancement of women's studies, gender NGOs, and lesbian activism[2] in the PRC.

---

1. The concept of gender mainstreaming was first proposed at the 1985 Third World Conference on Women and was formally featured at the Fourth Conference. It was cited in the document that resulted from the conference, the *Beijing Platform for Action*, which pushed partners at governmental and institutional levels to recognize and value the diversity among people of different genders through policy actions.

2. Hongwei Bao, "'We Are Here': The Politics of Memory in Narrating China's Queer Feminist History," *Continuum* 34, no. 4 (2020): 514.

2 Queer Chimerica

As issues of gender equality and women's rights firmly moved into public discourse, however, what lurked behind these triumphs remained rarely discussed. In their celebrated documentary, *We Are Here* (2015), filmmakers Zhao Jing and Shi Tou invited Chinese and international lesbian and feminist participants to recount their experiences at the conference. Many of the interviewed participants recalled the political hostility of the Chinese communist regime and the poor infrastructure and facilities at the NGO forum site, such as the Chinese government ordering married policemen and taxi drivers to bring white blankets to cover the activists in case of naked demonstrations and the heavy-handed surveillance and wire service at both public and private spaces.[3] The obstacles of communism and Third World underdevelopment nonetheless brought forth a strengthened global solidarity: despite, or perhaps, precisely because of these adversities, international lesbian activists refused to be deterred and rose to form a larger women's movement.[4]

One of the most widely circulated incidents that highlighted this type of bifurcation was about a Chinese volunteer working at the conference. When interviewed by Western media and asked about the living condition of lesbians in China, the volunteer self-righteously denied the existence of lesbianism and homosexuality altogether in socialist countries and ascribed it to capitalist corruption. Representing a prevalent (mis)understanding of homosexuality as Western imports at the time, her response was appraised by morality-defending state-owned newspapers, while being treated by Western liberal media as evidence of the lingering vice of communism. Agitated by the volunteer's response and the state's endorsement, the Chinese pro-lesbian and feminist activists at the conference immediately made public declarations to distinguish themselves from the alleged public ignorance and claimed global solidarity with international feminists.

The oppositional pair of the "enlightened lesbian activists" and the "ignorant mass" might look too familiar to transnational and anticolonial feminist and queer scholars, as the images of the modern democratic sexual subject and the brainwashed victim who defends the backward socialist ideology resonate well with the universalization of the Third World women as needing to be saved by White women under "Western eyes"[5] or the homonationalist promotion of

---

3. See Ara Wilson, "Lesbian Visibility and Sexual Rights at Beijing," *Signs: Journal of Women in Culture and Society* 22, no. 1 (1996): 214.

4. See Lisa Levenstein, "A Social Movement for a Global Age: U.S. Feminism and the Beijing Women's Conference of 1995," *Journal of American History* 105, no. 2 (2018): 354–55.

5. See Chandra Mohanty, "Under Western Eyes: Feminist Scholarship and Colonial Discourses," *Feminist Review* 30, no. 1 (1988): 61–88; and Lila Abu-Lughod, *Do Muslim Women Need Saving?* (Cambridge, MA: Harvard University Press, 2013).

LGBT rights as representing the "global good" and cultural superiority.[6] However, simply adopting the critique of "gay internationalists" hatched by Western imperialism[7] would eschew how the Chinese and US-led international activists came to a crossroads at the Fourth Conference and dismiss their shared agency in negotiating geopolitics for achieving individual and community goals, given the economic, cultural, and affective entanglements of the PRC and the US.

The US queer life in the late 1980s and early 1990s is characterized by a double bind of precarity and prosperity. On the surface, alternative gender and sexual expressions seemed to be reborn out of the debris of destruction—the decline of working-class masculinity since post-WWII[8] accelerated the rise of non-heteronormative cultures and identities, ultimately leading to a new kind of queer theorization in the 1990s; the "creative class"[9] revived the US cities, and cheap rent in some urban areas led to the blooming queer communities and neighborhoods; reduced cost of personal recording technology (mostly resulting from Japan's economic booms and bubbles) gave rise to more queer visibility on TV and new media; to just list a few.

On the other hand, the lives of the working class and racial minorities became increasingly precarious as the shift from Fordist mass production to flexible specialization replaced secured jobs and state welfare with contract work and commercial insurance. In the late 1980s, in response to the waning global hegemony caused by the dissolution of the Soviet threat that eroded US wartime nationalism, the right-wing government sought to expand its global war and existing military and prison industrial complex by creating new national "enemies" and "enemies within," such as the "terrorists," "illegal immigrants," and "gays" and "sexual nonproductivity." Despite the fact that mass LGBTQ political struggles and leftist social movements in the 1950s and 1960s shared a close tie in their battles against racism, imperialism, and global war, and early queer theorists were largely Marxists who urged to tie critiques of sexuality to political economy, this alliance was weakened by an increasing disillusionment of a global communist movement in the 1970s and a turning

---

6. Jasbir Puar, *Terrorist Assemblages: Homonationalism in Queer Times* (Durham: Duke University Press, 2007).

7. See Joseph Massad, "Re-Orienting Desire: The Gay International and the Arab World," *Public Culture* 14, no. 2 (2002): 361–86.

8. For the connection between the decline of working-class masculinity and the rise of queer theorization, see Kevin Floyd, "Performative Masculinity: Judith Butler and Hemingway's Labor without Capital," in *The Reification of Desire: Toward a Queer Marxism* (Minneapolis: University of Minnesota Press, 2009), 79–119.

9. See Richard L. Florida, *Cities and the Creative Class* (New York: Routledge, 2005): 3–4. Florida defines the "creative class" or "creative workers" as the roughly one-third of U.S. and global workers who have the good fortune to be compensated monetarily for their creative output.

4 Queer Chimerica

away from Marx in the wake of Edward Said and Michel Foucault in the 1980s. US queer theorization and the social movement in the 1990s departed from a Marxist critique of sexual capitalism and became disinterested in labor politics, turning to prioritize the entitlement of the LGBT citizens[10] and a gay "minority model."[11]

Placing queer theory's "thorough re-vision" to the "epistemological totalitarianism" of social-theoretical traditions in the context of the AIDS epidemic, the theoretical departure from early queer Marxist sexual critique also led to the devaluation, if not stigmatization, of earlier leftist sexual politics, reducing the rich history of collective resistance to merely identity politics of recognition. As Leo Bersani critiques, both Foucauldian and Butlerian queer theories abstract sex by politicizing it,[12] erasing "radical promiscuity" of nonreproductive sexual practices and communist/communal collective response to inequality under capitalism and commodification. The Cold War fear of communism and communal way of sexuality in tandem with the fear of AIDS "turned the militancy of resistance and mourning" into a "celebration of abstract fluidity and flexibility"[13] in the 1990s.

As the politics of redistribution was replaced with representation,[14] the US academe was struggling with its own paradigm shift under the pressure of postcolonial movements and the response to the heightened presence of scholars from Black, Latinx, and former Third World. Facing these global and domestic postsocialist predicaments, US queer and feminist scholars were desperately in search of international models and sites of revolution while LGBT activists found themselves marching onto the global stage to fight against dictatorship and to promote rights and freedom. At this moment, China as a "communist and backward Third World other" provided an ideal in-between space, where the US scholars and activists could find novel battlegrounds to reestablish their smashed political value at home.

The US queer feminists' outward search was reciprocated by the newly "awakened" Chinese women. Across the Pacific, the zeitgeist in the PRC was

---

10. Wendy Brown, "Resisting Left Melancholy," *Boundary 2* 26, no. 3 (1999): 26.

11. Steven Seidman, "Identity Politics in a 'Postmodern' Gay Culture," in *Difference Troubles: Queering Social Theory and Sexual Politics* (Cambridge: Cambridge University Press, 1997): 110.

12. Leo Bersani, "Is the Rectum a Grave?" *October* 43 (1987): 204–5.

13. Douglas Crimp, *Melancholia and Moralism: Essays on AIDS and Queer Politics* (Cambridge, MA: MIT Press, 2002), 137.

14. See Nancy Fraser, *Justice Interruptus: Critical Reflections on the "Postsocialist" Condition* (New York: Routledge, 1997).

gaige kaifang ("reform and opening" 改革开放) and *yu shijie jiegui* ("connecting with the world" 与世界接轨). Since the late 1970s, under the leadership of Deng Xiaoping, the state launched a series of nationwide projects that aimed to transform the state-planned economy into a market-driven one. Unlike many post-independent postcolonial countries that were forced into structural adjustment, post-reform China plunged into neoliberal restructuring through practices such as the disavowal of state socialism, flexibilization of the economy, capital accumulation through dispossession, and strategic collaboration with world powers such as the United States. In its post-1989 *Tian'anmen* era, the PRC sought larger global acceptance and greater economic opportunities by hosting international events such as the Asian Games in 1990 and the Fourth Conference on Women in 1995.

Similar to the US, the emergence of queer studies in the PRC is also thought of as antithetical to Marxism and socialism.[15] As the Cultural Revolution (1966–1976) ended with Mao Zedong's death in 1976, the previously repressed intellectuals rehabilitated themselves as agents of China's historical developments in the 1980s and turned to Western ideas to repudiate Maoist ideologies. Characterized by massive translation projects of Western works in social science, arts, and humanities, the tsunami of *wenhua re* (the "culture fever" 文化热) fitted squarely the *jiefang sixiang* ("thought liberation" 解放思想) movement launched by the Chinese state who also promoted traditions of Enlightenment and humanism to overturn Maoist class struggle. The early studies of women, gender, and sexuality were informed by the larger intellectual, cultural, and political climate that denied the specter of Marxism to advance the neoliberalization of economy and cosmopolitanism.

Instead of aligning with postcolonial positions of anti-imperialism and decolonization, Chinese feminists and LGBT activists—primarily urban intellectuals with foreign connections and scholar-activists within universities and state research institutes—abandoned the analytics of *funü* (Chinese Marxist and socialist conceptualization of women 妇女) in the 1990s and turned to the concept of "gender" and "female subjectivity" without contextualizing much the Cold War "biopolitical apparatus of gender."[16] Simultaneously, in the fields of women's studies and *funü gongzuo* (the cause of women 妇女工作), previous critiques of gender inequality in terms of political economy were largely replaced with the developmentalist model of women's

---

15. Petrus Liu, *Queer Marxism in Two Chinas* (Durham: Duke University Press, 2015), 1.

16. Jemima Repo, *The Biopolitics of Gender* (Oxford: Oxford University Press, 2015), 4.

6   Queer Chimerica

rights, liberty, and equality, and women's issues were primarily reframed in relation to men.[17]

Situated at the intersection of postsocialist changes in both the PRC and the US, the Fourth Conferences on Women is not about Western/American feminists "importing" ideas of lesbian identities and human rights into China and orchestrating gay imperialism; rather, it was the affect and social reproductive labor of the "native informants" that animated the reduction of differences into "oppression," "rights," and "identities" in the imagined community of global (queer) sisterhood, thus underwrote Western/American activists as representative of freedom and progress. Through elevating their status of superiority at the theater of international struggles and solidarity, whiteness and First World/ global North-ness get re-naturalized through the non-white efforts to denationalize hetero-patriarchal sexual norms.

The state-sanctioned homophobia, the erased existence of lesbians, and the violated homosexual subjects—the too-easily-called-upon metrics of "China's vice"—allowed the Chinese feminists and lesbian activists to sever their ties to socialism and step onto the global stage where they were previously excluded as both the Third World and communist others on the one hand, and granted a new front to the post-Reagan feminist and lesbian activists from the US to rejuvenate their agenda of liberation that was lost to domestic conservatism and gay backlash on the other. Ironically, as the seemingly homophobic state went in concert with the newly emerged queer subjects to produce the standardized LGBT identity, politics, and an imagined community for political and economic benefits, queer gender and sexuality became absorbed into the agenda of "international solidarity" and "national development" governed by both neoliberal nation-states and transnational institutes. Although LGBT rights were/ are not recognized in the PRC, turning queer China into both a symbolic other (communist and underdeveloped) and a neoliberal commodity that at once evokes fear, anxiety, anger, desire, and antinormative agency, strangely created a bond that intimately tied the individual, the state, and the transnational together, lubricating the transnational economy of queerness in the landscape of the late Cold War postsocialist transition. This contradictory entanglement through voluntary reduction of postsocialist experiences is a telling example of the book's central concept—"queer Chimerica."

---

17. Kristen Ghodsee, "Revisiting the United Nations Decade for Women: Brief Reflections on Feminism, Capitalism and Cold War Politics in the Early Years of the International Women's Movement," *Women's Studies International Forum* 33 (2010): 10.

"Chimerica" and Queer Fungibility

The portmanteau "Chimerica" is coined by historian of finance Niall Ferguson and economist Moritz Schularick in their 2007 journal article[18] to describe the economic symbiosis of China and the United States from the late 1980s to the financial crisis of 2007–08. Simply put, the massive influx of China's cheap labor and Chinese possession of US government securities enabled the US to accumulate without suffering from the usual consequences of high-interest rates, tax hikes, and currency crashes, leading up to a prolonged period of wealth creation for both nations. Although the scope of this book extends beyond economics, the concept of Chimerica has inspired my theorization of homopostsocialism, as well as my speculative writing on queer world-making.

The main portion of the book takes place in a fictional near future where China and the United States have merged into a super-empire known as the Mankind Unity of Chimerica. To quell unrest and reestablish order, the regime has implemented a project that rewards queer individuals for sharing their digitalized life experiences. Placing the oppressed in a position of prominence, the action has only fueled increased demands for violence and enhanced the government's ability to better track and predict the behavior of its dissidents. The protagonist, a queer activist turned cognitive engineer, must confront her own past as she learns about the erased histories of LGBT people, or else lose her best friend and lover.

In this story, Chimerica is a metaphor for a form of postsocialist biosurveillance capitalism, in which the authoritarian management of precarity operates in tandem with neoliberalist capitalization on queer consent and voluntarism. Resonating with the example of the Fourth Conference, the chapters in the book will show that under the banner of queer liberation, diversity, and emancipation, people of varying positions—the American Left, Chinese LGBT neoliberals, radical Queer Marxists, and so on—are complicit in the process of flattening complex trauma and injury, struggles, and life experiences of themselves and others, into standardized measurements of identity and formations of politics, that ultimately give rise to the industries of HIV/AIDS intervention, the NGOization of LGBT+ organizing, institutionalization of Queer and Feminist Studies, and the "pink economy." Different from the commodification of queerness for the purpose of generating surplus value, however, the "queer business" labors to turn lives into fungibility, allowing individuals and groups to be differentially managed as the Cool and the Uncool in respect of their ability

---

18. Niall Ferguson and Moritz Schularick, "'Chimerica' and the Global Asset Market Boom," *International Finance* 10, no. 3 (2007): 215–39.

8 Queer Chimerica

to foster the economy, to reproduce social norms, and to serve the nation-state.

Fungibility is a widespread concept in radical black and critical race studies. As Hortense Spillers[19] and Saidiya Hartman[20] have argued, the transatlantic slave trade reduced human lives to commodities by abstracting bodies into the metrics of property and capital, hollowing out any distinctive differences and contents. Turning black bodies into black cargo, fungibility rendered blackness exterior to the category of the human, exerting an ontological force that structured the emergence of blackness as a social category.[21] Although the postsocialist post-Cold War racial capitalism that this book traces emerged through very different routes, fungibility helps understand how the deduction of life into objecthood, experiences into data, subjectivity into identity, and histories into numbers under "queer Chimerica" has redefined "queer fluidity" and given new expressions to the economization of queer life with "Chinese characteristics."

Despite often being depicted as homophobic and anti-queer, China is no latecomer in terms of utilizing gender and sexuality for national building and development, as evidenced by various scholars.[22] In the post-Cold War era for instance, the Chinese state promoted women's and gender NGOs and urban cosmopolitan female subjectivity (the Cool) in the 1990s and embraced the HIV/AIDS intervention in the 2000s, in order to mine the potential of gender and sexuality issues for capital accumulation while relegating laid-off and migrant workers (Uncool) as shock-absorbers of the global economy and off-loading social security and reemployment responsibilities to civil societies. Riding the opportunities of global demand for Chinese culture products, against the background of the state policy shift from *yin jinlai* ("Bring in" 引进来) to *zou chuqu* ("Go Global" 走出去), the proliferation of androgynous expressions and gender non-normativity in public culture in the mid to late 2000s also sat squarely with

---

19. See Hortense Spillers, "Mama's Baby, Papa's Maybe: An American Grammar Book," *Diacritics* 17, no. 2 (1987): 65–81 and *Black, White and In Color: Essays on American Literature and Culture* (Chicago: University of Chicago Press, 2003) for more details on fungibility and black queerness.

20. See Saidiya Hartman, *Lose Your Mother: A Journey Along the Atlantic Slave Route* (New York: Farrar, Straus and Giroux, 2007) and *Scenes of Subjection: Terror, Slavery, and Self-making in Nineteenth-century America* (New York: Oxford University Press, 1997).

21. Shannon Winnubst, "The Many Lives of Fungibility: Anti-Blackness in Neoliberal Times," *Journal of Gender Studies* 29, no. 1 (2020): 105.

22. See Gail Hershatter, *Dangerous Pleasures: Prostitution and Modernity in Twentieth-Century Shanghai* (Berkeley: University of California Press, 1997); Lisa Rofel, *Desiring China: Experiments in Neoliberalism, Sexuality, and Public Culture* (Durham: Duke University Press, 2007); Susan Mann, *Gender and Sexuality in Modern Chinese History* (New York: Cambridge University Press, 2011); Wang, Zheng, *Finding Women in the State: A Socialist Feminist Revolution in the People's Republic of China* (Berkeley: University of California Press, 2016).

national demands for cultivating a middle class with strong purchasing power and consumer appetite, which will be further unpacked in the book.

On the surface, these strategies may seem indicative of societal and political openness in the era of the "desiring China,"[23] but from a perspective of political economy, they resemble financial assets in a speculative economy, where the state acts as an investor and distributes its capital across a variety of stocks and products in the hope of optimizing profits but with the risk of loss.[24] In this sense, women's NGOs, HIV/AIDS intervention, queer visibilities in public culture and similar initiatives become fungible as single metrics in terms of their ability to contribute to the national economy. Elsewhere,[25] I examined the "high-risk and high-return" industry of *dangai* (revised Boys' Love 耽改) to illustrate the speculative nature of capitalizing on queerness under the increasingly tightened regulation of LGBT content and anti-effeminacy policies in recent China. This experimental, flexible, and speculative economization of queer life and culture is a unique feature of homonormativity and homocapitalism in places like the PRC, where LGBT rights and recognition are not granted and legalized. It shows the synergy of neoliberal and authoritarian rules of queerness, not through the logic of privatization and commodification and "pinkwashing," but through financialization and risk management of "red capital." This perspective may offer a different lens to apprehend seeming oxymorons such as China's ten-million-dollar donation to UN Women while prosecuting domestic activists since managing "assets" is no longer more profitable than selling them and selling them out.

The transformation of life into fungibility also manifests itself at multiple levels beyond the state. As explored in the book with details, the economy of gender and sexuality, such as programs of HIV/AIDS intervention and LGBT outreaches, has created simultaneously homogenous and "diverse" communities legible for funding and intervention. NGO-ization necessitates regular reports on incidents of violence, simplified stories of victimization, and flattened accounts of sexual, national, and ideological contestations. As queer life becomes fungible to opportunities, money, and rights, as well as vulnerability, risks, and deprivation, the spectacles of fixed identities and positions of the Cool and Uncool become naturalized in the speculative queer economy and the speculation for a queer future. Yet the future and command for change often

---

23. Rofel, *Desiring China*, 3.

24. Uncertain Commons, *Speculate This!* (Durham: Duke University Press, 2013), 9

25. See Shana Ye, "*Word of Honor* and Brand Homonationalism with 'Chinese Characteristics': The *Dangai* Industry, Queer Masculinity and the 'Opacity' of the State," *Feminist Media Studies* 23, no. 4 (2023): 1598–99.

become futile when futurity is built upon the ontological grids and metrics of the present and its vapid inspirations for empowerment and empty promises of diversity, equity, and inclusion. The result is queer and feminist politics' "reheating the cold rice," conjuring up and paying homage to the histories of resistance and revolution without evoking concrete connections to specific forms of differences in both democratic and authoritarian neoliberal societies.

While black fungibility is originated from the history of the Atlantic and extends itself into the anti-black present and future, the "hollowing out of content" of postsocialist fungibility operates through the future-history of China as "becoming" and "yet to be." As shown in the example of the Fourth Conference, the differentiation of queer worth (the Cool and Uncool) to contribute to the "larger good of humanity," either defined as national prosperity or democratic ideologies, is inseparable from the affective and temporal construction of a "China" and the "Chinese" as "yet to become liberated," by both the agents in PRC and its US-led rivalries, after China's socialist experiments were announced dead and the Cold War ended. Like the abstraction of blackness into fungible units constrains blackness from entering the category of the human,[26] the abstraction of postsocialist Chineseness into "liberal" and "illiberal" markers prevents it from fully entering the future, always already marked by global capitalism and its "proper" ways of being, thinking, and feeling. From the post-reform era of Sino-US interdependence to the present time of delinking, this forever "lingering," sealed in the space outside the door, dead but undead, gets mixed with both the Chinese anticolonial and nationalistic aspirations for restoration, prosperity, domination, and expansion, galvanizing the movement of capital and labor exploitation and reworking colonial ontology, imperial relations, global (Cold War racial) capitalism, and hegemony.

The theoretical valence of queer fungibility conditioned by the rivalry and interdependence of "Chimerica" is not limited to providing new historical readings and evidence in the postsocialist regions. Rather, it offers some novel frameworks for the current field of Queer Studies in general and Global Queer Asia in particular, to engage questions of marginalization, precarity, coloniality, and the entanglement of empires.

Homopostsocialism as Critique

Facing global neoliberalism, many scholars in queer Sinophone studies have turned to queer Marxism to highlight the importance of political economy in

---

26. Hartman, *Scenes of Subjection*, 21.

reevaluating the Chinese queer emergence and genealogy.[27] Desirable as it is, the framework of "queer Marxism" has also brought up some problematics, especially when it comes to accounting for embodied queer experiences in the PRC. For instance, in a comparative book review, queer and trans historian Howard Chiang critiques Petrus Liu's theorization of queer Marxism as based on the experiences of privileged urban-based intellectuals, writers, and artists rather than the outcasts dwelling on the sexual margins of the PRC and Taiwan.[28] What Chiang's doubt reveals is perhaps the inconvenient fact that no matter how much queer theorists and activists of the PRC located in and influenced by Western and Anglophone academies want to see indigenous Chinese queer communities as embracing Marxist and socialist ethos, the "queer precariats" in China rarely pick up the rhetoric of Marxism and see themselves as explicitly drawing from socialist history and legacy. This dissonance reflects, on the one hand, the temporal and geopolitical differences in how social movement, resistance, and political identities are conceived; and on the other hand, persistent colonialist and imperialist impulses embodied in producing "valid" and "hot" knowledge to "sell to a theoretical savvy Anglophone readership"[29] in the field of queer studies. Different from reckoning radical queer history as a remedy to the neoliberal onslaught on queer social movements in the US, a "return" to queer Marxism in the PRC manifests more of a theoretical anxiety rooted in postsocialist colonial "double othering" than historicized connections between queer practices and Marxism.

Another trouble of "queer Marxism" in the PRC has to do with the relationship between the state apparatus, leftist politics, and the experience of existing socialism. Even though the PRC has gone far divergent from socialism in the last four decades, Marxism and socialism remain the official ideology used today by the ruling elites of the Party to justify its legitimacy, regulate the macroeconomy, and discipline citizens and populations. "Socialist politics," for the most part is understood at best as hollow state propaganda deprived of real meanings, and a means of oppression and control at worst. For example, in 2021 the state launched another round of campaigns against "sissy men" on TV and media sites to clean up the entertainment industry and to get the upper hand in the market competition with private capital, but official discourse utilized the rhetoric of "defending socialism" and "serving the interests of the people" to

---

27. See Liu, *Queer Marxism in Two Chinas,* and Hongwei Bao, Queer Comrades: *Gay Identity and* Tongzhi *Activism in Postsocialist China* (Copenhagen: Nordic Institute of Asian Studies, 2018) for discussions of queer socialism in the Sinophone context.

28. Howard Chiang, review of *Queer Marxism in Two Chinas,* by Petrus Liu, *The China Quarterly* 227 (2016): 848.

29. Chiang, review of Queer Marxism in Two Chinas, 848.

12   Queer Chimerica

justify the crackdown and framed the "distorted aesthetics of effeminate men" as a product of blood-sucking capitalism. A queer Marxist critique of neoliberalism could easily be repurposed by state conservatism on the one hand and fall prey to the fraught daily life of Cold War political discourse that regards anything "socialist" as "pro-state" and "pro-Communist Party" on the other.

The framework of homopostsocialism recognizes socialist histories and the significance of Marxist thinking to queer theorization without idealizing their political relevance, especially when it comes to accounting for the expansion of "global China." As an instance of homopostsocialism, "queer Chimerica" uncovers the dual process in which the ideologically oppositional powers could work in accordance to reformulate previous colonial legacies and accelerate the movement of capital and labor exploitation through sustaining the racialization of the communist world as "illiberal" and "unfree" and the internalization of "catching up" and "transitioning."

This conceptualization might seem counterintuitive at first; yet the defining feature of homopostsocialism is that the opposing differences in ideology, cultural and political values manifested through issues such as LGBT rights and legalization in fact function to displace social inequality and violence led by post–Cold War global restructuring and to conceal the interdependency of democratic and authoritarian variations of neoliberalism. If, as Grace Hong argues,[30] the epistemological structure of the US neoliberal selective affirmation of difference is a disavowal and relegation of racial and gendered violence to the past, the postsocialist incorporation of differences operates through a logic of abject assimilation as the future: on the one hand, former socialist countries are expected to become the same, and on the other, they will never be. One example of this oxymoron is that, as Suchland explains, social problems as results of global neoliberalization in postsocialist transitioning countries are often seen as the failure and lingering pathologies of state socialism.[31] It is also the case that China's 1989 Tian'anmen social movement has been (mis)understood in blanket terms of authoritarian state oppression and democratization, especially by the post-1989 generation, without differentiating that the protest was against the newly reformed neoliberal state, not the previous Maoist state.[32]

If the concepts of homonormativity, homonationalism, and homocapi-

---

30. Grace Hong, *Death Beyond Disavowal: The Impossible Politics of Difference* (Minneapolis: University of Minnesota Press, 2015), 7.

31. Jennifer Suchland, *Economies of Violence: Transnational Feminism, Postsocialism, and the Politics of Sex Trafficking* (Durham: Duke University Press, 2015), 12.

32. David Eng, "The Queer Space of China: Expressive Desire in Stanley Kwan's *Lan Yu*," *Positions: East Asia Cultures Critique* 18, no. 2 (2010): 478.

talism focus more or less on critiques of the US empire and its transnational political, military, and financial institutions, homopostsocialism calls attention to the interdependence and ambivalence of seemingly rival powers, such as "Chimerica," in producing hegemonic queer expressions, cultures, and subjectivities, that, in turn, reproduce colonial and imperial dominations. In responding to the global neoliberal restructuring since the late 1970s, Lisa Duggan's framework of homonormativity provides a compelling account that explains the shift from radical queer politics to individualistic, rights-based social movements in mainstream American political imaginaries. Yet, as queer geographer Gavin Brown[33] points out, the framework of homonormativity, both as a phenomenon and a theoretical vantage point, has too often been taken as an all-encompassing homogenous entity applied globally without geo-temporal diversity and particularity. Homopostsocialism therefore helps understand not only the variations of homonormativity but also how normalizations in US sexual politics are in fact entangled with political and economic changes in other locations.

Apart from homonormativity and homonationalism whose operation requires the state recognition of LGBT identities, legal protection of rights, and military and cultural coerciveness, homopostsocialism operates through a politics of opacity, marked by a dynamic equilibrium of fluidity and stuckness. Like a revolving door, it utilizes temporal and affective contradictions to govern the process of differential assimilation and social liquidation. Through sustaining the undead temporality of postsocialist future that is yet to (and will not) come, the cocktail of desire, labor, and capital is made and served. At a time when the Marxian concept of class was in dissolution, this revolving door effect reconfigures class formation according to one's ability to touch up the picture of the rosy future while justifying the lack of attention to new material inequality and genuine ambition to make changes.

In other words, a homopostsocialist queer subject is one who diligently replicates and disrupts the "crucial optimism"[34] of "becoming" and "transforming," embodying a new type of fluidity and flexibility apart from the poststructuralist fluidity of gender and sexuality. "Queer Chimerica," therefore, is not just about making visible the labor, affect, subjugation, and agency of the homopostsocialist queer; but calls for attention to what has sustained the imperative of producing fungibility, qualified and disqualified populations, and proper and

---

33. Gavin Brown, "Homonormativity: A Metropolitan Concept that Denigrates 'Ordinary' Gay Lives," *Journal of Homosexuality* 59, no. 7 (2012): 1066–67.

34. See Lauren Berlant, *Cruel Optimism* (Durham: Duke University Press, 2011).

14   Queer Chimerica

improper figures in the remaking of multiple empires, social norms, and capitalist relations, and how.

(Im)proper Subjects of Queer (Asia) Studies

In the field of Global Queer Asia Studies, the framework of Queer Sinophone has provided a compelling alternative to conventional analytics of the "Chinese" and "Chinese diaspora." As a dynamic theoretical praxis, it "exploded once and for all the possibility of any binary model of 'China and the West'" and "enabled works and concepts to be placed productively in dialogues without restriction by category, discipline, locations and convention" of China studies.[35] Recent publications tend to focus on the "frontier" and "borderland" of minor transnationalism in geographically diverse spaces, with a particular emphasis on the experience of the rootless, the nomad and in-transit, the abandoned, and the dweller, as these subjects are viewed as exemplifying queer displacement, transformative agency, and alternative modes of living.

While sharing the same commitment to transnational/transregional and decolonial praxis, the book seeks to reflect on the "subject matter" of queer studies and to expand "queer border thinking" by exploring relationalities, institutions, and practices that both enable and constrain queer's geographical and epistemological crossings. Being cautious of assuming the mobile queer as the self-evident radical subject of queer studies and activism, especially in the post-Covid era when mobility has a lot to do with privilege and class, the book is interested in how a queer subject becomes legible in both queer and Sinophone spaces, and what happens when they enter the stage that is not particularly designed for them.

The postsocialist postcolonial queers this book features might not look like the *mestiza* border-crossers who overtly embody decolonial antinormativity; on the contrary, they are "improper" and "inconvenient" with "politically incorrect" thoughts, feelings, and politics; immobility marks their daily lives, trapping them in geographical, historical, and epistemological fixities. Yet, the experience, knowledge and wisdom that anchor these improper queers could shed light on unexpected ways through which intertwined empires reveal and conceal themselves, prompting us to ask different kinds of questions and look elsewhere.

---

35. Ari Heinrich, "'A Volatile Alliance': Queer Sinophone Synergies Across Literature, Film, and Culture," in *Queer Sinophone Cultures*, eds. Howard Chiang and Ari Larissa Heinrich (New York: Routledge, 2014), 3.

Introduction   15

One of the "elsewheres" can be glimpsed from the following example of Steven Bognar and Julia Reichert's documentary *American Factory* (2019).[36] As a follow-up of their previous film, *The Last Truck: Closing of a GM Plant* (2009), Reichert and Bognar document the reopening of an automobile factory in Dayton, Ohio, purchased by China-based glass manufacturer Fuyao in 2014 till the workers' failed attempt to establish a union in 2017. At first, the narrative presents a reversed story of the "global saver," in which the Chinese private capital revives the US economy and enables opportunities for its laid-off workers. As the film proceeds, the "Chinese ways" of doing business—the robotic training procedures, hard-nosed business decisions almost solely made by the CEO and its management team, and the company's harsh anti-union harassment, and so on—are unraveled and pinned as what ultimately leads to the ill fate of Fuyao in the US. Reciting familiar discourses of ideological, political, and entrepreneurial cultural differences, the failed union organizing and American workers' unemployment are primarily attributed to the alienness of the Chinese and their inability to adjust to American (political) culture. Consequently, the true cause of the precarity of the American working class—the post-Fordist neoliberal capitalism finds its cheap scapegoat in the racialized other, as the American and Chinese working classes are pitted against each other.

Interestingly, although gender and sexuality are not the focus of the documentary, the tensions of capital accumulation are expressed through racialized queerness in many subtle ways. For example, the depiction of Chinese businessmen and factory workers as diligent, efficient, and dexterous is conveyed through their metrosexual appearance, soft, if not effeminate, masculinity, reserved humbleness, and sometimes flamboyant singing and dancing performances at the company's gala, in sharp contrast to the oversized, poorly dressed, slowly moving Midwest workers, who clearly no longer fit in the post-Fordist workplace. What underlies these contrasts is an odd triangulation: as the failed Fordist masculinity of American workers gave rise to the post-Fordist fluid and flexible queerness, hinted by Kevin Floyd's *The Reification of Desire*, the tensions between an anti-labor (or class blind) queer politics and an anti-queer (or sexuality blind) labor politics, both and simultaneously as results of neoliberal subsumption of life, are displaced onto the "queerly racialized" others. As the "proxy target" in the "Chimerica" world depicted in *American Factory*, the Chinese sojourners in suburban Dayton (not your typical queer site) nevertheless open up some possibilities for us to theorize queerness submerged from unnoticed afar folded in the hyperspace of the nearby, a space inhabited

---

36. I thank Christopher Fan for introducing this film to me.

16 Queer Chimerica

by the culturally and ideologically racialized subject who dis- and re-orients the "center" and the "peripheral, " the "proper" and "improper."

What I have found particularly helpful to tap into these spaces of fertility is through the lens of queer social reproduction. As scholars have repeatedly demonstrated, the "sexual revolution" to include nonmarital heterosexual relations, same-sex couples, and trans rights is in fact grounded in the "free" labor under capitalism. Building upon feminist scholarship on racialized unpaid labor,[37] a lot of the important recent work on queer social reproduction has focused on deprivatization, spaces of socializing and political organizing, and the kinds of collective labor that are essential to the constitution, not just of queer communities but of urban spaces in general.[38] As John D'Emilio notes, "the building of an 'affectional community' must be as much a part of our political movement as are campaigns for civil rights." [39]

Taking queer social reproduction to queer Global Asia and queer Sinophone studies, the book leans on the concept of resourcefulness,[40] as opposed to resistance, of the queer individuals and communities whose laboring and navigating through the rawness of life rejuvenate the meanings of agency, empowerment, and political pleasure. At a time when we are comfortably wired to see, feel, and be moved by certain violence while remaining cruelly indifferent to

---

37. See Evelyn Glenn, "From Servitude to Service Work: Historical Continuities in the Racial Division of Paid Reproductive Labor," *Signs* 18, no. 1 (1992): 1–43; Silvia Federici, *Revolution at Point Zero: Housework, Reproduction, and Feminist Struggle* (Oakland: PM Press, 2012); and Tithi Bhattacharya, *Social Reproduction Theory: Remapping Class, Recentering Oppression* (London: Plato Press, 2017).

38. See Martin Manalansan IV, "Queering the Chain of Care Paradigm," *The Scholar and Feminist Online* 6, no. 3 (2008); José Esteban Muñoz, *Cruising Utopia: The Then and There of Queer Futurity* (New York: New York University Press, 2009); Allan Bérubé, *My Desire for History: Essays in Gay, Community, and Labor History* (Chapel Hill: University of North Carolina Press, 2011); Max Andrucki, "Queering Social Reproduction, Or, How Queers Save the City," *Society and Space*, October 31, 2017; Nathaniel Lewis, "Queer Social Reproduction: Coopted, Hollowed Out, and Resilient," *Society and Space*, October 31, 2017; Alan Sears, "Body Politics: The Social Reproduction of Sexualities," in *Social Reproduction Theory: Remapping Class, Recentering Oppression*, ed. Tithi Bhattacharya (London: Pluto Press, 2017), 171–91; and Aniruddha Dutta, "On Queerly Hidden Lives: Precarity and (In)visibility between Formal and Informal Economies in India," *QED: A Journal in GLBTQ Worldmaking* 5, no. 3 (2018): 61–75.

39. John D'Emilio, "Capitalism and Gay Identity," in *Powers of Desire: The Politics of Sexuality*, eds. Ann Snitow, Christine Stansell, and Sharon Thompson (New York: Monthly Review Press, 1983), 111.

40. Thank Husseina Dinani for introducing this concept to me. Also see Husseina Dinani, "Gendered Migrant Labour: Marriage and the Political Economy of Wage Labour and Cash Crops in Late Colonial and Post-Independence Southern Tanzania," *Gender & History* 31, no. 3 (2019): 565–83.

others, when empowerment, consciousness-raising and solidarity primarily take the form of "pocket activism available at the fingertips," when intersectionality becomes a mere checklist and decolonization a buzzword, a turn to the social reproduction power of the "improper" is what orients the future-history of "queer Chimerica."

A Roadmap of the Chapters

Given the creative nature of the book, the remainder of the Introduction will not give a chapter-by-chapter description, but rather offer some contextualization of the book's themes, characters, and structures. Readers who wish to plunge into the speculative can skip ahead and revisit the following along with the Coda, where I explain the book's metaphors and narrative devices.

Although the history and dynamics of "queer Chimerica" can be traced back to at least the nineteenth century, this book focuses primarily on its contemporary development, spanning roughly from the 1970s to the post-2010s. The narrative is woven through the lenses of two main characters, whose stories also unveil the lives of five other individuals. These characters represent people of different backgrounds with various positions, showing queer subject formations and identities as processes of movement and mediation. The complexities of their personal histories and the interconnectedness of their lives correspond to the book's major research questions and lines of inquiry.

Most of the chapters are organized chronologically, with the exception of the first and last sections. Interweaving the protagonist's synchronization episodes with historical events, Parts I, II, and III unpack how queer Chimerica came to being through abstracting the thickness of life into fungible referents and markers. Revealing the protagonist's own memories, Parts IV, V, and VI examine the complicities and conflicts within the asymmetrical realm of transnational queer knowledge production and LGBT and feminist activisms. Chapters in the first three parts tackle a range of issues, including trauma narratives, the reduction of gender and sexual differences to identity politics, the Chinese invention of global whiteness through gayness, the flexibilization of labor, the roles of liberal intellectuals, and so on. The remaining chapters center on the tensions between radical queer politics and lived experiences of disproportionally marginalized and dispossessed people, to show the interplay between liberatory agency and violence conditioned by the postsocialist interdependence of the PRC and the US.

The book commences by reflecting on the double-edged sword of historical injury and the roles it plays in shaping contemporary LGBT identity formations and knowledge production. In the early days of the post-Mao reform, liberal-minded scholars and experts within state institutions, such as universities, research institutes, and hospitals, drew on their access to resources and networks and carried out research on homosexuality, HIV/AIDS, and women and LGBT. Straddling the boundary between the old socialist system and the new market-driven economy, early *tongzhi*, AIDS and LGBT activists/scholars/experts utilize the discourse of historical injury, collective trauma of communist oppression and Chinese backward traditions to leverage national developmental policies, carefully walking the line between approved and disapproved activities. By revisiting the discourse surrounding the "homosexual issues" and reviewing popular publications from the 1980s and 1990s, Part I and II demonstrate how these debates and controversies *pre*scribed rather than *de*scribed the stigmatization of certain queer experiences and socialites while nurturing others to better align with the ethos of global neoliberalism.

Part III reads Chinese *tongzhi* classic *Beijing Comrades* (1998) and its film adaptation *Lan Yu* (2001) in juxtaposition to the lives of the book's characters to show how the economic and sexual labor of the "intellectual class" and the urbanites are reordered and concealed for the accruement of capital. By doing so, I treat sexuality and gender as a set of relations of production and labor, rather than merely forms of identity, subjectivity, and cultural discourses, to trouble conventionally defined queer fluidity. This type of fluidity can also be found in other chapters, embedded in the sexual labor, eroticism, and pleasure of the sodomites, soldiers, communist Party cadres, and socialist workers that both uphold and disrupt the power and regulation of the state.

At the turn of the millennium, LGBT activism in the PRC welcomed its "golden age." Since the early 2000s, the concept of *duoyuan* (multidimension, plurality, or diversity 多元) began to replace *baorong* (tolerance 包容) in the lexicon of Chinese LGBT activism. In the wake of LGBT issues being recognized in the United Nations' agenda, Facebook's announcement of fifty-six gender expression options and intensified transnational connections through digital technology and media, *duoyuan* evolved into *duoyuan xing/bie* (diversity of gender/sex 多元性/别) in LGBT advocacy, corresponding to other buzzword labels such as "nonbinary" and "genderqueer" in the global queer market. The celebration of diversity as a value in and of itself forfeited the specific forms of difference and life. Although there seemed to be a proliferation of nonnormative expressions on the surface, the stratification and inequality within the *tongzhi*, LGBT, and queer communities became increasingly pronounced. This disparity was the result of the economy's growing need for a middle class with dispensable income while keeping the working class in place.

In 2008, after the Beijing Olympic Games, a fashion magazine published a special issue titled *Zhongguo Zhen Gaoxing* ("China is Very Happy," 中国真高兴) in Mandarin Chinese with an English title translated as "Gay China." Playing with the word "gay" as a pun, this issue brought whitewashed, middle-class, urban gayness, Chinese economic prosperity, and hyper-consumerist culture together, and sent the message that a post-Olympics China had moved past its socialist history and was becoming the equal counterpart to the Western world and especially the United States.

During this "queer renaissance" endorsed by racialized global capitalism, a younger generation of urbanites emerged as the backbone of various social movements. Part IV explores how the new class of queer individuals, as NGO workers, human rights activists, avant-garde artists, and social and political critics, presented themselves as "cultural outsiders," "political anomaly," and representatives of progressive culture under the scrutiny of "Western eyes," while being rewarded with upward mobility and the status of "honorary whites." Caught between Massad's concept of "LGBT Internationalism" and global informalization of labor, they promoted the universalized concept of "gay rights" by reorienting local sexual practices as "having problems" and in need of expertise and solutions provided by the NGOs. This particular activist strategy, informed by the contradiction of "becoming" and "othering," reveals the *conditioned* agency of queer individuals and communities in navigating the labyrinth of postsocialist queer life. Echoing Part IV, some chapters in Part V delve deeper into the conflicts among differently positioned LGBT politics and theorizations, arguing that the normalization of liberal strategies and identities could not be achieved without the flexible labor of LGBT individuals who constantly remake and mold themselves to fit the donors' agenda in order to survive the racialized transnational queer world miniatured in the NGO industry. Rather than viewing the tensions between gay activism and queer lesbian feminism simply from the perspectives of male privilege and sexism, these chapters provide nuanced accounts for global labor precarity and the economization of queer life in both queer political organizing and academic theorizing.

In contrast to the fluid/affluent Cool Child as China's new face, there came the denigration of other types of queer fluidity. In 2010, Liu Changshan (or Liu Xiaohui), a trans woman from rural China, received some media attention when she appeared on a local TV talent show. At the show, she was mocked by both the judges and audiences and eventually asked to leave the stage when the

20   Queer Chimerica

audience learned that Liu Changshan, the son of an extremely poor rural family, had been stealing from his disabled parents to buy gynecologist medicines in the hope of changing his sex and refused to work and fulfill filial piety. 2010 was also the year when the fabulosity of Liu Zhu, a crossdresser performer, as well as the *weiniang* ("pseudo girl" 伪娘) phenomenon, astonished the mainstream media and the Chinese public. Following the footsteps of the androgynous pop idol Li Yuchun who gained popularity in 2005, trans masculinity and male femininity were appraised as embracing self-expression and promoting the entertainment economy; but Liu Changshan's intention to change sex was depicted as a result of his frustrations with working in the city and wanting to become a woman in order to avoid hard labor. Eventually, a hospital offered free sex-reassignment surgery to fix Liu so she could be a "diligent daughter," contributing to both her family and the larger society. The paradox of Liu Changshan shows that while the "gender trouble" in China is often expressed through issues of proper labor, the sexuality of "the poor," "the rural," and the "ugly" does not make sense under the public gaze unless being subjugated to gendered labor.[41]

In Part III and V of the book, the reader will encounter more queer individuals like Liu Changshan, who exist within the paradoxical space of postsocialist queer economy. One has to put on a different "gaydar" to find these "low rung" "failed," and "dangerous" Uncool figures who distribute flyers, wait for jobs, or just hang out on the streets in the *chengzhongcun* ("village-in-a city" 城中村) hidden behind the dazzling city night. As the true protagonists of the book who embody "fluidity," "flexibility," and a sense of "fleeting" in their normative daily life, they would never be celebrated as the queer Cool Child wading into China's future of progress and prosperity. Bearing the tripartite stigmatization of men who have sex with other men, rural- and lower-class labor, and perhaps sex for money, they might be conjured up as proof of the "neoliberal *and* Chinese vice" here and there by scholars who eagerly search and celebrate "alternative

---

41. Subjugating sexuality to labor might remind us of the "vice of state socialism" so often critiqued by postsocialist feminist and queer theorists, yet this postsocialist relation between gendered labor and sexuality is rarely addressed in the LGBT agenda or Chinese queer theorization. Although early sociological research done by Chinese scholars of sexuality addressed issues of sex and migrant worker, rural, and lower-class populations, labor and class were treated as background information or sociological variance rather than foci of analysis. Many recent activist endeavors and scholarships have turned to the intersection of labor and queerness, but they often adopt an additive method to "import" LGBT topics and queer theory to labor organizations without taking serious issues of transphobia in relation to violence of commercialism and commodification. The reason I "deadname" Liu Changshan, rather than using Liu Xiaohui, is because the latter barely yields any search result, which further testifies to the erasure of rural queer subjects.

resistance"; but their precarious living condition, "ill-cultured" mannerisms, political incorrectness, lack of recognizable organized political action, alongside their marvelous skills and tactics for survival, prevent them from being assimilable to the photogenic "subaltern position" or sexy urban respectability.

As the economic growth of the PRC slowed down since the 2010s, the Chinese state began to seek novel models and directions to stimulate the national economy and sustain societal stability. These endeavors encompass the development of high-tech industries, global expansion such as the Belt and Road Initiatives, as well as experiments in detention/the prison industrial complex to offset the rising labor cost in coastal regions, evident in the recent Xinjiang Internment Camp scandals. Consequently, the anticolonial-induced national/ ist development ended up extending the familiar logic of racially gendered capitalism and feeding into new forms of coloniality, such as Han-centric nationalism, "China in Africa," and Islamophobia and anti-Muslim rhetoric in the guise of "Global War on Terror." Despite the rhetoric of delinking, China has grown closer to the United States, strengthening "Chimerica" through an assemblage of racialized surveillance capitalism.

Situated within these social, political, and intellectual nods, some chapters in Part V also reflect on the intersection of global China, the authoritarian-cum-neoliberal state and cyber queer feminism. From late 2013 onwards, the Chinese government imposed more stringent regulations on sexual content in virtual spaces and tightened its grip on feminist and LGBT queer organizations, an action that has been explicitly linked to the postcolonial and imperial reformulation of power and geopolitics. The crackdown on civil society and the end of the "golden age" spawned a new wave of feminist and queer outreach, at first glance, that indeed disrupted the repressive policies of the homophobic and patriarchal state and therefore Chinese global expansion. However, the glorification of visibility and representation, coupled with the reliance on sensationalist events and newsworthy incidents, rendered queer feminism susceptible to media capitalism, and further distanced activists from grounded experiences of economic asymmetry and resource inequality. The chapters in Part V unravel how social-media activism, an affect-driven "free labor" under capitalism, is hinged on insular groups of people sharing similar social, political, and economic ties, that prioritize internal conflict management over devising strategies and tactics for broader-scale empowerment and social change. As empowerment, consciousness-raising, and solidarity primarily take the form of "pocket activism available at the fingertips," the real crisis for liberatory practices under authoritarian neoliberalism is that we are comfortably wired to see, feel, and be moved by certain violence while remaining cruelly indifferent to

22   Queer Chimerica

others. Both the hyper-visibility in the US and the hypo-visibility in the PRC are the two sides of the same coin that not only erode queer's ability, but also the bodily sensation to grasp concrete experiences of oppression, dispassion, and necropolitical killing. In other words, we have become "way too cool"[42] to attach to the distinctiveness of social differences and histories.

Part VI envisions a future where queerness has lost its political edge and gets absorbed into the biopolitical management of geopolitical tensions. Yet hope is revitalized when an introspective look into our histories is enacted. Without searching for alternatives, the characters seek to unlock what is already present, creating conditions for understanding, connections, and mutual care. Together, *Queer Chimerica* weaves a tapestry of shared queer life through speculation, decentering of the autonomous liberal self, and attuning to the messiness of "dark matter" that refuses simple extrapolation.

---

42. See Shannon Winnubst, *Way Too Cool: Selling Out Race and Ethics* (New York: Columbia University Press, 2015).

PART I

Chimerica

They say you could still find Life Beets in China.
Where is China?
Wrong question. When is China.

CHAPTER 1

Here Comes the Cool Child

Every Monday morning, students were required to wear uniforms for the national anthem ceremony. The uniform of this *zhongdian zhongxue* (magnet middle school 重点中学) was a British-style suit: navy blazer, white shirt, crossover tie, vest for boys and skirt for girls. Students were excited about the uniform. None of the other schools in Beijing offered fashionable attire like this in the 1990s. But their naïve pride was soon crushed by their parents, who had the foresight to buy clothes one or two sizes too big, hoping their children would grow into them. The baggy uniforms on the thirteen-year-olds looked quite funny and out of place.

You wore a pair of brand-new Dr. Martens, sauntering the hallway and making yourself the envy of every onlooker. The dragon tattoo on your right arm leered beneath the revealing short sleeve. The industrial bar on your left ear laid bare under your two-toned spikes. What a misfit punk! You were hailed by the head teacher and questioned, "How could you dress like a rogue? Did you dye your hair? This is a *zhongdian* middle school!" You grinned and quibbled, making up whatever excuses you could come up with: the summer sun bleached your hair; you accidentally used beer as the conditioner (what kind of excuse is this anyway); or sometimes you would go a little more extreme, you shaved your head and put on a wig, so next time you were stopped by a teacher, you would take off the wig and reply unapologetically, *wo xuexi tai nuli, yijing tuding le* ("I studied too hard, and I have become bald" "我学习太努力, 已经秃顶了").

Teachers didn't like you but couldn't do anything about you. You napped in class, and your grades ranked the lowest five among your cohort. But when you tried, you could quickly get high marks on major exams. You were into postmodernism and psychoanalysis. A book by Fredric Jameson or Sigmund Freud was often spotted under your arm. You seized any writing opportunity in a composition class to give the teacher a lesson on famous homosexuals throughout Chinese history or opened the eyes of your classmates with sexual anecdotes and tales of well-known people and faraway places. When other students performed songs by Britney Spears and danced with the *Titanic* at the annual May gala, you used a *Waiting for Godot*-like drama to protest the educational system, drawing enthusiastic cheers and boos from the audience.

You were the "cool kid" at school, at odds with everything normative: Chinese familial traditions, exam-oriented education, and Communist Party authority, you name it. Oddly enough, cool kid, or *ku'er* (酷儿), happened to be the Mandarin translation of "queer." The rendezvous with queer theory was your destiny.

I learned about *ku'er* when you introduced me to the anthology *Queer Theory: Western Thoughts on Sexuality in the 1990s* (1999), translated by well-known sociologist of sexuality Li Yinhe. Unlike most of the publications and public discussions on the topics of homosexuality, *tongzhi*, *lala*, LGBT, and HIV/AIDS interventions that were meant to teach you to be a "good" gay (whether from the perspective of equality, tolerance, diversity, or human rights), the queer theses of antinormativity and gender performativity, along with the forbidden "puppy love" knocking at my heart, turned my world upside down.

In retrospect, we were drawn to queer theory, perhaps because its in-your-face defiance allowed the minor threat of punk teens like us to defy everything we hated about China. Like many Chinese scholarly and activist engagements with sexuality since the 1980s, we were deeply entrenched in the mission of "saving China" from its political alienation and cultural backwardness. As issues of gender and sexuality were barometers for measuring the nation's level of progress under the zeitgeist of postsocialist transition, the newly formed subjects such as the LGBT became the avatars of the heroic national saviors.[1] Even though queer individuals were not granted legal protection and citizenship in the PRC, the nation's future was, indeed, tweaking Lee Edelman's words, the "cool kid" stuff."[2]

Unfortunately, "the 'cool kid' saving China" was what severed us.

"Come on, it is not the end of the world!" You dismissed my silent pro-

---

1. Lisa Rofel, *Desiring China: Experiments in Neoliberalism, Sexuality, and Public Culture* (Durham: Duke University Press, 2007), 2–7.

2. Lee Edelman, *No Future: Queer Theory and the Death Drive* (Durham: Duke University Press, 2007), 2–3. Edelman discusses how the image of the Child imposes an ideological limit on political discourse that preserves the absolute privilege of heteronormativity.

test, "I will only be in the States for two years, and I will bring back the most cutting-edge knowledge from the West to set Chinese homosexuals free from the prison of heterosexist patriarchy!"

You certainly looked possessed by the spirit of Lenin or Che Guevara, "Queers of all countries unite! We have nothing to lose but our chains!"

"Sure," I sneered at the *proletariat* in the baggy private school suit in front of me and mocked, "I am sure you will be a great leader of the 'Queer Middle Kingdom.'"

It turned out the queer future you envisioned was no bullshit. In 2029 after dreary years of economic stagflation, natural disasters, global unrest and military standoff, two of the world's most powerful nations put aside their ideological differences and took a surprising turn to merge into one. In the hope of suppressing rebellions and restoring social order, the nascent super empire, Mankind Unity of Chimerica, launched a mass campaign promising to fight precarity and uplift the oppressed.

Among all the proposed plans, the Beijing Dome Project was selected. Optimizing resources and cutting-edge technology, the engineers built a neuro-computer interface that allowed its users to synchronize with others and "wine taste" their life experiences. The LGBTQ+ identified, racially marginalized, and economically dispossessed soon became the most wanted, because the visceral excitement derived from their oppression, violence, and struggle for equality not only evoked compassion and empathy but also revolutionary energy to transform the most privileged, allowing them to be proud allies in the fight against social ailments.

Breathing in Chimera Purple, tiny photon-upconverting implants produced from the Red Sun emitter, the donor projected their memory neurons onto an interface, forming biodata distillations called Life Beets. After a quick recoding by the engineers, Life Beets were ready to be transfused to the receiver, who waited eagerly in the Blue Sun Nano Pod to morph into their more progressive better self. The body of the queer became the medium of revolution and redemption; the pain of history in the fires and ashes of resistance quenched the multicultural thirst for diversity. The once deviant and despised in the old world were admired and sought-after in the herculean parade of liberation. As the "troublemakers" and "public threats" were put on the pedestal, and the ruling elites shielded against charges of -isms and -phobias with their queer amulets, there was no more fuss on the streets. Chimerica, the perfect unity of contradictions, became the best model of authoritarian surveillance with consent, dissolving precarity and resistance in a unified queer utopia.

Oh, did I mention it? It was me who created the Beijing Dome, so that I could meet you again and again in my dwindling memory.

CHAPTER 2

Zhang Shanping the Hooligan I

My name is Yang Xiaofei. No, not the *fei* with the "grass radical" (菲), too soft and feminine for my taste. I am the *fei* (飞) of flying, soaring above all constraints of convention. Some people say that in times of hardship, parents would give their children names that mean the opposite of what they wish for them. Did my mom hope that I would remain a baby bird without wings and not fly away from her?

Speaking of mothers, I was recently bestowed with the title "Mother of Immersive Synchronization" at the Confederation Celebration. Supposedly, it recognizes my key contribution to the Dome Project and my selfless sacrifice in service of the Unity. In this era where everybody spearheads to make the best use of their queer experience, I guess me swearing to conceal my past could be considered as heroic and admirable. But really, a mother? How cliché! Is the government still propagating the classic myth of patriarchy in 2029? Spare me! And who says a mother's sacrifice is always selfless? As a child of an abusive and neglectful mother, I . . . oh, I don't remember. Discarding painful memories has nothing to do with sacrifice; it's merely a matter of convenience . . . Enough! I shouldn't allow myself to get sucked into this thought loop again. Overthinking only muddles my mind. I need one hundred percent clarity to perform my job right, especially now that the "shrimp dumpling" incident has disrupted my work flow of recoding the damned Life Beets.

The name Dr. Andrei Lenkov pops up on the notification screen and rescues me from useless rumination.

"Thank Chairman Mao, we were able to recover some of the stolen Beets!" Andrei leaps into his work bay and projects a thumbnail in the left corner of my field of vision, "And guess what? They are treasures, my friend."

30 Queer Chimerica

A few days ago, a Beets donor was sent to the troubleshooting center. The report read that when she was found, her skin mysteriously lost melanin and her whole body turned translucent white. Some inconsiderate kid at the center blurted it out, "it looks like those shrimp dumplings you would get in a dim sum restaurant" without realizing what troubles the comment could get him into. Upon further examination, the rescue team was astonished to discover that despite the donor's own memory having disappeared without a trace, she had somehow compressed seven Life Beets from others into her own body, turning herself into a marvelous storage for biodata. The correlation between memory loss and turning white was unclear, but it became Andrei's and my job to extract and restore the stolen Beets.

This was not the first time we heard of accidents like this. A mere six months after the initiation of Beijing Dome, we had already noticed a troubling trend: good Beets that could efficiently transform the receivers were getting harder to find. This was not because the quality of the queer experiences was reduced, of course. Like any dopamine addiction, political ecstasy also requires an increasing dose of sensational materials as stimuli. The receivers were constantly searching for the next disaster, the next victim, much like short sellers waiting for the next market crash.

The donors soon learned to clay their experiences into certain kinds, spotlighting those that could elicit the most pain, anger, and tears while cutting out any unnecessary detail, psychic depth, and interior nuances that could derail the receiver from their sadomasochistic fantasy and endorphin high. Since the brain cannot reliably distinguish between recorded experience and internal fantasy, a little creativity is undoubtedly not a crime, especially when it serves the *greater good*. So there came the Beet Yourself Up movement, where experienced donors organized grassroots social groups to teach skills for Beets-tweaking. Gray industries of Beets production were flourishing, with their overwhelming slogan "Just Beet It!" Entertainments like the *Beeattles* became all the rage, with individuals competing to see who had the most painful experiences. As a result, the Beets began to look homogenized, losing their thorny specificity and flavors.

Driven by high rewards, some donors flirt with danger and steal the Beets of the elder and weaker, who are thought of as having lived harsher times of violence and oppression. Since they don't know how to trade their experiences for profits anyway, Beets thievery could be tolerated as "not wasting the resources." Isn't it ironic that when queerness is more normalized than ever, we need the suffering of the marginalized the most? Oh, let's not forget that Beets trading rarely brings material profit to the individual. While certainly there are high-profile celebrity donors who make inspiring and transforming others their full-time career, most people simply surrender their biodata to us in order to have their own sense of significance and self-worth bolstered. With little effort, the Unity has built a vast repository of information, tracking and predicting the actions of its citizens. But mind you, Chimerica is not your typical Orwellian world. Here, freedom and consent destroy what tyranny couldn't.

"I assure you, my friend, we won't *chao lengfan* (reheating the cold rice 炒冷饭) this time. The Beets are truly unlike anything we've seen before." Andrei interrupts my cynical self-rambling.

"Hope not." I roll my eyes as I settle into the trimming pod. As Andrei switches on the photon-convertor of the Blue Sun, a barrage of tiny purple lightning bolts rises and envelops my body like a silk armor. Soon the familiar feeling of ecstatic emptiness will wash over me, drawing me into the dark tunnel of the past.

"Buckle up, my friend, it is going to be a wild ride!"

OCTOBER 12TH, 1967

Quotations from Chairman Mao

> Discipline is the guarantee of our actions. Without discipline, the Party will not be able to lead the army and the mass to glorious victories.

My Confession
Under the leadership of the Party, the great enterprise of socialist modernization is rapidly moving toward prosperity. But class enemies from inside and outside have yet to come to terms with their failures. American imperialism is still ganging up with other world imperialisms, plotting to undermine our great nation. In this situation, we must enhance the sense of organization and discipline and always adhere to the Party principles. It is a must for the revolution; it is a must for preparing for the war. To forget the discipline of the Party is to forget the class struggle, to forget the regime of the proletariats. Discipline guarantees our righteous actions; any deviation from discipline is to assist the capitalist attacks on the proletariats.

Because my bourgeois worldview had not been completely transformed—in addition to the fact that I did not spend enough effort studying Mao Zedong's thoughts—and I was not well aware of the Party's goals and class struggle, I committed a terrible mistake. One night I came back from the city and did not return to my dorm immediately. Instead, I went to a workmate's dorm. It was late, so I shared a bed with

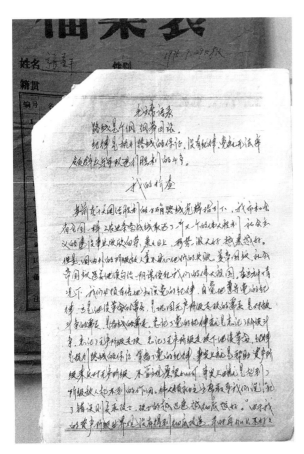

"The hooligan's Confession."

him. Then I started to touch his penis. At the time, I thought it was just fooling around. I didn't know it was such a severe problem.

The Great Leader Chairman Mao taught us that when we commit any mistake, we need to get re-educated and make changes. The sooner, the better; the more thorough, the better. I promise to keep Chairman Mao's wisdom in my heart and never repeat the mistake.

—Zhang Shanping[1]

---

1. This plot is based on the confession documents the author collected during 2015–2017. For a more detailed reading of the original material, see Shana Ye, "Reparative Return to 'Queer Socialism': Agency, Desires and the Socialist Queer Space," in *Power and Pleasure: Writing the History of Sexuality in China*, ed. Howard Chiang (Seattle: University of Washington Press, 2008), 142–62.

Zhang Shanping hands his confession to the Party cadre and fakes a bland smile. The yellow light from the lamp on the empty desk casts deep shadows on the boney face of the wrongdoer, conveniently disguising his anxiousness. The second hand on the clock moves loudly, but not loud enough to cover the annoying sound from him picking his fingernails under the desk. The Great Proletarian Cultural Revolution launched a year ago, and people are hyped for responding to the Chairman's call for "criticism and self-criticism." Exposing and reporting one another's wrongdoings is the most rewarding righteousness. What kind of storm is ahead of him? Will he be put into a struggle session and sent to a labor camp? Will the exposure to hooligan behaviors end his career as a promising technician? What will his family, friends, and coworkers think of him? Before his endless fear sends him down the rabbit hole,

"Explain how you touched his penis and why." The cadre interrupts Zhang Shanping's inner dialogue, jabbing his finger at the paper.

Zhang Shanping returns his eyes to the words "touch his penis," picks up the pen, and adds on the thin paper, "used my hands, and to measure whose penis is longer."

Two days later, Zhang Shanping was called in again to write another confession. To the Party administration, the cursory letter clearly indicates Zhang's avoidance of facing his crime and lack of commitment to be re-educated and transformed.

The cadre points at Zhang's previous confession, already underlined by the committee, "Here, write more with detail, tell the Party why you wanted to measure whose penis is longer."

Knowing there is no easy escape, Zhang Shanping dips the pen in the ink bottle and adds more lines:

The twin-size bed in the dorm is tiny, so we were very close to each other. My hand happened to be next to his penis, and I felt his erection. Out of curiosity, I held his penis to see if it was longer than mine. He moved a little, and I thought I had woken him up. So I stopped and went to sleep.

Seven days later, Zhang Shanping is requested to turn in the third confession. The Party committee was worried that the previous two letters were not strong enough to fully transform Zhang's bourgeois worldview and to bring him back to the correct revolutionary road.

In the third version, Zhang Shanping gives up the small bed excuse and completely discards the part about comparing penis sizes. He writes:

At first, Little Wang and I slept opposite in the bed. Then, around 3:00 or 4:00 am, I woke up and saw Little Wang sleeping soundly. I thought he must be sleeping heavily because he had drunk so much that day. So I sat up and turned to his side of the bed. I put my hand into his underwear and started stroking his penis. I got closer to him and started to put his penis into my anus. I wanted to make him ejaculate.

The cadre circles the words "penis," "anus," and "ejaculate" with a red marker. Other committee members underline the words with blue ink. When the confession is returned from the superiors, black dots are added to accentuate the severeness of Zhang's criminal behaviors.

In the hope of demonstrating his commitment to self-transformation, Zhang revises his story again. This time, he admits that the sexual incident was not spontaneous but planned:

When I went to Little Wang's dorm, he told me they had about four *jin* of liquor today after work. So I thought he must be exhausted and sleeping very heavily tonight. I could share the bed with him and play with his penis after he fell asleep. Around 11:00 pm, Little Wang asked me if I had a place to stay tonight. I responded immediately, "No, my place is taken by some guests." So I stayed.

Because of his hooligan behaviors, the man has been expelled from the Party. The dexterous bench worker is now transferred to operate the heater for the work unit. Compared to those who might die or go mad in the labor camp, the punishment of Zhang Shanping is undisputable proof of the generosity of the Party cadres.

Two years pass fast, and Zhang Shanping is caught again committing hooligan behaviors. Without hesitation and any meager attempt to "save face," Zhang Shanping picks up the pen and starts pouring audacity over the papers:

I asked Little Wang, 'Have you ejaculated before?' He said 'No.' Then I asked him, 'Can you ejaculate?' He said, 'I don't know.' I told him, 'Ejaculation feels better than the New Year celebration,' and I stroked his penis for a while. After that, he said he was too tired because of work and couldn't ejaculate.

But I knew he lied. Early that day, I walked past his dorm and saw him touching himself. He could not ejaculate because he had drained himself earlier, not because of work.

Two years of low-rank hard labor as a heater room operator, in addition to rumors behind his back and ridicules at his face, have put lines, dark circles, and gray hair on the young man. But hardship has also gifted him a sense of identity and the hopeless courage to *poguan poshuai* (smash the cracked pot 破罐破摔). If *gou gaibuliao chishi* (a dog cannot stop returning to its own vomit 狗改不了吃屎), why not sin and sin big? He has come to terms with who he really is; the hooligan has nothing to lose.

In contrast to Zhang Shanping's composure, it is the cadre who is uneasy this time. He tries hard to hide his blushing face in the shadow of his olive green hat, only to be betrayed by his stuttering voice when he asks Zhang Shanping to add more details about his ejaculation.

The Party cadre is Yang Zhongguo. A war veteran who, upon his return from Pyongyang, was assigned an administrative position at the factory. Although his official status is high, he is content enough to assume more or less the work of a clerk. Keeping his head low is the wisest thing when everybody else is letting the world burn. Thanks to the obscenity of Zhang Shanping's confessions, Yang Zhongguo has learned about illegally circulated hand-copies of banned booklets, affairs among coworkers at his work unit, and secret cruising sites that had "accidentally" slipped out of Zhang's mouth. Urged by an irresistible curiosity, he starts to initiate conversations with the hooligan under the guise of "promoting transparency of the confession and reeducation." And Zhang Shanping knows that well. Sometimes he leaves subtle hints here and there to lure the explorative mind; other times, he plays dumb only to keep the desperate more hooked.

For many people, Chinese communism might be synonymous with anti-sex. Still, same-sex behaviors were not uncommon among neighbors, colleagues, and soldiers, as long as discretion could be strictly maintained. It is perhaps a "Chinese characteristic" to live a dual-track life with a "double consciousness." After the breakout of the Cultural Revolution, however, trust was no longer a given, even between those who were supposed to be the closest. One must walk for a long distance, usually over kilometers, to places faraway from where they live in search of "their kind." Parks in remote areas or abandoned temples outside the city gradually became cruising spots for the "criminals." But ironically enough, the "culture of the hooligans" was given a virtuous name derived from socialist militarism, *zhangang* (standing guard 站岗), like a soldier fulfilling their daily duty of watching out for crimes and protecting the people.

Zhang Shanping frequents the cruising sites. But like everybody else, he does not know any name, personal information, or identity of his fellow "soldiers." He would walk back and forth at the same location, follow a potential

36 Queer Chimerica

"comrade" for a long time, and exchange eye contact with each other before striking up a coded conversation to make sure he finds the right type of folks. Sometimes people meet, find comfort in each other, and want to meet again, but they can do nothing except wait at the same spot, like an abandoned dog waiting for its owner's return, desperately hoping for another chance meeting. Zhang Shanping *diule hun* (lost his soul 丢了魂) to a young lad whom he had known nothing about yet felt he had known everything about. He went to the cruising park every chance possible for three months, but each time he ended up playing with somebody else to quench his insatiable longing.

One day Zhang Shanping learns that the barber's son was caught and sent to the struggle session. Having a bad premonition, he rushes to the neighborhood square. A man in a tall paper hat is kneeling at the center of the stage, hands tied behind his bent torso. A spear-shaped wooden board painted with big characters *niugui sheshen* (monsters and freaks 牛鬼蛇神) sticks out behind his neck, like a lightning rod eagerly waiting for the thunderous punishment from heaven. A Red Guard, a teenager, waves his military uniform belt in the air and yells, "*Ni zaigao nannanguanxi de shihou, xinli meibumei?*" ("Did you feel good when you had a male-male relationship?" "你在搞男男关系的时候, 心里美不美?") The young sodomite does not know how to answer and tries his luck, "Yes, yes." The metal buckle of the belt cracks his head, blood gushing out like water breaking a cheap plastic pipe. "What a capitalist corrupted thought!" The crowds cheer frantically. The young man immediately corrects himself, "No, no, it didn't feel good!" Metal buckle strikes again. "You dare to lie to the revolutionary avant-gardes! What punishment do you deserve?"[2]

The young man is the one for whom Zhang Shanping had been waiting. The holes on his head, the blood in his eyes, and the smell of iron in the air rob him of any recognizable form. Frightened out of his wits, Zhang Shanping buries his face and flees from the exuberated crowd, as if the menace would pull him into the devouring center of the vortex, the whips of the belt and the strikes of the buckle would disfigure his face like summer hail smashing corn, but worse. Suddenly he is overwhelmed by a wave of nausea and his throat gets tight. He just wants to run away and vomit out of him every piece of his dream lover.

He throws up.

---

2. This plot draws from Chinese *tongzhi* scholar, activist, and writer Tong Ge's recollection of the Cultural Revolution. The same story is also discussed in Wenqing Kang, "Seeking Pleasure in Peril: Male Same-Sex Relations During the Cultural Revolution." *Positions: East Asia Cultures Critique* 30, no. 1 (2022): 66, https://doi.org/10.1215/10679847-9417955

CHAPTER 3

History Is What Hurts

"Breathe! Take a deep breath!" I open my eyes and find myself gagging and sobbing in Andrei's arms. He strokes my back softly, "You are fine, my friend. You will be fine."

I don't feel fine. Crippling pain rips my chest, and the noise of the cheering crowds, the metal buckle hitting the bone, and the hopeless heartbeats of the sinful man still sound loud and constant in my ears, "What *is* this . . ."

"'History is what hurts,'"[1] Andrei hands me over the antidote, "Literally."

I shake the vial and mix the red and blue liquid sitting at its two ends, draining it in one gulp. As the purple drug coats my lips, tongue, and gums, a cooling sensation sips through my body. Then my lips tremble, my heart is a fierce fire, and my chest burns like the searing sun pelting its rays down upon a cracked desert. When I spill the contents of my stomach over the floor, Andrei recycles the nanobots with a small case made of barium copper silicate.

"Where did the 'shrimp dumpling' steal experiences like this?" As soon as I manage to crumple onto my chair, the sour taste of my bile and the spasms of my guts drag my quaking body back down to the floor, but this time I try my best to resist the urge to purge again. "I know what you are thinking Andrei. Sensation-wise, this sample is indeed stronger than those in circulation. I can recover it and make it into marketable Beets again, but it's not going to solve our problems in the long run. Not because experiences like this are rare, but Zhang

---

1. A phrase from Fredric Jameson, *The Political Unconscious: Narrative as a Socially Symbolic Act* (Ithaca: Cornell University Press, 1981), 88. The full quote is "conceived in this sense, History is what hurts, it is what refuses desire and sets inexorable limits to individual as well as collective praxis, which its 'ruses' turn into grisly and ironic reversals of their overt intention."

38   Queer Chimerica

Shanping is just not the right subject for the right thing. Admittedly, through the confessions, he did develop a sense of identity, but it was not a liberal identity that allowed him to rebel against communist suppression. Needless to say, he does not fit our basic category of LGBTQ+. How could his Beets be distributed properly and swiftly to meet the soaring demands?"

"You're not wrong, my friend," Andrei parts his lips in a cunning smile, "but we are not merely turning queer experience into 'human capital' and 'commodity' this time." He laces his fingers in front of his chin and continues,

"The 'shrimp dumpling' incident is only the tip of the iceberg. Recent investigations by the troubleshooting team have uncovered deeper issues with the Dome's infrastructure. Our use of photon-upconverting technology to project memories has led to unforeseen consequences. Mutations in the body and skin color, for instance, allow donors to absorb light more easily, thereby increasing the efficiency of transfusions. However, this very efficiency has created a feedback loop whereby the system reads accelerated transfusions as positive feedback, leading to the projection of the same memories over and over again. The result? A flattening of the rich experience of memory leaves donors alienated from their own past.

"But my friend, the scientific issue at hand is subservient to the political one. What does the Unity do with donors who continue to turn unremembering white? Without the experience of pain and suffering to transform consciousness, queers become mere vessels, hollowed out of essence, and ultimately nonproductive burdens for society to bear. The Unity's very public credibility rests on our ability to sustain the production of exceptional Beets."

"Honestly, what I really care about is not to lose my job."

"Save your worry for later. If anything, your job will be the most coveted." Andrei is a bit annoyed by my usual lack of enthusiasm. "Let's face the truth, we cannot rely on discovering new sensational Beets like the one we have currently stumbled upon. The only solution is to create them ourselves."

"Like those Beets Mafias who manufacture new violence?"

"Not like that. We are civil." Noticing the disapproving confusion on my face, Andrei adds, "Our job is not to dig out new experiences per se, but to upgrade the Dome to a self-generative system that reproduces queerness on its own."

"And how do we plan to achieve that exactly?"

"Well, the blueprint is already in our hand, the 'shrimp dumplings' had prepared it for us, my friend, and it is called 'Queer China'!"

"Uh?" I furrow my eyebrows in a frown, but Andrei raises the corner of his mouth and shows his teeth,

History Is What Hurts 39

"As I delved into the history of postsocialist China, I stumbled upon a curious phenomenon. That is, China seemed to be caught in a strange temporality between 'becoming' and 'never could be.' One example of this strange phenomenon is the way social problems resulting from global neoliberalization in postsocialist countries are often seen as failures and lingering pathologies of state socialism. Even the 1989 Tiananmen social movement was primarily misunderstood in blanket terms of authoritarian state oppression versus civil society democratization, without recognizing that the protest was, in fact, against the newly reformed neoliberal state, not the previous Maoist state.

"The result of this flattening is that history is forced to give up its grainy specificity, being repeatedly conjured up and recycled for the sake of an unattainable future. The future is thus determined by the past fallacy. Like vampires and zombies, postsocialism is an episteme of the simultaneously dead and undead,[2] a temporal collage of mortality and immortality embodied in an object, a fetish like cancer.

"In this picture, queer—its discourse, affective attachment, and apparatus—like many postsocialist fetishes such as the concept of woman and gender, plays an important role in keeping the 'stuck equilibrium' balance. These fetishes are not only effective tools through which progress is measured, but also agents that mediate the process of differentiation, where certain populations are incorporated into the neoliberal world while others are left as waste and surplus."

"Sure, Chimericans are certainly like vampires and zombies," I mock. "The only difference is we don't drink sweet blood and eat fatty brains; we suck that juicy essence of queer pain and suffering; what a postsocialist cybergoth world we live in!"

"You see," Andrei continues, ignoring my nagging sarcasm. "There are some similarities between the postsocialist flattening and how queer experiences are extracted for Beets. To ensure speedy and wide circulation, queer experiences with thorny specifications must be erased, and life must be streamlined. The queer Beets we have seen might be divergent, but in nature, they are the 'multiplication of differences without differences.'"[3]

"That's convoluting."

"Well, it is quite possible that the ideas that are expressed in the most con-

---

2. The idea of postsocialism as vampires and zombies came from a conversation with my friends Dr. Bogdan Popa and Dr. Erin McElroy in 2017.

3. Shannon Winnubst, "The Many Lives of Fungibility: Anti-Blackness in Neoliberal Times," *Journal of Gender Studies* 29, no. 1 (2020): 103.

40   Queer Chimerica

fusing fashion are the ones that were thought out most clearly."[4] Andrei replies obnoxiously. But to spare me from further confusion, he cuts to the chase,

"This postsocialist queer dilemma presents us an opportunity. We can reverse-engineer a paradoxical dynamism that sustains the production of liberatory agency, herculean resistance to oppression, and self-consciousness of identity, all while making the goal of liberation unachievable. Our first step is for you to synchronize with the Beets who have lived through China's past, collecting their biodata, studying their lives under oppression, and figuring out a set of metrics for the interplay between agency and violence. Next, based on our study, we will embed within the Dome a 'China' of illiberal backwardness, immersing our fellow Chimericans in it and reproducing those who are qualified and unqualified alike. This will conjure up injury and desire, resilience and gaiety, and lead us to step three: people devoting their labor to pursuing what cannot be achieved, caught in the curse and blessing of 'becoming yet could never be.' This endless loop, produced through a 'queer China,' will trigger a nuclear fusion among multiple actors and sustain the flow of investment and human capital required by the Unity. Our 'China' is a queer Tokamak, my friend."

Andrei tilts his head and darts his emerald eyes away. This look means Andrei is not telling the whole story. But I know him too well. What Andrei has in mind is that since his "queer China" could recreate labor of pain and suffering, so does that of hope. He wants to utilize the resources of the Unity to construct a simulation that would allow people to run through different scenarios of history, ultimately revealing alternative paths. As a devout believer in Lenin-Marxism, who actually lived through the heydays of state socialism, Andrei knows the dialectics of internal struggles that can lead to something new and revolutionary; and it is his destiny to resurrect the dead and call back that history.

When we first met in my darkest days, Andrei spoke to me about a Chinese plant, *chouchun* (ailanthus 臭椿). The tree with "foul-smelling flowers" was brought to America in the early nineteenth century, and its tiny seeds proved to be remarkably adaptable, able to grow in almost any environment. They sit quietly in sidewalk cracks for years, unnoticed, before one day pushing up through the blacktop and collapsing an entire parking lot.[5] Andrei sees him-

---

4. An idea from German poet Heinrich von Kleist in "On the Gradual Construction of Thoughts during Speech," published in 1805. The piece was translated into English by Michael Hamburger and first broadcast in the third program of the BBC on January 12th, 1951.

5. Thank Dr. Naomi Scheman for sharing with me the story of the ailanthus trees in 2016, when I struggled to write my dissertation and while coping and living with depression.

History Is What Hurts 41

"We are in this together."

self as the uncontrollable "foul-smelling tree" who has aced the game of *chugui* (derailing or cheating 出轨), having one leg in the cracks of the system and the other out, embracing institutional power yet waiting quietly for his day of a wild explosion.

But it is not the game I am interested in, not anymore. I admire Andrei's naïve idealism of the Chinese communist revolution and the socialist modernization of the "darker nations,"[6] but I have long been disillusioned with the Cause—whether it be communist or queer. The Chinese word for "revolution," *gemin* (革命), also means to cut off life.[7] I have learned the lesson the hard way. How much evil and unjust had been committed in the name of the sublime, the glorious, and the inevitability of history? Revolution is bound up with violence

---

6. Vijay Prashad, *The Darker Nations: A People's History of the Third World* (New York: New Press, 2007).

7. Thank my friend Dr. Weiling Deng for lending me this idea about the Chinese revolution.

to sever life from its grounded liveliness, erecting monuments of the heroes and digging graves for the villains, just like what we do, turning the unmeasurable life experience into measurable experien*ces* of life Beets. I might have fancied that type of violent strength. I might have banged the drum for what I thought was right and righteous. But now that I *have* the "hammer and sickle" in my hands to cut and clay lives, what I only care about is keeping my head down and doing my job right. I am in my forties; I just snapped out of a bout of bad depression. I have a family to feed. The past is behind me. History is no longer mine to shape for the future. Isn't the deal I made with God, with Hades, when I signed up for the Dome project so that I could avoid the fate of Eurydice, trapped in the underworld, or Lot's wife turned into a salt pillar?

But the truth is, I can't bear to let Andrei down, the only person I love and would still call a friend. I would have not made it so far if it was not for the bond we share. Wouldn't fulfilling his plan be the best way to deepen that bond and show my worthiness of his trust, to continue what has come to define our relationship?

"So, what do you say, my friend?" Andrei grants me access to a fresh batch of Beets as I make my way back to the Blue Sun Pod, "We are in the *business* of revolution together."

PART II

Life Beets

CHAPTER 4

Red Father, Pink Son

The journalist from the *Globe and Mail* presses the start button on her mini tape recorder. For a long while, Yang Tao sits there staring at the rolling cassette, before he turns his head to the window. He suddenly notices the deafening shriek of the cicadas outside the hotel room, and the buzz-saw siren of traffic on Chang'an Street begins to bring him back to the summer night two years ago.

> In 1989 I was a senior student at a university. Even calling it a university was too generous since all classes were canceled. The teachers and staff were either sent back home or slotted into "preserving the order." We were the "free lambs" grazing on the grassland. Except for those who were sweating for TOEFL and GRE exams, nobody was in the mood for their schoolwork.
>
> I also wanted to take the exams, I wanted to go to America. But I am the only child, and both of my parents are traditional and conservative. They did not want me to be "corrupted" by American bourgeois ways of living, I guess.
>
> My father is a Communist Party cadre. He had some *guanxi* (network 关系) at the National Department of Foreign Affairs and already landed me an "iron bowl" job. In the late 1980s, few iron bowls were left. "White foam plastic lunchboxes" were what you get.

Yang Tao squeezes out a smile and before waiting for the journalist's response, he continues,

> I was just living through the last days of my boring college life. Unlike many of my classmates and friends, I was not interested in politics.

45

46   Queer Chimerica

Growing up in a Party cadre's family, I was pretty much immune to "red washing." Politics, to me, were all about the game of power and manipulation. But for some reason, the word "revolution" excited me.

I heard that the hunger strike crowds were surrounded by tanks. A couple of buses were burned by the protestors. The Liberation Army was called to guard the square. The broadcast on TV warned civilians to stay off the streets. Rumors of all sorts flew. It just . . . sounded . . . interesting . . .

Out of curiosity, a group of buddies and I decided to check out the square on the third, disregarding the warning. None of us had seen real tanks before.

The whole Chang'an Street was blocked by people and troops, so we didn't get very far. When we were about to abort our plan, I heard a sudden sound like a firecracker. It stirred chaos, and people ran off like headless flies. A young man, face covered with blood, ran to me and almost knocked me over. I realized that something terrible had happened.

It was a narrow escape. If I had not run quickly enough, I would not be sitting here today talking with you.

Yang Tao pauses and raises his eyes, looking at the journalist. This young Canadian woman with an Asian face gulps and holds her breath, sometimes biting her lip. Certainly, she is deeply touched by the tragedy of China. *The tragedy of China is the halo we all wear.* He thinks.

At the moment of confronting state violence, Yang Tao's queer self fledges. He continues,

After the shocking, unforgettable night, something changed inside me. I could not get the bloodied face of the young man out of my head. I thought, life is so short and precious, why should I live with a mask? The three English letters I learned in books, magazines, and newspapers, kept jumping onto my head. They were like floaters I could not get rid of from my eyes. That night, I finally spoke the words I could only wish to whisper before, out loud to myself, I am G-A-Y. I am GAY! I wanted to tell the whole world, everybody I know, that I am gay! I wanted to tell my communist father that I am gay!

On the night that symbolized death—the demise of young bodies and lives, the broken dream of socialist ideals, and the collapse of democratic reform, Yang Tao was reborn. The English word "gay" not only promised Yang Tao a new sexual identity to make sense of himself but also a political language to convey and remember the collective trauma of China otherwise suppressed by the official narrative of the state and disbelieving fragile hearts of people.

Of course, Yang Tao did not "come out" to the whole world or his revolutionary party cadre father when the gravity of reality dragged him down. Instead, he found some short-lived emotional relief from the fantasy of a renewed self.

In the next few years after the political upheaval, Yang Tao lives in the darkness of confusion, despair, and intense struggle with himself. He does not want to disappoint his father and family who brought him up, he does not want to disappoint the society that educated him, so he must continue living with the mask of the successful well-behaved filial son.

Yang Tao is a *hong erdai* (red second-generation 红二代) by definition. His father was born to a Red Army family before the Liberation. As a teenager, Father joined *kangmei yuanchao* (Fighting America and Defend North Korea 抗美援朝) and lost a leg on the battlefield. He devoted most of his youth to the Party and the Communist Revolution, married Yang Tao's mother, the daughter of a high-up official, and gave birth to Yang Tao in his late thirties. In the Cultural Revolution, the family was brought down as Soviet revisionists. Yang Tao remembers being sent back to the rural village by his father when he was a little boy. He only agreed to go if his father promised to come along. He was devastated when he saw his father walk off the train after pretending to go to the toilet. This betrayal by his father still stings.

Surprisingly, Yang Tao's father does not seem politically ambitious. What he wants is for his son to have a stable and respectable good life. This life, in Father's mind, means following the ideology of the Party, getting a secured job in *tizhi nei* (inside the system 体制内), having a simple family, and keeping a low profile. Self-protection and preservation are the golden rules of life for the old man.

Besides sharing political indifference with his father, Yang Tao is nothing as the old man wished. Since childhood, he has desired a splendid free world. He is fond of foreign literature. Under the pen of great writers, the outlandish Western world contrasts sharply with the dullness and solemnity of Beijing that he is familiar with. In his eyes, the soul of Beijing is maroon, just like dirty, dark, dry blood, and lacking any zest of life. Through foreign literature, Yang Tao met Oscar Wilde, Plato, E. M. Forster, and Alexander the Great, who animated his longing for the love that "dares not speak its name."[1]

In 1985 the seventeen-year-old was accepted to Beijing Foreign Affairs Uni-

---

1. A euphemism for homosexuality. It is the last phrase of Lord Alfred Douglas's poem "Two Loves," written in September 1892 for Oscar Wilde and published in the Oxford magazine *The Chameleon* in December 1894.

48   Queer Chimerica

versity and majored in English Literature. He thought he might get a chance to go to the United States after graduation. But he knew his stubborn father would not support this silly idea in a million light years. So Yang Tao never even bothered to mention it.

Father does not like the Americans. In 1987 Beijing welcomed its first American restaurant, Kentucky Fried Chicken. Yang Tao dragged his parents to Qianmen to get a taste of democracy. After hours of waiting in line, they ordered a box of the Colonel's fried chicken, some buttered corn, a bottle of Coca Cola, and a side salad. The Coke tasted horrifying, like some overnight traditional Chinese medicine. Father picked the raw cabbage out of his salad, and this strange behavior caught the attention of the American couple next to their table, "So you don't like vegetables? They're healthy." Father was offended and turned his head to Yang Tao, "Healthy? So the *lao maozi* is telling me that raw cabbage is healthier than Chinese vegetable dishes? Why do I need to come to KFC if I want to eat healthily?" *Lao maozi*, the big old hairy 老毛子, is what the Chinese used to call the Soviet experts who were sent to help China's socialist modernization projects. In Father's eyes, both the Soviets and the Americans are the same evil imperialists.

Luckily enough, the job Yang Tao has at the Foreign Affairs department is an ideal compromise.

One day when Yang Tao finishes his work at Beijing Hotel, a handsome foreigner catches his eye. This tall English gentleman, blond with icy blue eyes, has wide shoulders and strong arms. Yang Tao makes up some cheap excuse and asks him about the time. He wants to accost the handsome man and also practice speaking English. One stone, two birds. In the 1990s, learning English was in fashion, but not everybody could get a chance to practice English with foreigners. To Yang Tao's surprise, the man responded in fluent Mandarin with a light Taiwanese accent. After a short conversation, the foreign man hands a business card to Yang Tao and says softly, "If you ever get a chance to visit London, ring me up." Yang Tao peeks at the card,

Eric Lee Thompson
汤文利 (Tang Wenli)
Assistant Director, BBC

Yang Tao tries hard to hide his excitement and says goodbye to Thompson without noticing that the business card was wrinkled by his trembling sweaty hands. This card, like Jack's ticket to the *Titanic*, brings Yang Tao the hope to leave behind the old world where his father dwells.

Red Father, Pink Son 49

That night he tosses and turns. He helplessly thinks about Big Ben and Buckingham Palace that he learned about in his middle school geography textbook. He sees the short Mrs. Thatcher in her blue dress suit or it could be the Queen of England, who knows, waving to her people. Then his mind jumps to Thompson's icy blue eyes. The eyes are like a chilly current piercing through every pore of Yang Tao's body, and then the coldness turns turquoise, like the warm Caribbean Ocean pampering him. Yang Tao hugs his pillow tighter as if it were the chiseled body of Thompson. His shoulders were wide, his veins popped out of the muscular forearms, and then his penis . . .

Huge!

Yang Tao thinks about the Western men he saw in pornography that circulated in dorms when he was in college. Classmates used to smoke, play poker, or Mahjong with pirate porn tapes playing in the background. Everybody pretended that they had watched enough and did not give a damn about the gigantic penises and big breasts on the screen. But in fact, they were all secretly scrutinizing with their peripherals the size, color, and shape of genitals, texture of pubic hair, and sexual positions they never possibly would have thought about before. The moaning and screaming often gave Yang Tao embarrassing erections; at those moments, he would thank Chairman Mao that somebody disrupted the porn with an ace in the hole.

Emerging media capitalism through pirate pornography in the late 1980s allows the "Sick Man of Asia" to negotiate hypersexualized whiteness. The awe for the "white penis" structures Yang Tao's sexual fantasy and inferiority, a proxy racialization through sexuality. He wonders what it is like to have Thompson's huge penis in his hands. For some reason, imagining this agitated penis, congested with blood, strangely reminds him of the bloody face of the young Chinese guy at the Square, who almost lost his life in Yang Tao's arms.

A few months later, I accompanied some officials from my work unit to London for business meetings. I dialed Thompson's number and met up with him at a local pub. During our high school sweetheart kind of flirting, Thompson pointed at a decorative painting of a Gothic-style building on the wall and joked, "Look at these tall architectures tearing holes in the sky, from the tower of Babel to the Empire State Building, they are the evidence of our Westerners' obsession with the phallus."

Apparently, Westerners are not the only people obsessed with the phallus. That night Yang Tao finds himself in bed with the charming British man.

Although I had long known about my lust for men, it is my first-time having sex with a man in real life. What surprised me was that I was not obsessively paying attention to Thompson's huge penis (whether it is huge, I cannot tell you). Instead, my eyes cannot move away from Thompson's broad shoulder. His shoulders remind me of those of my own father.

When I was a little boy, I used to climb up my father's shoulders and wrap my legs around his neck to pick peaches at an orchard. Father's back was not wide, but for a little boy like me, it was like a mountain swiftly lifting me up, as if it could lift up everything in the world. I was clumsy. I got peach fuzz all over Father's face, making him scratch like a monkey. The naughty boy I was smeared more fuzz on my father's face on purpose. His face turned red, like a monkey's bum. Father and I both burst out laughing, an endless laugh. This is one of the very few times that I remember Father laughing.

The romantic encounter with Thomson has brought up the "hooligan nature" of Yang Tao. The popular accusation in the 1990s that homosexuality is a Western capitalist corruption is perhaps not ungrounded.

If it was not for Thompson, I would not have known under the dull, lifeless maroon mask of Beijing there lies a vibrant queer culture. Thompson brought me to popular gay cruising parks, bathhouses, and nightclubs. In the 1990s, from Dongdan to Xidan, from Qianmen to Taijichang, the "Golden Triangle," the streets around Tian'anmen Square were filled with cruising spots. The most famous one, thanks to the novel by Wang Xiaobo and the movie by Zhang Yuan, perhaps was the "East Palace" and the "West Palace." Thompson used to joke to me, "Fucking under the eyes of the Great Proletarian leaders must be homosexuality with socialist characteristics."

He was absolutely right. Later I learned that in Moscow, gay men gather under statues of Lenin and fuck at public toilets around Red Square. They call Lenin "auntie" affectionately.

Thompson loves cruising at parks and public toilets. For this British culture junkie, these places represent the "real" China—the raw, blunt, sheer desires that couldn't be curbed by socialist ideology. Isn't it evident that Western dystopian novels seem to see "perverse sexuality" as key to disrupting a totalitarian regime like in Aldous Huxley's *Brave New World* (1932) or George Orwell's *1984* (1949)?

Yang Tao thinks.

In the 1990s, many foreigners with Orientalist fantasies came to China and ended up finding the queer Land of Oz at parks and public bathhouses.[2] They brought some of the "chosen ones"—usually good-looking, educated, and English-speaking—to private parties and "inner circles." When HIV/AIDS was first (mis)understood as being brought into China by foreigners, a prevailing heresy in the community was that it was a disease of the wealthy and beautiful because not every gay man was privileged enough to come into contact with foreigners.

Yang Tao despises the low culture of cruising grounds. People at the public park are rowdy folks with low *suzhi* (quality 素质), and they shame the reputation of gay men. He eyes the high culture of bars and weekend parties at foreigners' houses, where he meets more gay men and lesbians from Hong Kong and Taiwan, scholars and social activists from America and Europe.

> I started to get used to this double life. I was well-educated and could carry myself out with excellent manners and grace. I got my strong figure and tall, straight nose from my father, but my Mongolian folded eyes from my mother added an extra exotic charm. I was shy, but unlike my father, I tended to keep a polite smile on my face. Many women went after me, but my friends and colleagues were puzzled by the fact that I was single at the age of twenty-three. When my work unit's cadres introduced nice girls to me, I nicely turned them down with some excuses. Over the last year, I had gone on dates with a woman, bringing her to movies, amusement parks, and dinners, but never laid a finger on her, let alone made any "hooligan attempt."
>
> After work or during the weekend, I would replace my humble white work shirt and navy pants with tight jeans my "friends" got me from Guangzhou and Shenzhen—the first economic zones opened in the early 1990s under Deng Xiaoping's reform. Only "hooligans" would dress like that.

In proximity to the huge penises of these blond, blue-eyed foreign men, Yang Tao cannot stop thinking about the battle tanks and the type fifty-six assault rifles he saw in the unsettling summer evening of 1989. Having a man ejaculating in his mouth, he sees the expanding bullets exploding in the young

---

2. David E. Mungello, *Western Queers in China: Flight to the Land of Oz* (Lanham: Rowman & Littlefield, 2012).

52   Queer Chimerica

bodies of civilians at the square. Having a penis penetrating his thin body, he remembers ammunition holes left on the thin walls of Beijing's subway stations that soon disappeared the next day after the cleanup. He cannot wrap his head around the fact that in the age of peace, he has witnessed tanks, guns, and bullets so closely, just like he cannot believe how close these penises were right in front of his face.

Being gay is to live the visceral experience of desire and death. Sucking and touching these penises, putting them inside my body, owning them, mastering them; would it help me to reconcile with the memory of the tanks, guns, and bullets? Can it soothe the pain that I struggle to move past? Can I understand and make peace with it if I could make the unspeakable nightmare part of my body? Can the body be an archive for those muted and made invisible?

Every time I fucked, I told myself that there was no hope for China. The rich and powerful were merciless. There was no justice, no democracy, and no humanity. Lies and betrayals were the "everyday meals" of this country. So why didn't we just fuck the hell out of it?

And that was what I did. I fucked like there was no tomorrow. I wanted to fuck the memory of the tank out of me, to fuck the bloody face of the young lad out of me, to fuck the sad eyes of my father out of me . . . fucking is the key to unlocking the shut door of the unspeakable family conflicts I endure, fucking is the remedy to the shattered socialist dream we no longer dream about.

Unfortunately (perhaps fortunately), there *is* tomorrow.

I didn't tell my father that I went to the square and what I witnessed. Would Father defend the Party? Would I see the unbridgeable gap between Father and I enlarged even more? I was sure that Father would be mad and would not believe a single word, accusing me of being a liar or a punk as he always does. I was sure Father would be disappointed, not just with myself, but with his own disillusionment with the nation.

People who are like Father have devoted their whole lives to a sublime ideal. How much Father told me about how the communists defeated the Japanese invaders for the nation's independence and sovereignty, how my peasant grandfather joined the Party-led army and fought bloodsucking landlords for autonomy, how a generation of soldiers, farmers, and workers strived to build socialist modernity so their offspring could live in peace and prosperity. The last thing I heard from my grandfather was, "Thanks to Chairman Mao" on his deathbed.

Red Father, Pink Son 53

"Red Father, Pink Son."

How could these people believe what happened at the Square? How could they cope with the tragedy that the most beautiful dream of human liberation and egalitarianism ended in such a brutally violent and dehumanizing way?

They don't, perhaps.

I wanted to protect Father from the truth. I wanted to be Father's mountain. Lift him up. Pamper him. I wanted to smear peach fuzz onto Father's face again, so I could cover his face one more time, not letting him see what was in front of him. I wanted the endless laugh of him. Maybe not waking him up from the "red dream" was the only filial piety the unfilial son could fulfill.

---

54   Queer Chimerica

Yang Tao is overwhelmed by the joy and sorrow of memory. Two hours have passed quickly without his knowledge. The journalist taps the stop button and says, "Thank you so much for accepting my interview. It certainly was not easy to find gay people in China who wanted to be interviewed by Western media. I think you are probably the first one."

Yang Tao replies with a shy but complacent smile, hardly captured by the journalist.

Then she adds, "This report, how would you like to title it?"

Yang Tao thinks for a little bit before letting out his self-mocking answer, "What about 'If the Father is Red, the Son is Pink'?"[3]

From red to pink, you just need to add a little white.

---

3. This plot draws partially from a journalist report and my own interview with "Yang Tao" (pseudonym) in 2016. For the original report, see Jan Wong, "I Lived in Darkness, and There is No Way to Look for Hope," *The Globe and Mail*, November 14, 1993.

CHAPTER 5

The Noise

"'I Lived in Darkness, and There is No Way to Look for Hope,'" Andrei repeats the words as I step out of the Nano Pod. He types something on his work bay computer and turns to me, "I searched the data base and couldn't find the report with the title 'Red Father, Pink Son.' Guess what, it was changed to 'I Lived in Darkness, and There is No Way to Look for Hope'".[1]

"It does not surprise me," I reply, chugging the purple liquid, "You would expect the journalist to respect Yang Tao's decision and use the title of his choice. But it makes sense, 'darkness is the halo we wear,'" I quote Yang Tao, "the sensation of injury is generative."

I try my best to be smart and analytical, "To my knowledge, the Beets seemed to speak to a prevailing narrative of queer historiography in the PRC since the late 1980s. Yang Tao had an injured relationship with his father. Like many queer folks would feel, his father was the embodiment of a dual-oppression: the heteropatriarchal family on the one hand and its ultimate embodiment, the Chinese communist party-state on the other. It was at the moment of life and death of the 1989 Tiananmen upheaval, the moment of confronting state violence, and rising against his communist father, that Yang Tao's gay self was able to fledge. The emergence of modern identity requires the narrative of oppression. Suffering, pain, and violence are real, but what does that mean for queer history to attach to this type of narration?"

Andrei nods in agreement and adds, "The discourse of injury seems to be quite central to the formation of queerness. Recognizing and naming trauma,

---

1. This plot draws from Jan Wong, "I Lived in Darkness, and There is No Way to Look for Hope," *The Globe and Mail*, November 14, 1993.

56   Queer Chimerica

pain, and brokenness is not only a personal act of recuperation but a cultural and political object to call out violence and to serve justice. The desire to overcome historical injury and the commitment to 'progress,' are 'at heart of the collective project of queer studies and integral to the history of gay and lesbian identity'[2] across the twentieth century."

I am glad that my answer pleases Andrei and provokes him to say more,

"Injury, trauma, and pain are real, but they are also products of history and politics, subject to interpretation, contestations, and intervention. The attachment to queer injury enables politics and allows identity, but you see, the trick is that for the queers to be constructed as norm-resisters who carry the power to overthrow the tyranny of repressive regimes and respectability, the denigrated others must be in place.

"As evident in history, the abject 'lagging' queers in the past served as the others of Western modernity until they were assimilated into the liberal state. To facilitate modernity's imperialist global project, the advancement of neoliberal politics and technologies of biopolitics has created an image of the United States as queer-friendly by selectively including white homosexual subjects and excluding Muslims as sexual-racial others and even terrorists. This ideology installs an opposition between queers and Muslims, that fortifies US exceptionalism—political rhetoric that frames the US as epitomizing a 'higher' level of civilization, whereas the Middle East is understood as backward and uncivilized and therefore a national enemy upon whom to wage war.[3] In the

---

2. Heather Love, *Feeling Backward: Loss and the Politics of Queer History* (Cambridge, MA: Harvard University Press, 2007), 3. Love points out that the narrative of injury and progress that marks gay and lesbians as heroic norm resisters who overthrow the tyranny of repressive regimes, respectability, decency, and domesticity is in fact, citing Jack Halberstam, a "self-congratulatory, feel-good narrative of liberal humanism that celebrates homoheroism" in the article "The Anti-Social Turn in Queer Studies," *Graduate Journal of Social Science* 5, no. 2 (2008): 143. Then Love turns to Michel Foucault's concept of "reverse discourse" in *The History of Sexuality*, vol. 1, trans. Robert Hurley (New York: Vintage, 1978), 101 to explain how the impulse to damage and injure is rooted in the project of Western modernity, as the idea of modernity, with its suggestions of progress, rationality, and technological advance, is intimately bound up with the abject exaltation of the backwardness; see *Feeling Backward*, 3–5, for more detail.

3. Jasbir Puar uses the term "homonationalism" to describe how in a post-9/11 and post-*Lawrence v Texas* context, the advancement of neoliberal politics and technologies of biopolitics have created an imaginary of the United States as queer-friendly through selectively including white homosexual subjects and excluding Muslims as sexual-racial others and even terrorists. This ideology installs an opposition between queers and Muslims, which fortifies US exceptionalism—a political rhetoric that frames the United States as epitomizing a "higher" level of civilization, whereas the Middle East is understood as backward, uncivilized and therefore a national enemy on whom to wage war. For more detail, see Jasbir Puar, *Terrorist Assemblages: Homonationalism in Queer Times* (Durham: Duke University Press, 2007).

context of Chinese queerness, the abject queer repressed by the socialist regime serves as both temporal and spatial others of 'proper' modernity. The oppressive past promoted the desire to free one's gendered and sexual self from the socialist totalitarian state and evoked the hope for a liberal future."[4]

I start to drift off while Andrei continues his monologue. There was something strange I hadn't told him. During the synchronization, I heard some voices. At first, they were fading whispers, which I assumed were harmless noises from the photon-converter since we had yet managed to completely utilize the light without producing excess and waste, until the voices grew louder and began to distract me and interfere with my ability to navigate. For a moment, I even felt I was hurled into an alternative timeline only to be yanked back like a boomerang.

I could have raised the matter with Andrei, but I knew it would only give him another opportunity to give me shit. Oh, forgive me for my careless illogical mind that sometimes omits the most important information. I am regarded as the "Mother of Synchronization," not only because I invented the system, but more importantly, I also devised a way to trace and map memory neuron activities, a method that enabled us to select which memories to share. In essence, this breakthrough allowed us to turn biodata into measurable metrics and brought us ever closer to reconstructing bio algorithms.

Of course, there is always a trade-off. I had to relinquish access to my memories so that I could more dexterously navigate the trimming process and preserve the authenticity of the Beets without having my own queer experiences interfering with them. I couldn't imagine who else would make such a sacrifice these days since access to one's queer experience, especially those

---

4. If the abject "lagging" queers in the past serve as the domestic others of Western modernity, the technology to create and discipline backward cultural others through racializing "deviant" queer figures facilitates modernity's imperialist global project.

In the context of Chinese socialism, the abject queer repressed by socialist regime serves as both temporal and spatial others of "proper" modernity. As Lisa Rofel points out, the post-socialist collective project of neoliberal globalization relies on a revisionist historical account that views Maoist socialism as hindering China's capacity to embrace proper modernity because of its repression of sexuality; see Rofel, "Introduction," *Desiring China: Experiments in Neoliberalism, Sexuality, and Public Culture* (Durham: Duke University Press, 2007). This sly construction of socialist sexual past allows the emergence of a post-socialist allegory that presents the desire to free one's gendered and sexual self from the socialist totalitarian state. Marking China's proper, though belated, place within a cosmopolitan globalized world, this desire unfolds upon a political horizon of becoming, a political horizon of great significance for Chinese modernity and for Chinese citizen-subject alike; see David Eng, "The Queer Space of China: Expressive Desire in Stanley Kwan's *Lan Yu*," *Positions: East Asia Cultures Critique* 18, no. 2 (2010): 465, https://doi.org/10.1215/10679847-2010-010

58   Queer Chimerica

traumatic ones, hold such high value. Though Andrei has never expressed it explicitly, his passive-aggressive comments hide no secret of his disapproval of my decision. He interprets any occasion of my mind cloudiness or moments of thought rapture as undisputable side effects of my "selfless sacrifice" to the Unity, completely disregarding the possibility that they might simply be the expected things that come with the trauma I experienced before. It was not for any sublime reason that I severed ties with my past, as propaganda might have you believe. Not engaging with the painful memories has only done wonders for my health. It has freed up space for me to engage in other things with joy, small things, and ordinary things. Sometimes for survival's sake, forgetting trumps remembering. Andrei just does not want to admit the truth.

"So you think we can decode the Beets and recreate the conditions of post-socialist transition as infrastructures of historical injury?" The amplified voice of Andrei bursts into my thought meandering.

I don't remember what exactly he said, but I agree with him. "Historical injury" has played central roles in the formation of queer identity and activism both in the 1990s in the PRC and now in our Dome project. Yet, there is so much more about Yang Tao than what "I Lived in Darkness" could even capture. What about the experiences of desire and loving kindness that aim not to recuperate and transform? What about the knowledge and ways of knowing derived from tragedies that refuse to form an identity? What about the type of injury that does not appear "catastrophic" nor "spectacular"? Life could not be flattened into its representation through the narrow ways in which trauma and injury are recognized and made visible. The obsession with equating "visibility" with "political agency" could only excavate us from the "murkiness of memory" and "density of experience"[5] that constitute the intricacy of actions and social relations. This sanctioned history and experience

---

5. Jonathan Crary, *24/7: Late Capitalism and the Ends of Sleep* (Brooklyn: Verso, 2014), 34. In the context of discussing modern technologies of managing sleep patterns (such as urban streetlights, non-stop work sites, and 24/7 shopping malls), Crary points out that uncritically equating visibility with political agency not only deviates us from critiques of modernized panopticonism, in which a condition of full observation enables surveillance and control (16), but also from critiques of capitalism, whose techniques of profitability extend from the sphere of production (Fordist factories for instance) to that of circulation and reproduction (the Internet and the prosumers). Similar to the argument that Neferti X. M. Tadiar makes in her 2012 article "Life-Times in Fate Playing," Crary sees this shift as enabling the subsumption of nonmaterial forms of social cooperation, cognitive and affective labor, and individual and collective imagination to capitalist value renumeration. I find these observations helpful in thinking about the dilemma of making visible trauma and injury by recent online feminist organizing and activism.

functions as a potent form of forgetting in the name of remembering, a process of "unremembering."[6]

"Speaking out" and "making trauma and injury visible" have been regarded by queer and feminist advocates as the most desired and righteous way for the marginalized to address and work through the experience of woundedness, violence, and events of injustice. But what about the silence that may, in fact, be the intervention of normalcy?

The discourse of injury, or *chuangshang* (创伤) in the PRC, can be traced back to the late 1970s when the *shanghen wenxue* ("scar literature" or "the literature of the wounded" 伤痕文学) emerged during the campaign of *boluan fanzheng* (eliminating chaos and returning to normal 拨乱反正), a top-down political and cultural movement led by Deng Xiaoping to correct the mistakes of the Cultural Revolution. Although Freudian psychoanalysis and repressive desires gained vast popularity in the 1980s, followed by the cultural fever, the particular association of traumatic experience with political turmoil put much emphasis on the party-state to rectify social inequality and to redress the injured subjects through the political action of *pingfan* (rectify 平反).

Chuangshang faded temporarily in the 1990s and 2000s from the public as the collective affect of the two decades was characterized by the country's ascendance on a global stage, while the specter of historical injury lurked in people's daily life. For example, cultural production such as TV shows and propaganda movies about the anti-Japanese war and Chinese martial arts nationalism was given leeway to express this type of injury. Yet the meaning of *chuangshang* mainly shifted from "historical injury" to "personal trauma" in the 2010s, a time when professional counseling and psychotherapy started to become commonplace in China and the epidemic of depression gained public attention. This commercialized and consumer-based treatment of trauma was quickly picked up in the realm of LGBT advocacy and queer organizing as national and transnational founding fluxed into the profession of psychotherapy and popular psychology. In cyberspace feminist organizing, "trauma" also got paired with the discourse of "political depression" in the mid-2010s and later the rhetoric of "political burnout" and "care" in the 2020s. This change could be

---

6. For a more detailed discussion on how a sanctioned narrative of history constitutes a potent form of forgetting in the name of remembering, see Christopher Castiglia and Christopher Reed, *If Memory Serves: Gay Men, AIDS, and the Promise of the Queer Past* (Minneapolis: University of Minnesota Press, 2012), 2. There the authors distinguish "unremembering" from amnesia and claim that unremembering is "the direct assault on particular memories and on the cultural act of remembering."

60   Queer Chimerica

said to be caused by the uptick of the government's surveillance of civil societies on the one hand and the increasing exchanges between the Chinese queer and feminist scholars and activists and the transnational women's and gender studies and NGO networks in the era of social media on the other. Two landmark events were the "Feminist Five" incident in 2015 when a group of young Chinese feminists was detained by the police before International Women's Day, and the #MeToo movement in 2017, where feminists made "sexual trauma" visible and tied it to state-sponsored sexual and gender violence.

Queers indeed live through trauma, but does it mean they are entitled to talk about it? There was already enough "trauma dumping" in the form of memoir, autoethnography, or simply talking on TV and tweeting on social media, so how strange it is to see that the system I invented beefs everything up.

I could be a perfect subject of trauma and injury—queer, a child of an abusive mother, left behind by friends and betrayed by lovers, and disowned from the community that I devoted to—but there are dangers for damaged people to put their experiences to the page before they do their work. Without critical reflections, the words, narratives, and visuals of spectacular pain that attract eyeballs could only produce the bustle of motions to act, rather than resolutions and changes. And "motions" are exactly what revs up the capitalist engine, when we all live under the "politics of recognition" rather than the "politics of redistribution."[7] I refuse to be this kind of speaking subject, whose words could only perpetuate the . . .

Wait, I am getting sidetracked again. The point is that not all injury, pain, and suffering are denoted as trauma and receive attention. If trauma is a product of history and politics, it's about the power and language that narrates trauma. Which trauma narrative wins out is really "a matter of performative power."[8] The successful circulation of this trauma drama relies on "material resources and demographics, which affect, even if they do not determine, what can be heard and who might listen."[9] In other words, the materiality of trauma is uneven.

"What about the noise and the man?" Andrei saves me from this uncontrollable mind looping again.

When I was pulled into a hidden dimension folded in the Beets during the Synchronization, I saw a man sipping his tea at a restaurant table. Under the black designer dress shirt, he carefully hides the slight bulge of his belly,

---

7. Nancy Fraser, *Justice Interruptus: Critical Reflections on the "Postsocialist" Condition* (New York: Routledge, 1997), 2–3.

8. Jeffrey C. Alexander, *Trauma: A Social Theory* (Cambridge, MA: Polity, 2012), 3.

9. Alexander, *Trauma: A Social Theory*, 3.

The Noise   61

whereas the shy smile on his face leaves no mystery that this is Yang Tao at a much later time of his life. The older Yang Tao seems to be interacting with the Beets donor, but I couldn't reverse-image them nor restore more of their dialogue, except for the words,

"So you had your 'coming out' story written in English, refusing it to be accessed by your father?"

"No better way to kill the Father than by the sword of silence, am I right?"

"What man?" I pretend to be unaware of anything. I decide not to bring up the noise and timeline jump, at least not for now, so I can save myself from Andrei's preaching. I need to do some digging on my own as a scientist of sanity. I need to own my responsibility as a capable person.

I dismiss the aches and nausea running through my body and put myself back under the Blue Sun.

CHAPTER 6

Guang Hui's Box

Here in the coldest city of Northern China, night falls early. Dry air hugs the old Soviet-style architecture and sparkly ice sculptures, like a glinting snow globe magnifying everything in its transparency. Flakes start to fall.

Guang Hui slips back home. He wears a thin jacket, but one that is obviously too thick for the teenager—when he sneaks in, his t-shirt is drenched in sweat. He bounces into the bedroom and locks himself up, not minding the dinner his mother left on the table. What causes the young man to sweat, perhaps, is not the thin jacket but what is hidden underneath it. He pulls the warped booklet out of the inner pocket, *Anatomy of the Male Human Body*, and riffles through the pages. He locks his eyes on the chapter "Genitals and Reproductive System." The colorful pictures in the book give a vivid portrait of the dry medical terms—penis, testis, and erectile tissue—and his hand reaches his crotch. Before he knows it, his underwear is wet with a hot white stream.

After ejaculation, Guang Hui rushes to pull up his pants and slides the booklet under his mattress. There lies several medical textbooks and books for figure drawings with nude male models. For the youths in the 1980s, these medical, health, and art educational materials were their pornography.

As early as 1981, Guang Hui, an eleven-year-old in elementary school, had already learned the word *tongxinglian* (homosexual). One day he was browsing books at the school library, and an article titled "The Phenomenon of Homosexuality in *Red Chamber Dream*" in the mainstream medical magazine *Dazhong Yixue* (*Popular Medicine*,《大众医学》)[1] caught his attention. Spotting the words,

---

1. Zhang Mingyuan 张明元, "'Hongloumeng' zhong de Tongxinglian Xianxiang"《红楼梦》中的同性恋现象 [The Phenomenon of Homosexuality in *Red Chamber Dream*], *Dazhong Yixue* 大众医学 [Popular Medicine] no. 2 (1981), 42–45.

62

he could feel the blood rushing to his face, and he just knew this word homosexuality applied to himself! Sweat dripped from his forehead when he put the magazine back onto the shelf, terrified by the thought of being caught by the librarian. But he was convinced that the librarian already knew what he was!

Guang Hui does not remember much detail in the article. But this incident put a nail in the coffin, finally confirming what he already suspected. The sense of "being named," or a sense of identity, somehow relieved the boy. Guang Hui started to set up his gaydar, searching for anything related to homosexuality.

In 1985 the teenager came across another article titled "Homosexuality: An Unsolved Mystery," published in the medical journal *Wish You Good Health*. The author, "Hua Jinma," starts the piece with a rhetorical question, "Is homosexuality treatable and preventable?"[2] and then provides a brief introduction of Western studies and theories of homosexuality, as well as detailed accounts of the HIV/AIDS epidemic and histories of depathologization of homosexuality in the United States. Thirsty for an answer about his own sexuality, Guang Hui, however, is puzzled by the mixed message the article conveys.

At first glance, homosexuality is described as a "disease," "against the law of nature," and "shouldn't be promoted in socialist China."[3] But when reading between the lines, it is not difficult to tell the author's antagonism to the pathologization and criminalization of homosexuality. By framing the topic of homosexuality as a "mystery," the author invites the readers to further explore the homosexual world rather than rashly putting a moral judgment over it. At the beginning of the article, the author shows their compassion by pointing out that the death penalty for homosexuals in many countries is "a cruel fact of oppression of the minority by the majority."[4]Although "human sexuality is linked to reproduction," the author continues, "homosexuals should not be punished and discriminated against due to their non-reproductivity." The author further claims, "In the era of family planning and One-Child Policy, most sex has nothing to do with reproduction. Society not only does not blame it, but also encourages it, so how come on the earth homosexuals should be blamed?"[5] Guang Hui agrees with the author.

In the second section of the article, the author introduces several famous historical figures, such as Plato and Leonardo da Vinci, and studies of sexu-

---

2. Hua Jinma 华金玛, "Tongxinglian: Yige Weijie zhi Mi" 同性恋：一个未解之谜 [Homosexuality: An Unsolved Mystery], *Zhunin Jiankang* 祝您健康 [Wish you Good Health] 3, no. 5–6 (1985), 14.

3. Hua, "Weijie," 14.

4. Hua, "Weijie," 14.

5. Hua, "Weijie," 14.

64 Queer Chimerica

ality by Sigmund Freud, Evelyn Hooker, and Alfred Kinsey to further justify the "loving" and "harmless" homosexuals and to distinguish them from the "criminal-oriented, society-threatening" homosexuals who should be punished.[6] Guang Hui underlines the words "great famous historical people" with an orange marker. Knowing these homosexuals in history were great people makes him feel better about himself.

Guang Hui starts to wonder what kind of person the author is like. Obviously, they have a sense of justice for homosexuals and have faith in democracy, science, and law, and social order; they must be very knowledgeable and have a clear mind and superb analytical skill; they are probably a figure of authority, too.

"Do you know that 'Hua Jinma,' the author of the 'Mystery' article, is the pseudonym of Dr. Ruan Fangfu, the first person from the PRC who holds a Ph.D. in the study of sexuality and sexology?" My Synchronization with the Beets is jolted by the mysterious noise again. No surprise, I lose control as if pushed off the top of a tall building. Luckily, I get pulled into another timeline before the ground meets me.

"Yes, I learned it much later." In my vertigo, I see a middle-aged man taking a *zhongnanhai* out of the pack. He taps the end of the cigarette on the coffee table and sparks it up with a yellow plastic lighter. I summon my strength to focus on what he is saying.

"In the November of the same year when the article was published, sexologist Ruan Fangfu, who would later pioneer and chair the association of Chinese Sexologists, published a book called *Xingzhishi Shouce* (*A Handbook of Sexual Knowledge*, 《性知识手册》).[7] There was a whole chapter on the topic of homosexuality. The book was the first formally recognized legal publication in the PRC since 1949 on homosexuality, with the intention to introduce the topics to the general public with impartial scientific and decimal descriptions. I think Dr. Ruan wanted to use the article to 'test the water' of public opinion."

Guang Hui stretches his arms and blows a slow smoke ring, "Ah, the 1980s! I still remember that my body quivered when I first saw the scene of kissing on the silver screen in the movie *Lushan Lian* (1985) (*Love on Mount Lu* 《庐山恋》), and I got an embarrassing erection among the crowds cheering for half-naked male models at the Guangzhou Bodybuilding Competition!"

The noise giggles, "I heard that back then, many experts located inside the

---

6. Hua, "Weijie," 15.

7. Ruan Fangfu 阮芳赋, *Xingzhishi Shouce* 《性知识手册》 [A Handbook of Sexual Knowledge] (Wuhan: Kexue Jishu Wenxian Chubanshe 科学技术文献出版社 [Science and Technology Literature Press], 1985), 183–86.

Guang Hui's Box   65

system wanted to 'test the water' and 'push the boundary' since they had more access to internal information and connections ordinary people wouldn't have."

"Yea, there was an unprecedented cultural uptick of sexual mass media—print, radio, and TV programs and films—in the 1980s because of the 'insiders.' Some of those I knew would come out later and joke about themselves being the moles and spies who planted seeds for the visibility of gender and sexual variations in the minds of the mass audiences. In order to nudge the public gently while aiming to outwit state censorship, the authors during this period used ambiguous strategies of mix and match like playing tai chi to get their points across to a larger audience without stirring up too much public resistance."

From the exchanges between Guang Hui and the mysterious noise, I get access to a different archive of queer knowledge in the twilight years of the post-socialist transition that might have been obscured by the traumatic-dramatic queer historiographies.

After the Cultural Revolution (1966–76), the study of sexuality in China started to revive[8] and regained visibility in public space. Once suppressed and subjugated to Maoist ideology, sociology, especially the sociology of sexuality, became a new object of academic research in late 1970. From a perspective of the macroeconomy, this reenergized investment in sexuality was part of the state's Malthusian attempt to know more about its population and cohered with the restored census in 1982. Under Deng's reform mantra, *jiefengsixiang, shishiqiushi* (emancipate the mind, seek truth from the facts, 解放思想, 实事求是) to promote *shehuizhuyi jingshenwenming* (socialist spiritual civilization, 社会主义精神文明), scholarship of sexuality was strongly encouraged and sponsored by local governments and various state research institutes. As a result, there was an uptick of academic research published from 1980, which amounted to an explosion in the early 2000s. The majority of this work approached the issue of sex from the perspective of medical, public health, and sexually transmitted diseases, especially HIV/AIDS, and a minority explored sexuality from perspectives of culture, history, and psychology aspects.[9] Many scholars, like Pan Suiming would call the 2000s the era of the "belated sexual revolution" (2005),[10] which suggested that China's entrance into the global economy had

---

8. Elaine Jeffreys and Haiqing Yu, *Sex in China* (Cambridge, MA: Polity, 2005), 150.

9. Pei Yuxin, Sik-ying Ho Petula, and Ng Man Lun, "Studies on Women's Sexuality in China since 1980: A Critical Review," *The Journal of Sex Research* 44, no. 2: 203, https://doi.org/10.1080/00224490701263868

10. Pan Suiming 潘绥铭, *Zhongguo Xinggeming Zonglun* 《中国性革命纵论》[Sex Revolution in China: Its Origin, Expressions and Evolution] (Kaohsiung: Universal Press [萬有出版社], 2006), 1–2.

66   Queer Chimerica

ended a prolonged period of sexual repression since the socialist era.[11] But an increasing number of scholarships on homosexuality in the Maoist era had complicated the "socialist oppression" versus "postsocialist liberation" binary. They provided nuanced accounts of sexually and gender-variant people living in socialism, showing the intricate interplay between power and desire. For example, Mian Chen's innovative research on the development of psychiatry and homosexuality throughout the Mao and Deng eras revealed the continuity of global influence on the psychiatric discourse on the categorization of same-sex desires and practices from Republican to postsocialist China, breaking down the taken-for-granted "socialist closet" that not only secluded homosexuals from the norm but also the PRC from the world.[12]

Despite these works, arguments about the biopolitical management of homosexuality by the state and their agents, such as professionals and experts, were predominantly held by scholars to indicate the heteronationalism of the twentieth century. Within this context, accounts of homosexuality from medical professionals, psychiatrists, and state-sponsored scholars in the early *gaige kaifang* era were heavily criticized for their attempts to medicalize and "treat" homosexuality. Seen as exercising Foucauldian disciplinary power, these practices contributed to the pathologization and stigmatization of sexually and gender-variant individuals and their unjust treatments that did not exist prior and, therefore, were in service of the governmentality of the heteronormative nation. For example, Lu Longguang, a neurologist at Nanjing Medical University who pioneered nausea-inducing therapy in the 1970s and invented apomorphine injection, "treating" over one thousand homosexual "patients" from 1987 to 1997, had been often called among activists as the culprit of "conversion therapy" in the PRC, a dark chapter in the history of Chinese homosexuals that conjured up the excessive affect of injury. Additionally, Zhang Beichuan, dermatologist and venereologist at Qingdao Medical University, who advanced research on homosexuality and intervention of HIV/AIDS since the late 1980s, ironically identified homosexuality as a preventable and treatable disease.[13] Although Zhang played a pivotal role in China's HIV/AIDS intervention and social movements, he was also scolded for his internalized homophobia and heteronormative privilege given the fact that his public lectures in the 1990s and early 2000s often depicted gay sex as dangerous and needing to be handled

---

11. Jeffreys and Yu, *Sex*, 158.

12. At the time of finishing the book, Chen's article is to be expected for publication in 2024. See Mian Chen, "Homo(sexual) Socialist: Psychiatry and Homosexuality in China in the Mao and Early Deng Eras," *Gender and History* (forthcoming).

13. Hongwei Bao, *Queer China: Lesbian and Gay Literature and Visual Culture under Postsocialism* (London: Routledge, 2020), 39.

with extreme caution (for example, Zhang once suggested gay men to use double condoms for anal sex).

"I am so troubled by the ahistorical application of Foucauldian biopower to China's eighties and the black-and-white opposition between the 'heterosexual male authority' and the 'queer oppressed,'" the noise breaks in and protests.

Guang Hui takes another drag on his cigarette and raises the corners of his mouth, "Perhaps the library under my mattress could give you a more colorful picture of the knowledge production of sexuality by the 'sexperts' if I still have them."

As years passed, Guang Hui's mattress became too small for his growing collection. He tucked his treasures into a large cardboard box under his bed. As the teenager grew into a young man, his bedframe was too small to host his boxes.

Revisiting his collection, Guang Hui recalls, "Publications about sex from the early 1980s to the early 1990s in the PRC mainly consist of three kinds: academic research that was made accessible to the general audience, sexual education textbooks, TV and radio programs and pamphlets targeting adolescence, and literary journalism/journalist literature that mostly took the form of crime and detective fictions. Besides *Popular Medical* and *Wish You Good Health*, popular publications include *The Journal of Health* (*JianKang Bao*《健康报》), *Stories Club* (*Gushi Hui*《故事会》), *Harvest* (*Shuohou*《收获》), *Beginning of Human* (*Renzhichu*《人之初》), and *Journalist Literature* (*Jishi Wenxue*《纪实文学》). During this period, eye-catching titles could be frequently spotted even in Communist Party–sponsored mainstream print media and newspapers.[14] These three categories of publications often drew from one another, blurring neat lines among the genres."

Through Guang Hui's eyes, I capture the catchy titles on the covers of some of the magazines. The skimpiness makes me laugh:

"Homosexuality in China" (reportage literature)
"The Nun who Resumed Secular Life" (journalist fiction)
"Beria the Devil in Soviet Great Purge" (biography)
. . . [15]

The mix and match of different times and places of the magazine's content is no less bizarre than my inconsistent timeline jumps. For one moment, I am

---

14. For instance, an article titled "The Mysterious Female Ghost" was published in *Nanjing Daily* on August 13th, 1984.

15. This plot is based on the contents page of the journal *Jishi Wenxue* 纪实文学 [Journalist Literature] no. 1 (1989), published by Chuenfeng Wenyi Chubanshe 春风文艺出版社 [Spring Wind Art and Literature Press] in Shenyang.

68   Queer Chimerica

"Death of a Lesbian."

so browbeaten by the feeling of being out-of-control. Am I still in the Synchronization troubled by the noise, or is it myself who has lost my mind again and conjured up these illusions?

"Wait, 'The Death of a Lesbian,' did I see it somewhere else?" The inquisitive noise seems to comfort me that I am not imagining the conversation, so I collect myself and keep making mental notes, ". . . Yes! It was featured on the cover page of *jishi jingcui* (*Essentials of Journalist Literature* 纪实精粹)[16] and cross-published in the anthology *Bingfei "Liumang"* (*Not a "Hooligan"* 并非"流氓")[17]!"

---

16. *Jishi Huicui* 纪实荟萃 [Essentials of Journalist Literature] no. 6 (1989), published by Huanghe Wenyi Chubanshe 黄河文艺出版社 [Yellow River Art and Literature Press] in Anhui Province.

17. See *Bingfei "Liumang"* 并非"流氓" [Not a "Hooligan"] (Beijing: Tuanjie Chubenshe 团结出版社 [Solidarity Press], 1989).

"AIDS and Homosexuality."

"Apparently, lesbianism was hot!" Guang Hui points at the cover with a sexy woman and some nude drawings of women on the inner cover.

"Hey, look! Two men kissing!" The noise points to the cover of another magazine published in 1989. Two men hold each other in an awkward position, obviously cut and pasted from different sources, revealing the public's imagination about gayness in the late 1980s. "Now I understand why you said the publications were the *Playboy*s with Chinese characteristics!"

Opening these magazines, it is not hard to notice that the writing style of these articles shares a very similar pattern to Ruan Fangfu/Hua Jinma's article. They usually start with tabloid-like stories that depict homosexuality as bizarre or mysterious, such as through openers like "Homosexuals? China has homosexuals?" or "The wonder of homosexuality," and the hooks are followed by rhetorical questions such as "Is homosexuality a disease?" "Should it be treated?" and "Can it be cured?" and then quickly move to suggest tolerance and a posi-

70   Queer Chimerica

tive attitude toward it. The main body of these publications is generally divided into three separate sessions: detailed depiction of the stories/examples with highly sensational and provocative language, review of the conditions of homosexuality worldwide, and/or scientific research in advanced Western countries (usually the US), and a general introduction of present-day (the 1990s) gay culture and the AIDS epidemic. Finally, the publications either end with relatively positive questions, such as whether homosexuality should be accepted as crucial to socialist development, or "safer" conclusions like "Socialist China shouldn't promote homosexuality for the sake of promoting spiritual health."

A twenty-page article that collages six stories of gendered and sexually variant individuals is an on-point example.[18]

Following the propaganda-like disclaimers that describe homosexuality as "intolerable," "socially threatening," and "perverted" at the beginning, the author nevertheless labors to depict the stories of homosexuals with a highly artistic writing style, in which the romanticization of the homosexual encounters and pity for the tragic love that ended up in murder and death reveals the author's tremendous compassion for the individuals and anger toward the ill and unjust social situations they face. Although these stories also utilize the injury of gendered and sexually variant people to attract the readers, the attitude toward homosexuality is almost always expressed through concerns with other social issues, such as ignorance of feudal thoughts, misogyny, gendered labor, urban-rural inequality, and class-based discrimination.

Next to the stories of tragedy, the author deploys a bright affective tone and positive wording to introduce homosexual cultures worldwide, including literature, scholarly research, and social movements. In their description, the inviting world of the homosexual is saturated with seductions and lures. For example, the author writes,

> San Francisco is a blessed paradise for homosexuals. At the end of June each year, homosexuals all around the world who are hiding in the "glass house" meet in San Francisco, show themselves under the sun and hold the Pride parade. This extraordinary parade, attracting 300,000 participants and audiences each year, is a tourist wonder of the city. The march is like a pageant, where participants wear outlandish clothes or cover their bodies with feathers and metallic accessories. Some of them are nearly naked . . . [19]

---

18. Wu Baosheng 吴宝生, "Zhongguo de Tongxinglian 中国的同性恋 [Homosexuality in China]," *Jishi Wenxue* 纪实文学 [Journalist Literature] no. 1 (1989), 4–23.

19. Wu, "Tongxinglian," 23.

The writing style of the above excerpt resembles many travel and tourist guides and TV programs prevalent in the late 1980s. It does not merely provide an introduction to the life of homosexuals in the West but also constructs a colorful picture of the desirable outside world, teasing the imagination of the Chinese audience.

At first glance, this longing for consumerist cosmopolitanism seems to testify to queer subjects' conformity to neoliberal globalization, but the word choice shows something more complex. For example, the affective undertone of the term "glass house" (*boli wu* 玻璃屋)[20] that the author uses to refer to the "closet" is different from that of the dark and gloomy "closet" in the Western context. The glass house indicates the world of homosexuals as unrealistically dreamy yet fragile, something desirable but needing to be handled with caution and care. Along with this affect doubleness, the author further claims with rationality, "I believe modern China is open and humanist, and should respect science. To the question of homosexuality, we should learn from foreign experiences and treat it with progressive ethical values."[21]

Sometimes these publications are sandwiched by editors' words, disclaimers emphasizing the journal's position to not promote homosexuality but to understand the phenomenon from scientific perspectives of sociology, psychology, and anthropology. In the end, the author also draws on scientific research from abroad to suggest decriminalizing homosexuality and promoting social acceptance for a better socialist society.

———————

The more I sync with the Beets, the less convinced I am that I will ever be able to carry out the project Andrei has in mind. Who is able to turn the vast number of experiences into metrics, measurements, and grids? The complexity only renders the attempt to build a backward "China" with suffering people waiting to be liberated naïve and insulting. With the noise that has become louder and more frequent lately, I also notice that uninvited memories of my own start to surface and impede the Immersion, like jitters in a beat-up VHS tape. I just need to focus more and to block the noise from accessing my memory. Do the work you are assigned, Yang Xiaofei, and let others worry about the rest. So be focused! Go back to work!

I temporally relieve myself from the thought loop and continue my observation in the Beets:

---

20. Wu, "Tongxinglian," 23.
21. Wu, "Tongxinglian," 23.

72 Queer Chimerica

"Guang Hui's Box."

It might appear absurd at first, but the publications in the 1980s, in fact, express deep concerns about the course of socialist modernity, marketization, and consumer culture. Through introducing research in the West and comparing the situations of homosexuals worldwide, the discussion of homosexuality aligns with many conversations that both the intellectuals and the general public in China had in the early stage of the reform, such as population control, nonreproductive sex, changing gender roles, as well as despotism, political trauma, and the dismantling of social security.

As Guang Hui and the noise revisit the "Mystery" article by Ruan Fangfu, it is apparent that "homosexuality" didn't emerge through identity politics and as an identity at first, but instead as a portal through which the Chinese masses reflected on history and aspired to the future in a depoliticized way (since popular magazines are the primary medium for these discussions) against the more considerable climate change from Maoist hyperpoliticization to post-Mao depoliticization, from class struggles of Marxism to the centrality of "culture" of Max Weber.

In "Mystery," Ruan tells the readers, "We should not discriminate against homosexuals only because homosexuals cannot reproduce their offspring.

Many heterosexual couples are infertile, but society does not blame them."[22] Advocating for approaching homosexuality through the perspective of science, not "the tyranny of the majority," he rebuttals, "[a]lthough there is no clear law against homosexuality in China, once discovered, homosexuals usually are treated with brutality by the police . . . but we should believe that the new China ought to be an open society, that is obliged to respect humanism and science."[23]

Ruan's pleading for science might come across as endorsing institutional power to discipline sexuality in service of socialist modernization, yet given the choice of word in the article, such as the "tyranny of the majority against the minority," [24] Ruan's suggestion clearly points to the historical lesson of the Cultural Revolution, without explicitly referring to it. The return to the "rule of science" bares significance to the cultural and political shift after the Cultural Revolution. Briefly speaking, in the late 1970s, what was later called *lao sanlun* (the "old three theories" 老三论), theory of system, theory of cybernetics, and theory of information, arose as a set of scientific methods of engineering to rectify the "rule of person" of Maoism. Drawing from American sociologist Talcott Parsons whose theory of social "equilibrium" and "oneness" was introduced into China and highly regarded as a practical means of statecraft in the 1960s,[25] the post-Mao intellectuals prevailed in the idea of a "general design" in the pursuit of socialist modernization (*lao sanlun*, along with Taylorism and Fordism as scientific methods of governance and managing the state, was not only deeply ingrained into the PRC's national projects such as national defense and military development but also in social management and organization of social activities such as population control and the One Child policy. Its long-lasting effect can be observed in the later "Chinese Prometheans," or *gongye dang*, literally translated to the "Party of Technology," which arose in the post-2010s rise of China.). Although Parsonian theory is clearly a product of Cold War geopolitics, the ardent embrace by Chinese intellectuals and agents of techno-statecraft shows an adamant determination to move past the ideological rivalry internationally and the "cult of the icon" domestically that wounded the Chinese society and national psyche.

With enthusiasm for the Weberian thesis of "culture" in the 1980s, scientism and developmentalism became a pillar of the national project to leave behind historical injury and pursue a new route to modernization. Seen in the context

---

22. Hua, "Weijie," 14.
23. Hua, "Weijie," 14.
24. Hua, "Weijie," 14.
25. Xiao Liu, *Information Fantasies: Precarious Mediation in Postsocialist China* (Minneapolis: University of Minnesota Press, 2019), 124–25.

74   Queer Chimerica

of national affect and material changes in culture and politics, statements such as "let the socialist modernization decide on the 'homosexual issue'" were the authors' attempts (even though they might have failed) to reconcile with the history of sexual prosecution and to bring humanity to the violated social and political subjects. The reflection of and reconciliation with history through the "issue of homosexuality" seems to be made possible by a mutually constructed queer-medical subjectivity enabled by the post-reform print media.

The conversations between Guang Hui and the noise also point out something I had never thought about before. Although the "tyranny of the majority against the minority" was detrimental to Chinese society, the dramatic disruption of social hierarchy during the Cultural Revolution tore a hole in heteropatriarchy and planted some seeds for the emergence of queer culture in an unexpectedly strange way. Conventional figures of patriarchal authority—the father, the teacher, the Party cadre, and so on, can be and indeed were brought down from the unshakable pedestal of power, leaving medical authority one of the very few that remained. Since those with the scalpel have a say over life and death, doctors and medical professionals were the primary embodiment of symbolic authority to the post–Cultural Revolution ordinary people who simultaneously mourned the personal loss and longed for a life of stability. The eruption of medical and public health discourse, including the care of the body (such as the emergence of advertising for plastic surgery and "expert advice" for exercises and dieting), the medicalization of sexuality and sexually transmitted infections, and pathologization of homosexuality in the 1980s, is a cocktail of desire and agency for a good life mixed with historical injury and present anxiety experienced by both ordinary people and experts who witnessed the violence of power yet submit to its protection. Agency and violence are intricately entangled.

Guang Hui leafs through the pages with a sort of nostalgia, and his hand stops at a Q&A session in the magazine.

"Oh, that's right, many publications on the topics of homosexuality in the 1980s took the form of Q&A between the readers and the experts, a popular format at the time in print media, where the reader or the 'patient' sought professional help through correspondence. Many of the 'readers' and 'patients' themselves were intellectuals, experts, or people interested in the topics of homosexuality who wrote to journals and magazines with the intention of making homosexuality public. Using the excuses of 'seeking cures' and 'being treated,' the homosexuals squeezed themselves into the straitjacket of the 'criminal' and the 'pervert' to 'come out' under the public gaze and to share their personal experiences. This chosen path differed from their Western counterparts.

This might explain why many 'reader's letters' appear similar in terms of their questions, narratives, and writing styles, as the correspondence could be seen as fabulation that agglomerates personal history, imagination, and longing for a community. In other words, the format of Q&A on medical and popular magazines with their patient/reader/writer was a virtual cruising site across time and space that heralds a national queer network."

"How did you know?"

"Because I used to write these letters!" Guang Hui grins, "I should be a writer since I stretch the truth when I see fit!"

The form of correspondence between the experts and the homosexuals would soon evolve into live hotline consultation aired on midnight radio programs in the 1990s when telephone and small-sized personal radio devices became more affordable. The innovations made new subjects that could be more suitable for shifts in the workplace and at school, especially in the context of urgent labor restructuring (note here that the background and origin of *yanda yundong*, or the intensive crackdown campaign 严打运动 in the early to mid-1980s was to regulate sent-down youth who returned to the city, migrant workers and "free" laborers unemployed within the socialist state working system. The "homosexuals" were among an extensive range of the population regarded as *liumang*, or hooligans 流氓.). Purchasing magazines at the street vendors after work or burning midnight oil with a Walkman in hand under the quilt to see if their questions were answered was a life change when the youngsters began to reorganize their daily routines and activities around newly available knowledge, providing diversified circadian rhythms from the monochromatic life routine in the old socialist time. These "queer subjects" were more likely to embrace nightlife, irregular work schedules, or take the risk to *xiahai* (jump into the sea of business 下海) and become initiative *getihu* (self-employed business owner 个体户) in the first years of the 1990s.

The interactive space enabled by scientific knowledge on sexuality and reproductive health in the publications and programs also provided a counterpublic that enabled the postreform urbanites to discuss and digest social issues in the disguise of "education" and "popularization of science" that were otherwise missing or constrained in the official discourse. For example, in an anonymous letter sent to a state-run journal on June 30th, 1985,[26] the author starts by condemning Western sex liberation but quickly turns to cite Chinese history to

---

26. Gong Huimin 龚惠民, "Kuajin Diandai de Shijie 跨进颠倒的世界 [Stumbling into the World of Inversion]" in *Bingfei "Liumang"* 并非"流氓" [Not a "Hooligan"] (Beijing: Tuanjie Chubenshe 团结出版社 [Solidarity Press] 1989), 37–39.

76   Queer Chimerica

justify homosexuality and to confess his own same-sex behaviors. Nevertheless, his confession is intertwined with critiques of the Cultural Revolution and continued state violence, such as in the "intensive crackdown campaign" in 1983,

> . . . in the 50s and 60s, the Party's conduct was good, and politics was wise, so I was able to constrain (my homosexual impulse). But after the Cultural Revolution was launched, and the society became chaotic, my evil tendency started to grow.[27]

Weaving personal history into the social and the historical and blaming the deterioration of socialist politics for his own same-sex behaviors, the author continues,

> Since the central government enacted stricter punishment in 1983, I have lived in worry and despair. Days feel like years, and I truly felt that death might be easier than living like this . . . I have become jumpy and shuddered with fear even when I hear the wails of police alarms . . . I pity the harmful folks while abhorring the opportunists in the society who take advantage of and blackmail them . . . [28]

"So let me recap," interrupts the noise, "if I am following you correctly, what you are saying is that the medical professionals, experts, and scholars in the institutions were not necessarily oppositional to the homosexuals, but rather we can regard them as sharing an interrelated position of desire and deviancy when it comes to 'speaking the truth' of sexuality and the construction of the 'homosexual species.' Both became adept at utilizing the discourse and rhetoric that were immediately available to them, such as the revived *De xiansheng Sai xiansheng* ('Mr. De' and 'Mr. Sai' 德先生赛先生, referring to Democracy and Science used in the New Culture Movement in the early twentieth century), 'socialist spiritual civilization,' and cultural novelty under globalization. The experts spent much labor on 'testing the water' and 'pushing the boundary' since they were located 'inside the system' whose internal information and connections are wind barbs of governmental policies."

Guang Hui nods, and the noise cannot hide its exaltation, "Can I also say that using seemingly self-contradictory arguments in their writings is a tactic to take advantage of the ambivalence of Chinese composition that requires

---

27. Gong, "Kuajin," 38.
28. Gong, "Kuajin," 39.

both the writer and the reader to be flexible in guessing the subtextual meanings. In other words, can I say that the very fluidity of 'queer theorization' in China by the 'politically incorrect' subjects is not rooted in poststructuralist deconstruction but from flexible labor embedded in the postsocialist material world of everyday negotiation with culture, politics, and language?"

"That sounds spot-on like a graduate student's comment for the sake of writing a dissertation!" Guang Hui gives a rumbling laugh and teases. The light of enjoyment in his eyes shines through the softly lit tearoom. I envy this kind of interaction between them.

In the early 1990s, a new category of literature, *tongzhi wenxue* (literature on homosexuality 同志文学), appeared in Guang Hui' s box. *Niezi*, (Crystal Boys《孽子》) (1985; 1988 mainland) by Pai Hsien-yung and *Taose Zuichun* (*Pink Lips*《桃色嘴唇》) (1997) by Cui Zi'en lay next to scholarly publications *Tamen de Shijie* (*Their World*《他们的世界》) (1989) by Li Yinhe and Wang Xiaobo, *Tongxinglian zai Zhongguo* (*Homosexuality in China*《同性恋在中国》) (1993) by Fang Gang, and *Tongxingai* (*Same-Sex Love*《同性爱》) (1994) by Zhang Beichuan. In 1998 Guang Hui became an HIV/AIDS intervention volunteer and *tongyun ziliao* (*tongzhi* liberation movement materials 同运资料), for instance, *Aizhi Jianbao* (*Love Knowledge Newsletter* 爱知简报》) and *Pengyou Tongxin* (*Correspondencesof Friends*《朋友通信》)—were added to his growing collections.

"Here, take a look at this. It was a landmark!" a pink palm-size pocket magazine pops up in front of me.

"Yes! I remember that, the legendary *Hope* magazine!" The noise gets excited but soon softens in sweet memory. "I remember hearing about the magazine on a gay web forum, and I was scouring the city's newsstands with this girlfriend searching for it! I also learned about the songs 'Come Out' by the Grasshopper band and 'DNA Gone Wrong' by Leon Lai Ming. So funny now you mentioned it. I can almost hear the melodies escaping from my pirated cassette in the cheap silver Walkman I had!"

Hope magazine was a Guangzhou-based fashion magazine. In early 1998, the chief director, Hao Jia, contacted Cui Zi'en, a well-known queer-identified scholar, director, and public speaker, for a special section on the topic of homosexuality. After three months of preparation, Cui collected articles, interviews, and materials from soon-to-be-well-known scholars, artists, and cultural producers such as Chou Wah-shan, Pan Suiming, Ye Guangwei, Fang Gang, and Li Yinhe and compiled a twenty-page introduction to the topics of homosexu-

"Hope."

ality.[29] Many people would later recall this special issue as their first point of entry into the queer world, as the magazine not only made the homosexual, LGBT, and queer legible subjects through sharing literature, arts, music, and news from the United States, Hong Kong, and Taiwan but also brought into public information that was previously circulated within a small circle of LGBT activists and scholars, such as the 99575 hotline (later evolved into the first registered gay and lesbian and HIV/AIDS intervention organization *Ji'ande* 纪安德 or the Gender and Health Research Center), as well as information about the two global Chinese LGBT conferences held in 1996 and 1998. What to highlight is that the contributors of this special issue, for the first time, provided a

---

29. Cui Zi'en et al., "Renshi Tongxinglian 认识同性恋 [To Understand Homosexuality]," *Hope Magazine* no. 6 (1998), 53–73.

clear distinction between *tongxinglian* and other terms such as *tongzhi*, gay, lesbian, transgender, queer, and S/M to the general public and offered a brief introduction of queer theory.

The writing style and pattern of the special issue also set a precedent for later popular publicity and pamphlets circulated by LGBT activists. For example, it places the Chinese LGBT community within a brief global queer history and encloses data and results from surveys and questionnaires both from China and abroad,[30] followed by a "useful LGBT dictionary."[31] These publications are meant to show that the "homosexual" is a clear-cut subculture with its own history, genealogy, and "differences within" as part of the liberatory agenda to raise consciousness and advocate for legal representation and social acceptance.

"Do you know what is interesting?" Putting the *Hope* magazine side by side with the publications in the 1980s, Guang Hui suddenly seems a little unsettled. "The early publications are absurd and pathologizing indeed, but the 'homosexual issue' was taken as one of the 'social issues' entwined with other pressing social concerns. Although written in such ways that treated homosexuality with (un)friendly curiosity or denigrations, these publications are mash-ups of theories, expert adversaries, commentaries on pressing social issues, and everyday life questions and struggles of ordinary people. The topics diverge, ranging from critiques of legacies of the Cultural Revolution and feudalism to urban-rural economic inequality, from police harassment to anxiety and excitement about marketization and globalization, from gender ratio imbalance to disability issues, from unemployment to rumors of love triangles among neighbors, and so forth. Under the canopy of 'the homosexual issue' was the porous social densities breaking into and spilling all over one another. The 'homosexual' was seen as a bizarre 'something else,' but not so much from other 'new phenomena' and 'social outsiders' rendered visible by China's reform and entrance to a globalized world. In these stories, the 'strangeness' and 'outlandishness' of homosexuality were mainly expressed through concerns and curiosities about the 'estranging society' that puzzled postsocialist subjects at the time of economic and political restructuring.

"On the contrary, the queers in the *Hope* Magazine were clearly taken as 'sexual minorities,' a group of people who stand out against the social mural. As the discourse of sexual diversity and sexual rights emerged in the 2000s,[32] the social issue-oriented discussions gave way to a more single-lens identity and

---

30. Cui et al., "Renshi,"64–68.
31. Cui et al., "Renshi," 69–70.
32. Jeffreys and Yu, *Sex*, 154.

80   Queer Chimerica

sexual orientation–focused approach, a change that bears striking similarity with the shift from Marxist *funü* to 'gender' and 'female subjectivity' as far as Chinese feminism is concerned. If we take the moment of 1998 as the consolidation of identity, can we say that queer identity emerged against the intersectionality of other oppressions?"

It is the noise that laughs at Guang Hui being the dissertating graduate student this time. He draws his eyebrows together and further explains,

"As the collaborators of the 1998 *Hope* magazine special section define *tongzhi*, appropriated from the Communist lexicon as 'comrade' by Hong Kong playwriter Edward Lam and gained its popularity in the larger Sinophone communities since the 1990s, is an 'absolutely politicized' and 'highly self-conscious' concept that moves beyond the narrow focus on sexual orientation and behaviors. Not unlike 'queer' in the English context, anyone who identifies with anti-heteronormative hegemony and binarism can be called a *tongzhi*. Throughout the pages, sometimes *tongzhi* is a political position against normativity; other times it is an identity that congeals differences; sometimes it claims a fantasy of unitary liberation; other times it emphasizes absolute autonomy and individuality . . . Framed as a 'cultural identity' unbridled by 'gender, sexual orientation, sexual practices, race, nationality, age, and skin color,' the contributors, however, interestingly left out 'class' in their redefinition of *tongzhi*. [33] This omission is very much aligned with the dominant ideology of postsocialist China that renounces 'class struggle' and the analytic of 'class' from the national level to the public and individual everyday life. Although claimed as anti-identity and anti-normativity, I found it ironic that the previously class-focused communist concept *tongzhi* is actually depoliticized when appropriated into a queer umbrella of multiculturalist cosmopolitan ideal."

I see his point. The disarticulation of class from race, gender, and sexuality has been central to the success of the neoliberal project in Western industrialized countries such as the UK and the US since the 1970s, which gives an illusion that, in some ways, neoliberalism is a precondition of the gains in anti-racist, anti-sexist, and anti-heterosexual struggles. Similarly, the postsocialist, postcolonial Chinese articulation of *tongzhi* that hollowed out "class" and separated it from other social densities can be said as inheriting the logic of global homonormativity as the emergence of Chinese *tongzhi*, LGBT, and queer cultures have been conventionally thought of as influenced by, if not derivative of, the "global gay" metastory. The self-claimed anti-normative anomaly of *tongzhi* and queerness seems not to originate from fragmented experiences of

---

33. Cui et al., "Renshi," 69.

postmodern poststructuralist subjectivity but from the exclusion of class and material anomaly.

Yet, what I resonate the most with Guang Hui's observation is not so much how *tongzhi* is appropriated without a class difference but rather this liberalized identity and politics seem to be predicated on the constant production of pathological anomalies, namely, the "improper" and "premature" knowledge production that is deemed to disappear in queer historiography or to be relegated as an example of "mass stupidity and ignorance" of the 1980s. How were the two trajectories of queer knowledge production separated and set as oppositional, to begin with? One was deemed as "improper" and "premature," and the other "righteous" and "celebratory." How did this differentiation reproduce different formations of identity, political agency, and politics? Would queer historiography be different if the life and experience of the "nonidentity" and the "politically incorrect" could be taken seriously?

A thought flashes in my head: What is it like to build Beijing Dome based on the improperness, a "China" that maps and projects queer absence and disallowing?

Well, Andrei is going to hate me.

———————

The *Hope* magazine, along with the dialogues between Guang Hui and the voice, start to fade away. Without the aches I usually get at the end of each Synchronization, my body is floating into a rather calming trance. A strange feeling of warmth pampers me.

Peeling through the dreamy unclarity, I capture the back view of a teenage girl in her indigo middle school uniform and brand-new Dr. Martens boots, cruising the streets in ecstasy; the melodies of "Come Out" and "DNA Gone Wrong" in the headphones of her Walkman grows louder and louder in my ears, muffling the deafening sadness of her/my lonely world. I nudge my body to chase her so that I can see her face, only to find that the scenery is about to change again. This time the noise is gone, leaving me wandering in somebody's dream world.

PART III

One Is Not Enough

CHAPTER 7

The Genital Squad

Dongdan People's Park is one of the most well-known gay cruising sites at the center of Beijing. Next to Tongren hospital and not too far from Beijing Railway Station, Peking Union Medical College Hospital, and other attractions, its convenient location and fame attract curious *tongzhi* and non-*tongzhi* from all over the country. It was Guang Hui's first stop when he moved to Beijing in 2003.

Unlike others, Guang Hui is not looking for "quick fun." He comes to Beijing for what he believes is the *chonggao de tongxinglian jiefang shijie* (the sublime enterprise of homosexual liberation 崇高的同性恋解放运动), or *tongjie* (同解) for short. While most men are busy looking for potential partners and fuck buddies, Guang Hui searches for young people with backpacks and pamphlets in their hands. Those are HIV/AIDS intervention volunteers from local grassroots groups.

In the late 1980s, medical doctors Zhang Beichuan, Wan Yanhai, and Chen Bingzhong started to work with *tongzhi* leaders for HIV/AIDS intervention within the men who have sex with men (MSM) communities. In 1991 Shanghai Public Health Education Institute conducted unpublished research on HIV/AIDS among urban gay men. At the same time, scholars of sexuality, such as Fang Gang and Pan Suiming, also conducted research across locations. With limited funding resources, ranging from private donations and individual savings to international funds provided by foundations—such as the Barry & Martin's Trust, the Ford Foundation, and UNAIDS—these pioneers ran hotlines, published journal articles, and established preliminary networks that would soon turn to community-based organizations and grassroots groups for later HIV/AIDS intervention and LGBT movement.

China's AIDS epidemic is typically thought of as coming from three sources. The first is a localized epidemic among intravenous drug users in southwestern

86   Queer Chimerica

Yunnan Province since the 1980s, the second is from illegal plasma trade in rural Henan in the 1990s, and the third is from sexual transmission.[1] After a decade of dodging the AIDS issue, the Chinese government eventually acknowledged the urgent need to tackle the AIDS crisis in 2001 and promoted cooperation among transnational donors, state health agencies, and local grassroots groups.

Given the deep-rooted social stigma surrounding homosexuality and the history of prosecution of male same-sex behaviors, at the onset of AIDS intervention, the government faced tremendous difficulty reaching out to the target populations and conducting effective research and education.[2] As a result, the government and international donors had to rely on recruiting "insider volunteers" in *tongzhi* and MSM communities to carry out their projects. Like Guang Hui, many *tongzhi* men and women are motivated to be HIV/AIDS volunteers in the hope of educating themselves and their peers. The insider volunteers provide medical experts, researchers, and transnational donors knowledge of where *tongzhi* men gather, tactics of how to approach them, and build trust between community, state, and international sectors. This model of mobilization, later termed *tongban jiaoyu* (peer education 同伴教育), was the primary strategy in discovering, testing, and confirming HIV-infected individuals and promoting education.

Guang Hui quickly gets himself familiar with the park. The total area of Dongdan Park is about 450,000 square meters. Near the eastside entrance, it is where middle-aged sex workers and rural immigrants gather. Following the pathway up to the north, Guang Hui finds the legendary *kuaihuo shan* ("hill of pleasure" 快活山) for gay men. The rumor is that the hill is made of excavated soil from nearby bomb shelters. In fact, the whole area is above hidden tunnels and underground pathways built in the 1950s, through which the nation's leaders could be safely transported from the city center to the suburbs in case of foreign attacks and national emergencies. It is funny that any gay story must have something to do with war, militarism, and the Party. Walking past men who

---

1. Casey J. Miller, "Dying for Money: The Effects of Global Health Initiatives on NGOs Working with Gay Men and HIV/AIDS in Northwest China," *Medical Anthropology Quarterly* 30, no. 3 (2016): 418. https://doi.org/10.1111/maq.12300

2. Wei Wei, "Queer Organizing and HIV/AIDS Activism: An Ethnographic Study of a Local Tongzhi Organization in Chengdu," in *Queer/Tongzhi China: New Perspectives on Research, Activism and Media Cultures*, eds. Elisabeth Engebretsen, William Schroeder, and Hongwei Bao (Copenhagen: Nordic Institute of Asian Studies, 2013), 197.

exchange flirtatious looks or hand jobs, Gaung Hui finally arrives at the pagoda where the HIV/AIDS volunteers station their outreach activities. Guang Hui is welcomed by the shining smile of a handsome man.

"Want to learn about HIV/AIDS intervention and testing?" The man is soft-spoken, but his words are affirmative and convincing. His smiling eyes are like sunshine lighting up Guang Hui's heart.

"Call me Yang Tao. Here are some pamphlets about HIV/AIDS prevention. You can grab some condoms too." Guang Hui takes the materials from Yang Tao's hands, noticing that his black leather shoes are covered by a light layer of dirt.

A few days later, Guang Hui finds himself sitting in Yang Tao's office. The warm sunshine through the windows makes the small room much more spacious than it seems. Behind a steady desk, two tall bookshelves stand against the wall, packed with booklets and pamphlets. There are only two foldable chairs, indicating the limited number of regular personnel. But the desktop computer with a dial-in modem elevates the office to a "luxurious level." Perhaps Yang Tao catches the surprise on Guang Hui's face and explains:

> "I am the only 'personnel member' here. The donor agencies usually don't sponsor office supplies, meeting places, and the cost of personnel. They didn't know much about the Chinese conditions. There are barely any established NGOs in China. The foundations give money based on the projects. That's why most community-based groups either don't have a regular office or have to borrow some volunteers' homes. We will have to 'play smart' to support the daily operation of the group."

Yang Tao opens the lower drawer of the cabinet of his desk and hands over a plastic bag full of condoms to Guang Hui, "Join me for the training tomorrow at the bar!"

The governmental promotion of AIDS projects and NGOs is as much a public health concern as an economic one. Many activists and scholars believe that the motive behind the Chinese government's participation in AIDS intervention is economic gain [3] due to the unique situation of arranging transnational

---

3. Timothy Hildebrandt, "Development and Division: the effect of transnational linkages and local politics on LGBT activism in China," *Journal of Contemporary China* 21, no. 77 (2012): 851–54, https://doi.org/10.1080/10670564.2012.684967

funds. Funded by the United Kingdom Department of International Development, the China-UK HIV/AIDS Prevention and Care Project launched in 2001 was the first pilot cross-sectional partnership, aiming to develop replicable models of HIV prevention, treatment, and care. Started in Sichuan and Yunnan provinces, the project identified male homosexuality, along with drug use and sex work, as high-risk behavior for vulnerable groups. This program was aimed to inform and develop a national policy framework for HIV/AIDS intervention. But in the early 2000s, there were almost no legally registered LGBT NGOs in China that would directly accept funding from transnational donors. Most LGBT groups in China were, and still are, not officially registered as either NGOs or commercial companies due to a plethora of issues, such as lack of sustainable funding, instability of personnel, underdevelopment of civil organizing mechanisms, avoidance of government surveillance, etc. Some more prominent and influential organizations registered as commercial companies, such as Work For LGBT in Shanghai and *Aibai* in Beijing. By the year 2015, there were only two LGBT organizations registered as civil organizations, including Shanghai *Qing'ai*, an HIV/AIDS-focused LGBT group affiliated with and obliged to report to the government. NGOs' ambivalent status was due to, on the one hand, that sodomy as "hooliganism" was just decriminalized in 1997, and the identities such as homosexual, *tongzhi*, *lala*, and LGBT were relatively new; and on the other hand that the financial mechanism and infrastructure of local NGOs were still underway. To ensure more unrestricted movement of funding and government surveillance of foreign donations, the China-UK project initiated a "filter model," whereby international funds are directed first to the Chinese government and then passed to community-based organizations and groups. Government agents, local Centers for Disease Control (CDCs), or government-organized NGOs (GONGOs) have first-hand knowledge of dealing with transitional funds (examples of GONGOs are the Chinese Association of STD and AIDS Prevention and Control and the Chinese Preventive Medicine Association, organizations registered as nongovernmental but constituted of retired governmental officials, state-hired experts, and professionals). Despite a number of potential problems of naming the Chinese government and its agents officially as the "primary recipient," and local CDCs as the second-level sub-recipients, this model has mainly been followed by other international donors in the field of HIV/AIDS intervention, such as the China Global Fund AIDS Program started in 2003, and the China-Gates Foundation HIV Prevention Program begun in 2007.

By putting the AIDS intervention under the motif of China's health reform, at best, the Chinese government was experimenting with different modes of reforming the health system through collaborating with transnational capital, expertise, and professionals; and at worst, AIDS intervention allows the government to shift the financial burden of troubled health reform and repurposing resources for profits. China's neoliberal restructuring of the economy started to deepen in the field of medical and health care in the early 1990s. Set in motion in 1994 by the central government, the health reform aimed to replace state-funded health care coverage with commercial health insurance, local government, work unit, and the individual altogether. To solve problems of low efficiency and bureaucratic management of state-owned hospitals, the government implemented a series of market strategies to cut resources and governmental support. The former public good of health care, in the project of marketization, was subsumed under the "service sector" in the market economy.[4] To make up the budget cut and make profits, hospitals have developed new services such as "special care" and "high-rank cadre room" and doctors often prescribe expensive medicines and order unnecessary examinations to treat the patients. Privatizing health care led to pricey medical care, low service quality, and severe corruption, which significantly deepened social inequality and broadened class and rural-urban disparity.

The HIV/AIDS intervention and the transnational capital flows in China have generated a vast amount of financial and human resources. For example, as data from Shanghai *Qing'ai* shows, from 2004–2009, the China Global Fund AIDS Program created 708 community-based intervention organizations; in the 2012–2013 annual report, 845 organizations and 973 local intervention programs were operating, and about ¥61 million ($10 million at the time) was spent on these programs. These resources have created some casual, unstable, and flexible jobs, such as social workers and volunteers for AIDS prevention, service, and advocacy. It allowed the states to channel some laid-off workers, and unemployed populations resulting from the economic reform into "flexible labor," as well as off-loading the burden to revitalize certain "non-profitable" sectors within the postreform medical and health system. Take the operation of local CDCs as an example, the transnational money was used to subsidize infrastructure, expand offices, hire personnel, and organize conferences, which are supposed to be sponsored by the central government since CDC is a governmental institute. At the same time, the use of condoms was repurposed from "family planning" as promoted by the socialist state's One Child policy to

---

4. Mei Zhan, "Human Oriented? Angels and Monsters in China's Health Care Reform," in *Health Care Reform and Globalisation: The US, China and Europe in Comparative Perspective*, ed. Peggy Watson (London: Routledge, 2013), 79.

90   Queer Chimerica

disease prevention, leading to the booming economy of sexual commodities. The governmental management and regulation of HIV antiviral medicine also benefited from reforming the pharmaceutical industry and reviving other public health sectors. Since 2012, both the Global Fund and the Gates Fund have started to withdraw from China, leaving the Chinese government the largest sponsor of the HIV/AIDS intervention. Yet the previously established model of fund distribution and organizational structures continue to allow the governmental agency to have a tighter hand on allocating money and managing profit.

The "filter model" has led to several issues. Because of the lack of funding for essential daily expenditures, CDC officers and activist leaders work together to appropriate the project money to sustain the groups' operations or else fatten their own wallets. At first, representatives from the donors kept their eyes half shut but soon requested more detailed financial reports from local groups. Circling the transnational donors, CDC officers, and volunteers, an attractive smart-ass like Yang Tao soon learned how to put on different hats—his good English and network with foreigners bestowed him standout skills in proposal writing, while he learned where to purchase fake invoices by following the lead of illegal lamp pole advertisements. Unless a group is blessed with somebody like Yang Tao, they barely survive. As CDCs and their long-term partner NGOs monopolize the HIV/AIDS funds, small groups die out or become scavengers fighting each other for breadcrumbs.

The volunteer job is not as easy as Gaung Hui had imagined. Three times a week, he takes the bus to the cruising parks and bathhouses, stopping men with his enthusiastic lectures about the history of AIDS, the policies of free testing and treatment, and proper condom use. When questioned by the patrolling police at the park, Guang Hui straightens his back and speaks sternly, "HIV/AIDS intervention is the national health policy." Then he softens his voice and puts on a faked cute face so out of his character, "*Jingcha shushu tongzhi* (Comrade Uncle Policeman 警察蜀黍同志),[5] HIV/AIDS is a public health issue. The government has been paying lots of attention to it. Our work is not only legal but encouraged. Here, take some of the flyers and booklets, and please help spread the word. Join our meetings if you want to learn more." Guang Hui is

---

5. The word 蜀黍 is the homophone for "uncle" 叔叔 in popular expressions. It indicates that the activist uses it to play cute, a strategy to downgrade the tensions between the cruising gay men and the police.

not a people pleaser, certainly not a police pleaser. But he understands that for the purpose of activism, sometimes one will have to be tactical and not act their personality out.

Besides the routine checks from the police, what surprises Guang Hui is the resistance from the MSM community. The cold shoulder is common. Many men at the cruising parks blame the volunteers for exposing them to societal scrutiny. One day Guang Hui gets into a quarrel with several men at Dongdan Park.

"AIDS? Where is AIDS in China? AIDS is the disease of the rich. As long as you don't get in contact with foreigners at those bars, you are not gonna get AIDS!"

"In the past, nobody noticed us, we were happy here. Thanks to the activists like you, now we are like mice scurrying across the street, chased by everyone. You made us in danger!"

"Go away, I am not gonna wear a condom! Who the heck wants to think about the disease while fucking a butthole?"

Guang Hui's sex education flyers and pamphlets are defenseless weapons facing right-in-your-face harshness. The anger of the scolding men finally cools down when Guang Hui mentions that the testing is compensated and each of them will receive twenty yuan.

In the early 2000s, due to the stigmatization of AIDS, *tongzhi* men rarely go to hospitals for routine testing. *Tongzhi* volunteers must strategically work with open-minded and nonthreatening doctors and bring them to gay bars, providing a relatively safe and private space for MSM. These doctors are usually women and middle-aged or older who come across as professional yet caring. For example, Professor Xu Zhilian at Beijing *You'an* hospital (one of the designated AIDS care hospitals in Beijing) is well-known as the "AIDS mom" among positive gay men and volunteers. She not only provides exams and treatments for those who are infected but also spends holidays and vacations caring for the poor and sick.

To gain trust, many *tongzhi* volunteers start their community mobilization with the men they sleep with. Young, devoted, and physically attractive with an agreeable personality are indispensable features to "lure" other men into either testing or being an insider-volunteer. That is perhaps why Yang Tao thought that Guang Hui would make a great volunteer leader with his exotic sexiness, when he said "Welcome to our *yi shengzhiqi wei niudai de fanzui tuanhuo* (the squad of genitals 以生殖器为纽带的犯罪团伙)" the first time they met.

One of the most effective yet problematic strategies for mobilizing is to provide cash for people who provide blood samples. For example, the Global Fund

92 Queer Chimerica

projects would pay thirty-five yuan to the contrasted grassroots groups for each vial of blood they collect (this is the price around 2005 and 2006) and the local groups usually give out twenty to twenty-five yuan to the person who undergoes testing, and then keep the rest for their own groups. In 2007 when the China-Gates Project entered the landscape, the price paid to local groups for each test conducted increased to sixty-two yuan, and the cash bonus for a positive test was three hundred yuan.[6] The Global Fund Projects also increase their bonus to sixty yuan to match the Gates projects. Typically, the blood sample providers would receive around fifty yuan as compensation. Since HIV testing before 2012 did not require a real name for registration, one person could "sell" several vials of blood to receive compensation or share their blood with others to help them pass the tests, which caused significant inaccuracy in data collection. This bonus system also led to competition among local groups and corruption among the group leaders.

Guang Hui has feelings for Yang Tao. Even though they have become travel buddies doing outreach work together in other cities and provinces, Yang Tao keeps Guang Hui at arm's length. This is before Guang Hui discovered Yang Tao's taste for white foreigners.

With the help of Yang Tao, Guang Hui soon built an extensive network of his own with people in the circle. He has become a regular at bars, bathhouses, conferences, and training workshops, excelling at lectures on the difference between HIV infection and AIDS, "Four Frees and One Care" policies, and tactics for comforting positive patients. Sometimes he brings fruit and *dianxin* (traditional Chinese cakes 点心) to the CDC doctors who provide testing at the bars or hospitals. Other volunteers start to recognize him as an HIV/AIDS intervention leader. But unlike Yang Tao, who already purchased an apartment on the east side of Beijing and a car, the middle-aged *waidi ren* (people from outside Beijing 外地人) from Harbin lives off the ¥1,500 allowance received from his organization, in addition to the generous help from his mother. For him, HIV/AIDS intervention is a sublime revolutionary cause, not an occupation. *Chi aizi fan* (feeding off of HIV/AIDS 吃艾滋饭) is impure and shameful.

The HIV/AIDS intervention has fertilized a series of lucrative industries at the juncture of China's postmedical reform pharmaceutical industry, government-sponsored NGOization, and increasingly visible LGBT culture

---

6. Miller, "Dying," 422.

and activism. But one of the important but overlooked aspects of the rise of the HIV/AIDS economy is its reliance on unpaid work by people like Guang Hui. Yet the labor and expertise of *tongzhi* are often essentialized as part of their nature or something they are supposed to have simply as being a member of the community in a way, like how racialized women who are naturalized as docile dexterous workers for the global economy. Naturalizing the "homosexual differences" in service of the HIV/AIDS economy also goes hand in hand with an internalized logic of homophobia, that is, fear of "gay sex," running deep through the intervention industry. It is often said that because *tongzhi* are at the "forefront of risk" or already "affected by HIV and doomed" due to their promiscuous lifestyle, volunteers' affective and intellectual labor is framed as "self-interest" and "self-serving" for basic survival. Hinting at the "guilt" of causing AIDS, this homophobic view prevalent in the HIV/AIDS intervention reduces structural inequality to individualist, idiosyncratic responsibility, and justifies the erasure of the "dirty job" *tongzhi* men undertake.

Yang Tao picks up Guang Hui at Dawanglu subway station and drives off to his new office at the city center. Over the years, Yang Tao has worked for different projects, assuming positions in various groups. His versatility has landed him a job at a well-funded donor agency as the Chinese-side representative. He once sent his father a picture of himself standing in front of his workplace. The prominent characters "联合国" (*lianheguo*, the United Nations) took the center of the photo while the words "艾滋" (*aizi*, AIDS) are blocked off by his head.

"I can smell the leather of a new car!" Guang Hui tries to break the awkward silence with exaggerated excitement. The two friends have not seen each other for a while. "What kind of car is it?"

"Honda Accord." The answer is brief. Yang Tao hates when Guang Hui goes out of his way to bridge their enlarged gap.

The meeting place at Yang Tao's new office is much larger, brighter, and more modern. It can host twenty to thirty people at a given time. Guang Hui sees many familiar faces—former colleagues, volunteers, and friends he met at the parks. Guang Hui is a little surprised by the sight of Lao Zhang (Old Zhang). Usually, older men at the park do not participate much in activist activities unless it is the rare meeting about reaching out to the elders. When the concept of "participatory community organizing" was first introduced by donor agencies, elders, along with other *tongzhi*, would be invited to meetings and asked about their needs to inform strategy making. Other times they would be interviewed by researchers from institutes or journalists and reporters who look for newsworthy stories, and their needs are recorded and reported. Most times, changes in their living condition rarely happen.

Lao Zhang is a walking queer encyclopedia. Rumor is that he survived both the Cultural Revolution in the 1970s, and *yanda yundong* (the anti-crime campaign 严打运动) in the 1980s; he was sent to conversion therapy and labor camps; he was discharged from the army and was expelled from his working unit because of his same-sex behaviors; he was a hero who protected younger men from being arrested by the police and he acted shamelessly begging the *chengguan* (municipal management officer 城管) on his knees when he was caught selling counterfeits at the Tian'anmen Square . . .

A voice of a squawking crow interrupts Guang Hui's thoughts, "Sis, long time no see!" Xiao Yao (meaning "Little Faerie") makes his appearance like a model catwalking in his debut fashion show. Just like his nickname, Xiao Yao is a lousy effeminate man who loves giving uninvited hugs and kisses. His oversized black denim jacket hangs loosely over a tight yellow T-shirt. His asymmetrically cut hair is styled like those in the Korean band H.O.T. "Korean style" is a euphemism; in other people's eyes, he is at best a *shamate* (the "smart" folks 杀马特), a derogatory word used by urbanites to describe rural migrants with eye-catching colorful hair and copycat punk fashion. His narrow eyes disappear when he laughs, making his crooked gray teeth more noticeable. He often introduces himself as one of the *jingcheng sida mingji* (Beijing's four hetaeras 京城四大名妓), but his fellow *tongzhi* men have not endorsed this title. After asking around what this meeting is about, Xiao Yao sits down next to Lao Zhang with crossed legs and a pouting face, "Is this event paid? I'd rather suck some old cocks than sit here wasting my time if there is no money."

Yang Tao slightly raises one eyebrow, barely captured by anyone. He despises people like Xiao Yao. Not only because he is a "money boy" who tarnishes the reputation of *tongzhi* but also because these people have been destroying the wholesome community that activists like Yang Tao have worked hard to build. When Yang Tao started his community organizing work, his peers, men and women, were all motivated by helping and caring for each other because *dajia dou henqin* (everybody is linked like a close and intimate family 大家都很亲). When there were activities—making dumplings together, hiking, singing and dancing competitions, or salon discussions—no matter how far away, people showed up and offered their time and labor. People used to chip in money just for hanging out and being there for each other. But since the groups started to pay for testing and vials, many *tongzhi* expect compensation for attending community gatherings.

In Yang Tao's eyes, Xiao Yao also does not take the volunteering work seriously. Perhaps Xiao Yao only uses the opportunity of being a volunteer to develop his *kehu qun* (circle of clients 客户群) or to increase his chance of having a one-night stand. He attends many training sessions but barely learns anything useful. He still could not distinguish between the HIV virus and AIDS. He does not follow the instruction and instead uses his own analogy when talking to other *tongzhi* and often misinforms them. Now his job is reduced to distributing condoms and pamphlets only. Simple as that. But one day, Yang Tao caught Xiao Yao *danao* (playing around 打闹) at the park. He made a scene by blowing a couple of condoms like balloons to entertain the crowds, inviting attention and laughter from passersby both *tongzhi* and non-*tongzhi*. Another time, Xiao Yao put on a rowdy show by showing his audience how to give a blow job to a banana with a condom on it.

"China's LGBT activism is hopeless." Yang Tao sighs bitterly. Because of the disappointment with volunteers like Xiao Yao, Yang Tao is a firm believer in the professionalization of activism and NGO works. Efficiency, high-quality paid work, and ability to follow instructions are key to success.

On the other side, Guang Hui finds Xiao Yao's work intriguing. Despite the overwhelming education about safe sex, an unpublished report in 2015 shows that the percentage of condom use among MSM is extremely low. A major reason that might explain the resistance to condom use by men at parks is that condoms have been associated with disease and death. This connection might be due to the medicalization, especially the pathologization of gay sex, through which anal penetration is constructed as dangerous and needs to be handled with extreme care. Many community-based *tongzhi* volunteers have been advocating for an alternative method of sex education, whereas condoms could be treated as a sex toy, primarily associated with pleasure and fun, not as a protective tool. Far from "being useless," Xiao Yao's tricks show the labor to rewire the connection between gay sex and condom use through the "pleasure principle" and expand the narrow definition of activist work. Guang Hui also thinks that it is a special talent Xiao Yao could translate jargons into the layperson's language. The vulgar expressions somehow are more memorable than a doctor's advice that often requires a Ph.D. to decipher.

Xiao Yao reminds Guang Hui of something that pushed him to rethink what volunteer work means. In the early- and mid-2000s, *fanchuan* (drag queen 反串) performances were very popular at gay bars across China. Several of the volunteers Guang Hui just met through training programs were amateur drag queens who were trained as Peking Opera performers. Guang Hui disliked this type of low-brow performance, which for him, denigrates the image of gay men

96 Queer Chimerica

and contributes to the stereotypes of gay men as "feminine perverted people."
Yet trying to be friendly and open-minded, he accepted their invitations.

On the stage, three *meinü* (beautiful women 美女) in Chinese traditional
fineries were making dirty jokes and flirting with the audience. When the audience was pumped up, the fourth queen walked out with three *xiuqiu* (silk balls
绣球)[7] and suggested an interactive game, "Gentlemen and handsome boys,
whoever catches the balls, I will marry my 'daughters' to you." The three drag
queens then threw the silk balls to the audience and asked those who caught
the "love crafts" to read the "love letters" inside to the audience. The love letters
were doggerels that read like this:

帅哥帅哥你真帅 (*shuaige shuaige ni zhenshuai*, "Hottie, hottie you are so
   hot"),
小弟弟想把你来爱 (*xiaodidi xiangba nilai ai*, "my penis wanna give you my
   love"),
为了咱两能恩爱 (*weile zanlia neng xiangai*, "but for our love to last"),
帅哥一定把套带 (*shuaige yiding ba tao dai*, "I'll get you a condom to put
   on")!

The queens' interactive performances were welcomed by both the audience and the gay bar owners. In the past, when volunteers reached out to gay
bar owners for HIV/AIDS intervention and condom promotion activities, the
owners rarely participated, fearing that their activities would impact the business or be misunderstood by the police as promoting illegal sexual activities.
But the performances brought more patrons to the bars, and many bar owners
became supportive of the intervention activities. Like the drag queens, *tongzhi*
Peking opera, crosstalk, and skit performers also worked hard to incorporate
HIV/AIDS-related knowledge, including condom use, national policies, and
how to provide care for positive persons and each other into their shows, even
though they were not the official volunteers. These strategies helped to build a
closer community through intimate labor and improved the self-identification
and a sense of belonging among many *tongzhi* and gay men.

In three months, the activist-drag queens created a series of AIDS
intervention–related performances and games, touring different bars, before
they were accused of being "not scientific," "not serious," and the monkey business of the low *sushi* (quality 素质) people. Within the volunteer communi-

---

7. *pao xiuqiu*, or "throwing the silk ball" 抛绣球 is a traditional game in the Guangxi
region where young women show their affection for men by throwing the ball at them.

ties, people discussed whether their activities should be considered volunteer work. After *qingshi* (asking for advice 请示) from some activist leaders, Yang Tao included, the conclusion was that their activities were *not* proper volunteer work. The volunteers of high *sushi* created some other activities at the bars, such as AIDS trivia, and offered prizes. But the patrons were not buying into it, complaining "We are here for fun, not for taking exams," and asking for refunds of the entry fees and drinks from the owners. As a result, the volunteers were asked by the owners to just leave their outreach material and condoms at the bar for those who were interested, significantly reducing the quality of the intervention. Nevertheless, as long as the task of distributing certain numbers of condoms was finished, the work was considered done, and the rewards collected.

The training today is about how to design and organize *shequ canyushi ganyu* (community-based participatory interventions 社区参与式干预). Unlike the "top-down" expert-led model, the participatory model aims to inspire community members to share their wisdom and needs in the intervention, regardless of their class, occupation, and location. Many activities are organized around how to desensitize the taboo of AIDS and raise consciousness through creative and entertaining designs. Expert labor often focuses on the professional "dry knowledge" inaccessible to many ordinary *tongzhi* audiences; participatory labor is to translate this knowledge into lay-person language. The professionals are more interested in teaching the mechanism of AIDS and advocating for rights and legalization, but the community participants are more curious about proper ways of condom use, the differences among lubricants, and so on.

Yang Tao starts the meeting with his signature smile and soft voice, "The leading principle of participatory intervention is to promote equality. We respect opinions from all walks of life. We will discuss issues like '419' (one-night stand), 'MB' (money boys), and rights and responsibilities of positive individuals, and so on. Please keep in mind that we need to actively listen to others even when their views are different from our own. There is a feedback board called 'the Parking Lot' outside the room, where we can leave the unresolved debates and unsolved problems from today's meeting there and revisit them next time we meet."

Then he hands out some cards to the participants for the introduction session. On the cards, there are word combinations such as "肛/交" (anus/intercourse), "艾滋/病毒" (AIDS/virus), and "安全/套" (safe/ noose). Each person introduces themself to the person who receives the card with the matching

98   Queer Chimerica

word. Some first-timers blush and giggle, but experienced oldies like Xiao Yao and Lao Zhang initiate the introductions with confidence. This game is called "speed dating." After the introduction, each pair goes to another pair for a role play. For example, the couple with the "安全/套" (condom) plays the protectors for the couple who receives "肛/交" (anal intercourse). Warm-up games like this one have been used to *xinli tuomin* (psychologically desensitize 心里脱敏) and *yong pingchangxin duidai* (treat with an ordinary mind 用平常心对待) the discussions of gay sex and AIDS.

Although Yang Tao does not like these games as he believes entertainment derails the agenda of education, he is good at putting aside his own opinions in public, separating his personal identity as a gay man from his work role as a community leader. Unlike Yang Tao, many volunteers do not see their work and pleasure as compartmentalized. They prefer to *wan zhe jiu ba gongzuo zuole* (do their job while playing 玩着就把工作做了).

Xiao Yao shares with the group, "I admit I am *feng* (lousy 疯) and *nao* (mess around 闹) in 'the circle' a lot, and I like to amuse people at the cruising parks and bathhouses. I do not like to analyze too much and put a burden on my own shoulders. I like to listen to lectures by scholars, doctors, and professionals, but I myself do not understand much and don't know how to teach the big principles to others. I have my own ways of raising consciousness. When I go to the bathhouses, I often make a big scene, yelling at people, 'Condoms, condoms, no condom, no play!' Everybody knows about my flamboyant personality and tolerates my lousy behavior. I can be versatile as well. When I meet 'newbies,' I play the experienced big brother and show my *xinteng* (care 心疼)[8] for the young people; when I meet masculine tops, I play cute and feminine, acting like I need their protections. In the past, sex among them was something under the table, done secretly. But now, buying condoms from the bathhouse owners is as common as buying a pack of cigarettes. I cannot say if my way is effective, but at least what I do makes gay sex and AIDS something aboveboard. Most *tongzhi* men at parks and bathhouses are not going to attend lectures. I come to those places to mess around twice a week, so at least they can hear some condom-use and AIDS prevention reminders."

Xiao Yao is a pro at being flexible and wearing different faces. A drag queen of life. The value of Xiao Yao's work is praised by some, among whom are also sex workers, immigrants, or low-income folks. But this type of "shoddy" labor is difficult to be recognized and measured by rubrics and protocols of activist leaders, or donor sponsors and therefore rarely compensated. The "looking

---

8. The direct translation of the word should be "heartache," meaning being protective or showing care for someone.

for fun" approach is not only "hardly presentable" to the transnational NGO donors but also "nonprofitable" in terms of attracting stable sources of funding, compared to the "rights-violation" approach.

After the meeting, Yang Tao answers a phone call. His phone buzzed several times during the meeting, but he left it unanswered. At the other end, is a high-pitched female voice. The indistinct conversation seems to irritate Yang Tao at first, and his impatience soon turns to annoyance, "I already told you. I am busy next week and won't make it to the family dinner. I have a meeting abroad!" He lies. "How about you order a cake for him, and I will pay for it. And help me to give him a red package. I will give you 2000 *kuai* tomorrow. I beg you, sister."

Yang Tao quickly resumes his tenderness after he hangs up. This smile he gives to everyone he meets is such a luxury for his own family. The last time he went back home was on his father's birthday. He bought the old man a Motorola cellphone. Cellphones were young folks' privilege in the early 2000s. Father must be overwhelmed by this unusual present. Yang Tao showed him how to set up ringtones, save contacts, dial numbers, and send and receive text messages with rare patience and excitement. In rejoicing, Father commented, "Tao Tao, you are my portal to a new world. Without you, how will I keep up with the changing society? You should get married and have a child of your own before it gets too late. When you get old, who will show you the latest technology and be your doors and windows to a new world?" Yang Tao stormed out of the room and regretted ever stopping by.

Yang Tao tucks his Nokia in his belt case and sees Guang Hui, Lao Zhang, and Xiao Yao walking out of the office building. He offers the gang a ride to the subway station. Diving into the front seat right away, Xiao Yao flips down the sun visor to check his hair in the vanity mirror. When Yang Tao opens the rear door and invites Lao Zhang in, Lao Zhang smiles at the handsome man, "Your name is Yang Tao? The 'ocean waves.' *Jingtao hailang, chushi bujing* (amidst the raging waves, remain calm and composed 惊涛骇浪, 处事不惊). I guess the one who named you must have hoped you to keep a level head even in the face of greatest adversity."

Yang Tao is caught off guard by the strange comment, not noticing that Guang Hui has drifted away. He drives up, signaling Gaung Hui to get in the car. But Guang Hui waves his hand as he continues his pace, "It's okay, I'd like to take a walk by myself."

CHAPTER 8

Zhang Shanping the Hooligan II

"To infiltrate the enemy's core," thought Yang Zhongguo, as he trailed Zhang Shanping through the dense pine forests that guarded the land of prohibition. The sneaky sodomite had always managed to slip away, leaving Yang with nothing but disappointment. Tonight, it is different though. As Yang prepares to leave empty-handed once again, a sudden burst of light illuminates the hillside. In a billowing curtain of opaque clouds, a heptagon-shaped object shoots out seven shafts of purple light from its bottom. Is it a secret weapon from the Soviets or the Americans? Before Yang Zhongguo can make any sense of it, the men and women in the woods are lifted like helium balloons floating in the air. In the light beams, he spots Zhang Shanping. Their eyes cross. Afraid of being sucked in or, perhaps even more, of being recognized by Zhang Shanping, Yang Zhongguo turns around and dashes away like a headless fly. Then the ground tilts. In unconsciousness, his head meets the earth.

When Yang Zhangguo opens his eyes again, he finds himself in a stark white room. Minimalist in design, the room offers no clue as to where or when he is. But the line of Mandarin characters etched into the wall gives him some comfort: "一不足矣"—One is Not Enough.

When he awes for the electroplate work of the words, a technology that seems out of place in his own time, he is suddenly spooked by a holographic screen quietly shimmering behind him. The display recognizes Yang's face and unlocks itself automatically, projecting a catalog on the screen: history, arts, culture, and lifestyle. The list goes on. As Yang Zhongguo's eyes stop on the "lifestyle" tab, subcategories unfold alphabetically. He scrolls up and down the list and makes its final haul at the word "anus."

Options under the tab "anus" read like the following:

"What is it like to have hemorrhoids?"
"What is it like to have anal sex?"
"What is it like to have anal sex with hemorrhoids?"

Yang Zhongguo feels his ears burning, but out of curiosity, his eyes stop at the last line. "What is it like to have anal sex with hemorrhoids in the Cultural Revolution?"

No time to be embarrassed by his selection, a vivid purple holographic armor materializes around his body, snugging him like an electrified noose. Then a woman in her thirties shows up on the screen. Black leather jacket, white shirt, and bristle short hair, nothing resembles the look of Yang Zhongguo's own time. What she *does* resemble to Yang Zhongguo, however, is her silent rebelliousness behind the faked confidence and her forced smile. Yang Zhongguo steals a glance at her name tag: Dr. Yang Xiaofei.

The name takes him by surprise. Were he to have a daughter, "Xiaofei" would be the name he had always envisioned for her. To fly above all life's constraints. But just as he is about to utter a word, the scene shifts. Now, he finds himself floating above another white room, observing himself from a God-like vantage point. Doctors and nurses scramble around, attaching paddles to his chest. A middle-aged man joins his hands, crooning a ballad about the Volunteer Army crossing the Yalu River. A small box with wires charged up, hummed with electricity. The sudden jolt of energy causes the lifeless body to convulse, but the heart monitor shows no beep. As the doctor administers one final shock, Yang Zhongguo is jolted awake, drenched in cold sweats. In the deafening thuds and lingering echoes of anguished sobs, he soon realizes that somebody is indeed pounding on his door.

"You . . . you gotta help me, comrade Yang!" Zhang Shanping gasps, glancing around. "Something strange happened here," he points to his head and lowers his voice, "it's . . . like many people are living in my head!"

"You are delusional, Comrade Zhang. Seek a doctor's aid." Yang Zhongguo steps one foot back, wary of the agitated man.

"I can't go to a doctor! Won't they lock me up and treat me like a lunatic?"

Yang Zhongguo offers no solace. "Well, I fail to see why lunacy is worse than thuggery. At least you will be locked up in a hospital, not a labor camp or a prison . . . But I am sorry, Comrade Zhang, I cannot help you." He begins to shut the door but feels a grip on his arm. Zhang Shanping's grubby hand clasps a crumpled piece of paper, which he unfurls, revealing a time-worn certificate of Honorary Communist Member. The certificate bears Yang Zhongguo's own name, but with a future date.

102   Queer Chimerica

"What is this? How did you obtain such nonsense?" Yang Zhongguo jerks his arm away from Zhang Shanping's sweaty filthy grasp.

"Comrade Yang, I know you can help me!" Pleads the desperate hooligan. "Because . . . because I saw you there. You were one of them, one of us!"

"You know not what you speak of . . ."

Years have passed. Yang Zhongguo cocoons himself in the warm glow of an overhead light. He opens an envelope and basks in the joy upon glimpsing the photographs of his family. He hasn't seen his wife since last Spring Festival, and his children have grown unrecognizable.

A decade ago, the couple was stirred by Chairman Mao's fervor to build the Third Front and moved to the Mountain City. Yang Zhongguo's wife was soon transferred back to Beijing as her spinal disc herniation worsened, leaving Yang Zhongguo alone to pursue his great career of building socialism. The distance granted him a reprieve from the duty of being a husband and a father; though he grappled with guilt, he could not deny the pleasant relief it brought him. But the end of his carefree days is drawing near since a rising-star engineer from the capital is eager to put socialist principles into practice with his own hands.

Yang Zhongguo carefully sits the letter and pictures into the tin box, joining the other letters he has received over the years. Immediately his mind jumps to another box, "What am I supposed to do with Zhang Shanping's confessions now that he is gone?" He gazes at the sage-colored wall that looms above his bed, adorned with a jumbled display of certificates of merit. Finally, he plucks one from the left, revealing a minuscule keyhole hidden beneath. He unlocks the pigeon-cage door-sized lock and reaches for a puzzle box.

Zhang Shanping gifted it to him.

Coworkers were convinced that Zhang Shanping must have descended into madness amid the tumultuous confessions and struggle sessions. Some colleagues lost interest in the "exposing crimes" frenzy that had overtaken the Party, while others were empathic and suggested sending Zhang to Nanjing where he could be treated by Dr. Lu Longguang, an expert in sexual perversion and conversion therapy.

Yang Zhongguo had a different theory. Taking advantage of his cadre position, he conversed with Zhang Shanping for a long while without raising any unnecessary suspicions from his coworkers. It was clear to him that Zhang Shanping was implanted with artificial memories after the strange encounter at the hill. The idea sounded scandalous to a Marxist atheist like himself, but not

Zhang Shanping the Hooligan II   103

entirely impossible. After all, hadn't the Soviets and Americans experimented with mind transfer on animals? And China had already succeeded in launching the "Two Bombs and One Satellite" in the 1960s; *chaoying ganmei* (catching up with the British and Americans 超英赶美) would be just around the corner. Who knows about other secret advancements that had been made?

So, Yang Zhongguo had been studying Zhang Shanping like a science project. Sometimes Zhang Shanping would look off into space with darting eyes, this was when the flashbacks happened; other times, he seemed more coherent and talked about others in the first person. Sometimes he made up words or spoke languages Yang didn't understand, and other times, he buried his face crying in his sleeves nonstop. The headaches and heartaches brought by implanted memories also caused Zhang Shanping to lose his own, and that was when the records of his confessions became handy. As they grew closer through the confessions, Yang Zhongguo discovered that being a hooligan was not Zhang Shanping's only sin. They had found their shared interests in banned books, *ditai* (enemy's radio stations 敌台), and bird catching.

One evening after curfew, Zhang Shanping met Yang Zhongguo in the heater room to share another confession about his implanted memory:

"I was twenty years old in 1949. Chairman Mao said that the youths are like the eight o'clock sun, the world belongs to us. The civil war just ended not long ago, and we were sent to chase Chiang Kai-shek, or so we thought . . .

"We were cramped in the tank, and I sensed the air getting colder. When the sun was made seen to us again, I realized that we were on the bank of the Yalu River, sent to Pyongyang to support the Volunteer Army! . . . *Kangmei yuanchao* (fighting Americans and supporting North Korea 抗美援朝) was the most brutal war I had ever seen; it was a war between humans and machines. At least you have seen the Japanese, right? But you don't see the Americans at all. There were only fighter jets, bombs, tanks, mortars, and machine guns . . . The whole time I was there, I didn't see a single American face. When you don't see faces, you would doubt whether you are fighting with other humans, right? You would fear and demonize them, right? . . . Except when a group of injured captives was sent to our clinic. When the helmet was removed from the young soldier, to my surprise, he was black.

   . . . . . .

"I lost a leg in an air raid and was sent back to Dandong. After returning, my rank was raised, and my disability rewarded me with a comfortable position. Soon I learned that some nemesis got jealous and wanted to denigrate me when my supervisor threw a report of an allegation of male-male indecent behavior in front of me. I had to be transferred again."

104 Queer Chimerica

"Did you have male-male indecency?" Yang Zhongguo interrupted.

"Of course not! I swear to Chairman Mao, I was born to be loyal to the nation, how could I . . ."

Zhang Shanping scratched his head and closed his eyes, overwhelmed by the implanted life that didn't belong to him. The pain surged through him, flooding his senses.

"Well, during wartime, we had to save anesthesia for surgeries. One time, I received a young soldier whose injury was beyond heaven to help. No need to waste medicine on someone who was in the hand of *Yanwang* (Lord of Death 阎王). But how could I leave him in agony like that? As he lay in my arms passing, he asked me if I had met Chairman Mao. I had not. But I told him that Mao's son was here in Pyongyang too. For some reason, I couldn't help touching his face, chest, legs . . . and he fell asleep against my chest, coldly.

"After that, I became sick. Images of blood, shit, and cum haunted my mind, like the resentful specters haunted the Yalu River. Touching the dying soldiers quenched my anguish, the anguish and agony that only numbness and self-destruction could contain, and eventually, I was caught by a supervisor. I knew I would be discharged and lose everything. The dark spot of my soul will be put on my taintless record for everybody to see and gossip about, and the stigma of a disguising pervert will be my ghostly shadow chasing me till my days' end. My family would despise me, and the young woman I was fond of would not marry me . . .

"One day, a bomb hit the hospital I worked at in Sinuiju. In the debris, the superior cried out for help, but his mouth was muted by pouring blood. And I, the only one under Chairman Mao's ubiquitous eyes who heard his desperate silence, who could save him or end his suffering, just laid still, witnessing his bitter passing in front of me."

Head bowed, Zhang Shanping shivered. His eyes fixed on his shaking hands as if he could see and smell the blood. When he raised his head again, he suddenly noticed that Yang Zhongguo was missing his right leg! A shabby prosthetic limb hung listlessly in his pants. How on earth had he never noticed it before?! Now he understood everything.

Zhang Shanping inched closer to Yang Zhongguo. In the cacophonic damp air of the heater room, he placed his hand on Yang's leg, at the very end where his teardrop and the prosthetic met. Their boundaries dissolved into each other as if the shared memory of betrayal and guilt could melt metal into water, reformulating what could be new and stronger. A very long time passed before a sigh escaped from Yang Zhongguo's lips.

"How ironic," he said. "My name is Yang Zhongguo (杨忠国), to be loyal to the nation, but I ended up being a traitor to the country, to my own comrades. Years later, I learned that the superior never reported me at all. No matter what I do now, I will never be able to *xibai* (wash clean 洗白) myself."

Zhang Shanping squeezed out a self-taunting smile and offered his comfort, "My name is Zhang Shanping (张善平), to be kind and have a peaceful life, but my life ended up nothing kind and peaceful. That's probably why there is an old saying that you should name your children the opposite of what you wish them to become."

"Perhaps it is a true blessing to place oneself in the shoes of others, to learn from the pain and betrayal that life can offer, and to become better equipped to care for those around us," Yang Zhongguo whispered, his face stricken, his heart broken. "I remember trembling with fear each night during the war, deprived of sleep and plagued by anxiety. The only time I could fall asleep was when I was surrounded by my comrades. Maybe for truly becoming kind and at peace with all things, one person alone is not enough."

"But why me? A shameless hooligan, a damned sodomite!"

"Even I have seen inexplicable things, Comrade Zhang. My son blooming into adulthood, a granddaughter yet to be born, and the finish line of my one lifetime . . . . . . Perhaps they are the glitters from the future, harbingers of our resilience, our survival, our capacity to overcome obstacles."

The words had their power. Zhang Shanping rose to his feet and slipped behind the growling heater. Emerging once more into the dim, yellow light, he presented a small coffer to Yang Zhongguo. Deftly solving the puzzle lock affixed to the box, Zhang Shanping revealed its contents: a handful of Chairman Mao icons, some small tools, and a collection of metal rods and mineral rocks.

"I don't need these anymore." His voice was soaked with sadness. "The 'model of labor' bench worker in me has been long gone." Zhang Shanping tossed the junk into the furnace. Their dull glimmer was consumed by the bright, ephemeral flames that danced before them, red, blue, then purple.

"This is your confession now," Zhang Shanping extended the puzzle box toward Yang Zhongguo, "how about you keep the vault so that you can look after the past."

My damned hallucination! A hexagon flying object? A coffer with a puzzle lock? A certificate with a future date? And my grandfather with a sodomite? What is this made-up bullshit that is playing tricks on me?

106   Queer Chimerica

My first instinct is to reach out to Andrei for help before my senses get completely shredded by the out-of-control noise and distorted reality jumps. Or should I? A suspicion creeps into my mind. Why are the stolen Beets and the noises bleeding into one another? Why have I never experienced interference with my perception before? And why has Andrei not even mentioned once the identity of the donor, whom I am also unable to reverse-image? It all seems too strange, too convenient, too orchestrated.

My mind is getting murkier. Faces of people I know and don't know crowd upon one another. In a wild roar of voices, there rise two scenes. One seems like a bird, an eagle, or an owl, with its wings stripped of feathers, grayish pink bones revealing its fragile ugliness. The other, exactly like in the movie *Inception* (2010), the whole world opens up, and the skyscrapers fall upon one another, swallowing me with their horrid emptiness. Suddenly sorrow and fear turn to rage; I am enraged. I can't even make sense of the system I invented, can I?

What comforts me in this helplessness is the music. The vapid noises from a distance turn into melodies. The bass drum is jumpy, and the broken lyrics of "Come Out" from Grasshopper become coherent.

It is in the orgy of images, phantoms, and sounds that I see the schoolgirl in the indigo uniform and Dr. Martens again. I stand up to follow her, to chase her. When she turns her head, I see that the girl is in fact myself, a self I can no longer recognize.

CHAPTER 9

Beijing Comrades I

The teenager pauses the cassette and pulls out her earbuds. She rubs her back against the pole at the bus station and peeks at her Swatch sporadically. The reflection of her face on the large navy dial looks anxious but exciting. Her appearance needs to be flawless. A black Mercedes pulls over, the window rolls down, she smiles, and asks the man in the driver seat, "'Lipstick Lan Yu'? Hop in!"

Yang Xiaofei met Boss Jiang at "Beijing Tongzhi," the largest gay online chat room in China in the late 1990s. "Lan Yu" and "Handong" were two popular usernames in many gay chat rooms. They are the protagonists of the popular gay-themed novel *Beijing Gushi* (Beijing Story 《北京故事》).[1] In this gay Cinderella story, the profligate son of a retired Communist official Chen Handong falls fatally in love with college student Lan Yu who comes from a small town to Beijing to attend university. Handong showers Lan Yu with extravagant gifts including clothes, cars, and villas while maintaining sexual relationships with other men and women. Despite Handong's realization of his true feeling for Lan Yu after the Tian'anmen upheaval, the man decides to break up with Lan Yu and marries a woman. Years go by but the love remains, and Lan Yu eventually bails out Handong, who commits financial corruption, from jail. Finally, the decades-long love story ends with Lan Yu's tragic death before the couple settles down for a stable life.

Beijing Gushi was written by a woman under the pseudonym "Beijing Tongzhi." The novel was first published on Chinese American-based gay BBS www.

---

1. The novel was translated into English as *Beijing Comrades* by Scott Myers and published in North America in 2016.

108   Queer Chimerica

csssm.org, also known as *taohong man tianxia* (桃红满天下)[2] and republished on mainland literature website *yifan wang* (亦凡网) in 1998. It was later adapted into the film *Lan Yu* by well-known Hong Kong director Stanley Kwan in 2001.

In 1999, Boss Jiang was twenty-eight years old, and Yang Xiaofei sixteen, just like when Handong met Lan Yu in the novel. In his Mercedes, Boss Jiang was allured by the smooth face of the beautiful "boy." The boy was shy, and unlike on the phone, he only replied when a question was asked. It was almost dangerously love at first sight. Boss Jiang tried to press a kiss on the boy's lips while reaching between his legs, but Yang Xiaofei dodged and pulled away, face blushed. Boss Jiang interpreted this reaction as the "innocence and purity" of a virgin teenager; he *was* the perfect Lan Yu for the successful businessman, except it was not a *he*.

———————

"It worked out!" Yang Xiaofei whooped and pulled the rolled socks out of her crotch, a trick she had just learned from the film *Boys Don't Cry* (1999), "I don't think these are necessary!"

Yang Xiaofei was my partner in crime in high school. We dressed up like boys to date gay men we met in online chatrooms. I constantly worried that my face was too girly, my voice too high, and my breasts too perky, but she pulled off the stunt easily every time. The truth of gender didn't matter, as long as the fairytale was fulfilled.

"You get what you want if you deliver the fantasy right," she was as wise as an owl, "gay men are men, after all."

Classmates gossiped that we were homosexuals. But I never saw her as my girlfriend. "Girlfriend" was too pale to describe what we had. She was the only one with whom I enjoyed endless conversations and arguments, from history to geography, black holes to Marxism, Michel Foucault to String Theory. Even in her most naïvely hysteric moments, she took hold of me more powerfully than any others did. She was the only one there who patiently stood with my shameless adolescent anger, despair, and insecurity, listening with great curiosity to

---

2. "CSSM" stands for the "Chinese Society for Sexual Minorities." It was a group of diasporic Chinese scholars and professionals based in North America with the goals to promote the depathologization of homosexuality, introduce international research to China and facilitate cross-regional collaborations. It was founded in September 1997 by Er Yan (pseudonym) in Los Angeles, and *taohong man tianxia* was both an online journal and a website with an interactive Bulletin Board System (BBS) created by the group. This website has remained inactive since 2007.

my narcissistic dream of saving the world. When she eventually turned her back on me, she remained significant to me for the many years that followed.

But now, we are standing in the chilly morning at the observatory mounted on the hilltop. The indigo glow of the sky is giving way to pinkish purple. The orange sun behind the mountain range sends its velvety warmth to the cold setting moon. Soon there will be two suns. One red, the other blue. She turns and whispers to me, "Sometimes our most brilliant moments come from reflecting the radiance of others." Her words stir something within me, "Perhaps we are quantum entangled," I think to myself.

Yang Xiaofei grew up in Shenzhen, one of the four Economic Special Zones opened after Deng Xiaoping's 1992 southern tour, before moving back to Beijing for middle school. Her dad spent half of the year idling in the rural areas hunting inspirations for his books nobody would bother to read, and couldn't care less about his untenured university position. Her mom, a model-drama dancer at a state-run art troupe turned businesswoman, amassed a fortune through investments in stocks and real estate. Despite divorce being uncommon in the 1990s, it was inevitable for this unmatched couple.

I envied Yang Xiaofei's fluent English, as well as the cool pencil sharpeners, erasers, and backpacks her mom got her from Hong Kong, which she often dismissively gave away. At fifteen, she passed the TOEFL exam with ease while I struggled to distinguish between the pronunciation of "keys" and "kiss." She dressed fashionably, but her tight floral "chicken-leg" jeans were a subject of ridicule among classmates who gossiped about her "family misfortune." Her privilege of having seen the world outside mainland China at a young age intimidated us, the "Mainlander bumpkins."

I wasn't a fan of her chicken-leg jeans either, but I fell in love with her immediately after our chit-chat about the affairs between French poets Arthur Rimbaud and Paul Verlaine in a PE class. Knowing that someone else in the world had heard of "The Drunken Boat" lifted me out of the shithole we called "adolescence." From that point on, we started calling each other "A" and "W"[3] and exchanged coded love poems in class. In 1996 American fast food restaurant A&W opened its first franchise in Beijing, and without a doubt, it became our favorite spot for trading "tales of anal sex" and meeting other queer folks. We loved people watching, inventing their gay affairs to entertain each other; we giggled, we cracked up, and we strictly followed the law that everyone is gay until proven otherwise. The root beer float tasted like mosquito repellent to our Chinese taste buds, but it gave us an excuse to skip school and act out our bratty

---

3. The Chinese translation for "Verlaine" is *weierlun* 魏尔伦, starting with the letter "W."

110 Queer Chimerica

protest against the overwhelming educational system. Sometimes we walked for miles to check out pirate vendors at subway stations, hoping to find another banned queer movie. We had watched *Farewell My Concubine* (1993), *East Palace, West Palace* (1996), *Velvet Goldmine* (1998), *Total Eclipse* (1995), and *Interview with the Vampire* (1994) together. But the dream was to hear our favorite lines from *Beijing Gushi* spoken aloud on the silver screen, and thanks to the blood-sucking media capitalism, it didn't take long for that dream to come true.

At the illegal street vendor, Yang Xiaofei pretends to sift through the box of VCDs wrapped in flimsy plastic, and after the fruitless search, she blurts out: "So . . . do you by any chance have the movie *Lan Yu*?"

"*Lan Yu*? The blue universe?" The vendor raises an eyebrow, "We don't sell educational documentaries here."

"No, no," Yang Xiaofei leans in closer and covers her mouth, "You know, the . . . the . . . homosexual movie that just came out."

"Oh . . ." the vendor smirks, "Well, we are not *that* kind of seller either . . ." Assuming that the girl is looking for pornography.

Luckily enough, we did end up with a *qiangban* (枪版) copy, one recorded by someone with a hand-held camera from a Hong Kong theater.

The film was such a disappointment!

The next day, Yang Xiaofei stormed into the classroom, snatched the math homework I was struggling to finish before class started, and shouted out loud, "What an inauthentic portrayal of life in China! How could they use '*jichengche*,' instead of '*da di*' to refer to taking a taxi?[4] And why did they replace the socialist 'Eighth Route Army's Song' that Chen Handong sings to Lan Yu with a Taiwanese love ballad by Huang Pin-Yuan?"

I agreed. Despite the fact that the film was shot in our familiar hometown,[5] *Lan Yu* was not intended to be an "authentic" depiction of queer life in postsocialist China. Only in hindsight did I realize how much this "transregional Sinophone production" from "outside of the geopolitical China proper"[6] was at odds with the immediate world of the two schoolgirls we were, and how much she felt, once again, that something belonged to her was snatched away.

---

4. The former is the Hong Kong expression for calling a taxi while the latter is the Beijing dialect.

5. The film was shot without an authorized permit by the State Administration of Radio, Film and Television, therefore making it "illegal."

6. See Howard Chiang, "(De)Provincializing China: Queer Historicism and Sinophone Postcolonial Critique," in *Queer Sinophone Cultures*, eds. Howard Chiang and Ari Larissa Heinrich (New York: Routledge, 2014), 37.

Beijing Comrades I 111

In the late 1990s and early 2000s, when the novel and film were first popularized, the PRC shifted from the "world factory" to the "venture capitalist investor." The changes from the cheap "yellow" labor to valuable "red" capital in the processes of racialized capitalist accumulation heightened long-lasting national anxiety intertwined with nationalist pride that could be (and in fact had been) turned into national aggression. The economic wonder of the PRC reigniting the century-long myth of the Oriental menace in the white, Western world is mixed with an internalized consciousness of civilizational inferiority in the awakening Chinese mass. These changes in material conditions of the late 1990s and early 2000s onwards evoked queer scholars and cultural producers to ask what the "Chinese characteristics" of queerness really are, thus informing Chinese queer cinema for years to follow.

Briefly speaking, queer cinema in the PRC and its international reputation emerged at a time when three prominent transnational phenomena overlapped in the early 1990s: post–Cold War reconfiguration of global economy, postcolonial revitalization of the "subaltern" knowledge, and the institutionalization of queer studies and the NGOization of LGBT and feminist activism. Arguably, the earliest queer films could be traced to Chen Kaige's *Farewell My Concubine* (1993) and Zhang Yuan's *East Palace, West Palace* (1996), the first couple to broach the topics of male same-sex relationships in China. These innovations are often highly praised not only because they make visible marginalized subjects of cinema but also for disputing the socialist state studio system and setting precedents for the international distribution pattern of mainland Chinese films. Before the 1990s, the continental Chinese art cinema auteur was played by the "Fifth Generation" directors, such as Chen Kaige and Zhang Yimou whose films were produced within the state studio system. Beginning in the early 1990s, however, the "Sixth Gens" started to replace the Fifth Gens representing Chinese art house on a global stage, as directors began to step away from the *zhuxuanlü* (main melody, meaning "official propaganda" 主旋律) films and received funding from multiple international sources.[7] Since the Sixth Gens' films are not produced by state-owned studios, and therefore not recognized officially, they are labeled as "independent" in a sense that the directors have one foot in and the other outside the system, not in a sense that they are

---

7. Zhang Yuan's *Mama* (1990) was the first to disrupt the socialist state studio system and to receive funding from international sources. See Jason McGrath, *Postsocialist Modernity: Chinese Cinema, Literature, and Criticism in the Market Age* (Stanford: Stanford University Press, 2008), 131–32.

112 Queer Chimerica

"nonprofit driven."[8] Shaped by the market logic of the international art house that demanded particular types of "Chinese cultural products," artistic innovations in the 1990s invested greatly in exploring the "raw and unpleasant reality" of post-Mao China through the aestheticism of "postsocialist realism" largely distinct from propaganda-like "socialist realism."[9]

Around the same time, the PRC witnessed a "cultural fever" in the fields of social science, literature, and arts, and humanities that aimed to dispute the Maoist ideology of class struggle and to turn Western liberal humanism into means of statecraft. Under the zeitgeist of post-1990 "reform and opening," the "homosexual," not unlike other "fringe figures" such as women, migrant workers, villagers, and underground artists and musicians, were treated as raw material of a modernizing project,[10] and their visibility was regarded as the barometer against which the nation's progress level could be measured. Informed by both the convention of the international arthouse and the Chinese "cultural fever," directors in the 1990s naturally found the homosexual an ideal actor to soothe their ache for humanist liberation as well as for fame and profit. One prominent feature of this postsocialist development of non-*zhu xuanlü* arts and films is its reliance on the production of a distinctively pronounced "homosexual identity" and their conflicts with social norms—sometimes ending up tragic and other times revolutionary—to be consumed by a curious mainstream audience who *lieqi* (hunts for the bizarre and the exotic 猎奇) to simultaneously sympathize with and to keep a safe distance from.[11]

---

8. The early Sixth Gen directors should also be distinguished from the later "independent," "urban generation," and "underground" directors who have diminishing connections with the state studios.

9. McGrath, *Postsocialist Modernity*, 132.

10. See Rey Chow, *Primitive Passions: Visuality, Sexuality, Ethnography, and Contemporary Chinese Cinema* (New York: Columbia University Press, 1995) for more details. In Chow's analysis, the underprivileged people, women in this case, often become "a source of fascination that helps to renew, rejuvenate, and 'modernize' . . . cultural production in terms both of subject matter and form" (21). Using Zhang Yimou's films in the 1980s and the 1990s, Chow goes on to explain how women's bodies are used to display a simultaneous primitive and liberating sexuality that represents "China's 'barbaric' cultural institutions" (47). Although Chow's original formula does not address queer and sexual minorities, I think her observation on the relationship between sexualized primitivity and the discourse of the transition from oppression to a progressive enlightenment can be applied to the representations of queerness in Chinese cinema as well.

11. The enormous public appetite for consuming the "bizarre and the exotic" in the late 1980s and 1990s is evident in the growing number of tabloids and popular magazines that featured stories of queer sexuality, discussed in Chapter 6.

Concomitantly, stemming from the "new documentary film movement,"[12] queer documentary films and docudramas also contributed to an "alternative archive"[13] that raised the consciousness of queer invisibility in the heteronormative society. Against being represented by men and straight women filmmakers who often highlight the sadness of the homosexual characters with dark, slow, and melancholic auteur styles, [14] queer-identified filmmakers emphasized the specificity of LGBT identities and often possessed blatant political appeal.[15] Sharing similarities with the Sixth Gens, many queer documentaries in the 1990s and 2000s invoked notable sensitivities to the sociopolitical situations of LGBT subjects and political activist responsibility, and incorporated liberalist and feminist overtones in conceptualizing identity formation and agency of women and the marginalized.[16] Among all, Shi Tou, Cui Zi'en and He Xiaopei (and later Fan Popo and Wei Jiangang) are often thought of as the most acclaimed artists and filmmakers who not only provided sharp critiques of normative gender and sexuality, but also pioneered LGBT organization and film festivals under strict authoritarian rules. They make visible the tensions between heterosexual family and individual freedom, Chinese traditions and globalization, and questions of individual identity and kinship, but more prominently utilize queer intimacy, sexuality, and body as forms of feminist and queer intervention within contested political spaces.[17]

In addition to the proliferation of queer representations in the international arthouse cinema and Chinese independent films, queer visibility in the post-2000 media was shaped by cross-geocultural flows of androgenous idol cultures

---

12. Chris Berry, Lü Xinyu, and Lisa Rofel, eds., *The New Chinese Documentary Film Movement: For the Public Record* (Hong Kong: Hong Kong University Press, 2010).

13. Berry, Lü, and Rofel, *Chinese Documentary*, 137.

14. Chris Berry, "Happy Alone?: Sad Young Men in East Asian Gay Cinema," *Journal of Homosexuality* 39, no. 3–4 (2000): 187–200, https://doi.org/10.1300/J082v39n03_07. In this article, Berry gives a thorough account of how the prevalent representation of the sad young East Asian gay men is associated with a particular type of signification of the East Asian individual as a lonely outcast without a role in the traditional family system (197). He also notes that this trope seems to have been mostly invented for mainstream culture rather than by and for gays themselves, adding to "the range of circulating and visible potential models and images of oneself to negotiate with and work off" (198). One of the goals of my book is to show different kinds of queer representations beyond the "sad model."

15. Shi-Yan Chao, *Queer Representations in Chinese-language Film and the Cultural Landscape* (Amsterdam: Amsterdam University Press, 2020), 249–50.

16. Chao, *Queer Representations*, 250.

17. Hongwei Bao, *Queer China: Lesbian and Gay Literature and Visual Culture Under Postsocialism* (London: Routledge, 2020), 53.

in the inter-Asian regions as well as by Western LGBT and queer media.[18] A growing number of Chinese-language LGBTQ films and TV/web shows are transnationally coproduced, posing questions about the stability of "Chineseness" and "queerness."

Scholarly readings of the film *Lan Yu* and its original version of *Beijing Gushi* so far are mainly situated at the intersection of these three trajectories. For example, while David Eng reads *Lan Yu* as representing a queer space of socialist and capitalist modernity in China which he calls a "discrepant modernity,"[19] Chiang suggests that reading the film as a queer Sinophone production would redirect attention from both China-as-the-center and China/West binary to a broader horizon that connects the legacy of British colonialism, American neoimperialism, and communist China's role in the Cold War–structuring of transnational East Asia.[20] Grounded in a diverse transregional space, scholars in transnational and Sinophone queer studies often anchor their critical analysis in the "frontier" and "borderland" of minor transnationalisms, such as locations of Hong Kong, Taiwan, and Southeast Asia. This is perhaps because, as Amy Brainer observes, cross-border and cross-continent flows are integral parts of queer space in these locations.[21]

While these works have brought center stage experiences of mobile subjects inhabiting these spaces as embodying queer displacement, transformative agency, and alternatives, queer Sinophone studies also need to caution against the romanticization and generalization of the "rootless," since a rootless existence is also a kind of life that neoliberalism favors with its nationalization of precarity and the dissolution of security. The homogenization of "China as the center" itself reduces the social historical differences of the PRC into the Cold War geopolitical conceptualization of "China proper" and works very well with neoliberalist reduction of people into labor and opportunities for capital and market. These reductions could impoverish queer Sinophone studies as the desire for and idealization of mobility prescribe particular subjects as the ideal queer subject while dismissing asymmetries within the realm of queer Sinophone knowledge production, risking the pathologization of what is "trapped in the center." One example could be seen in the one-way flow of queer knowl-

---

18. Jamie Zhao and Alvy Wong, "Introduction: Making a Queer Turn in Contemporary Chinese-Language Media Studies," *Continuum* 34, no. 4 (2020): 476.

19. David Eng, "The Queer Space of China: Expressive Desire in Stanley Kwan's *Lan Yu*," *Positions: East Asia Cultures Critique* 18, no. 2 (2010): 462, https://doi.org/10.1215/10679847-2010-010

20. Chiang, "(De)Provincializing China," 37–40.

21. Amy Brainer, *Queer Kinship and Family Change in Taiwan* (New Brunswick: Rutgers University Press, 2019), 6.

edge from Hong Kong and Taiwan to the mainland, not the other way around. Since queer experiences and subjects in the PRC are predominantly seen as repressed by Communist authoritarianism and the illiberal state, activists and scholars from Hong Kong and Taiwan usually go to mainland China to share their queer experiences but see the mainland experience as irrelevant to their own locations. Queer scholars and activists in the mainland are also incentivized to identify with this affective inclination in their politics as a result of both their own embodied precarity of doing LGBT and queer work in China and their "epistemological inferiority" and "theoretical inadequacy" coming from an "illiberal regime."

The direct reason that *Lan Yu* was "banned" in mainland China was not for it being gay-themed nor its content about the 1989 massacre, as many critics and viewers would assume based on a Cold War–orientalist presumption of homophobia in Communist China; the direct reason was because the production did not obtain the domestic label of production and distribution.[22] As film scholar Jason McGrath explains, although China started its market-driven reform in the late 1970s, it was not until the early 1990s that the fundamental cultural logic underwent a basic marketization.[23] Regardless, some Fifth Generation art films such as Chen Kaige's *Yellow Earth* (1984) and Zhang Yimou's *Red Sorghum* (1987) were internationally acclaimed and were China's most noticeable cultural exports in the early1990s; these films were solely produced within the existing socialist studio system with the filmmakers and crews being salaried employees of the state.[24] In the 1990s, the culture industry was for the first time placed on the front lines of economic restructuring, making it both part of the state public development imperative and a private enterprise for market competition. This led to a hybrid film production system rather than wholesale privatization: private film companies needed to work with state-owned studios in order to obtain official labels and have the film distributed domestically, and state-owned enterprises made profits not by creating products but by selling its official legitimacy and sharing with the product's success. Pointing out this historical difference is not to prioritize a state-centered view nor to suggest that China in the early 2000s was homo-friendly, but it is to caution against the ahistorical "cookie cutter" simplification when it comes to understanding Chinese surveillance of queer spaces and state-sponsored homophobia and to promote

---

22. As will be explained below, "being banned" in China means many things and could be caused by multiple reasons. But my intention to show the complexity behind the economy of "being banned" does imply that China mainstream media and state were not homophobic.

23. McGrath, *Postsocialist Modernity*, 2–3.

24. McGrath, 5–6.

a method that pays more attention to the intricate and changeable dynamics of how sexuality and state shape each other. It is important to note that the censorship of sexually related content (including homosexuality, BDSM, and pornography) was much looser, and the online surveillance mechanism of "netizens" much less organized in the Jiang Zemin and Hu Jintao eras compared to the later era of Xi Jinping due to many economic, cultural, and geopolitical factors. Similar to the state-promoted HIV/AIDS industry and gender and development NGOs, an increasing official emphasis on culture as statecraft to promote economic development led to a relaxation of homosexuality in the first decade of the 2000s. Queer culture started to gain prominent, if not positive, public representations in mass media and the budding Internet space, exemplified by the popularity of gender ambiguity and gender-bending in the *chaonü* (the "Super Girl" 超女) singing competition show and *weiniang* ("pseudo girls" 伪娘) phenomenon, as well as in the proliferation of online fan fiction community.

The particular decision to not obtain an official label to make *Lan Yu* "legal" could be speculated as a marketizing strategy that plays up the global economy of the art-cinema market, whose increasing desire to know about marginalized life in PRC intertwined with persistent repetition of the anti-communist Sinophobia. Cooperating with a mainland official studio was an option that the directing team originally considered,[25] but given the predictable bureaucratic hurdles and the estimation that the topics of homosexuality would not yield much profitability in the Chinese market (the major types of box office hits were and still are Hollywood blockbusters and Chinese New Year's films), keeping the production "illegal" and targeting the international audience made the most economic and political sense.

In many ways, despite *Lan Yu* being a transregional Sinophone production, its "logic of capital" shares similitude with what has been known as the Sixth Generation or independent films from the PRC. At the turn of the century in Chinese intellectual and cultural life, second-guessing, self-critique, and an inferiority complex in relation to the "advanced" Western culture that underlined the social psyche of the 1980–1990s were mixed with confidence regained

---

25. This claim is based on "personal information." During 2002 to 2005, I was in a relationship with the celebrity agent of Liu Ye, the actor who played the role Lan Yu in the film. Through personal conversations, I learned about the original plan of collaborating with a mainland-based film studio and the screenwriting progress. This information was also disclosed to me by another "insider" from the production team during my doctoral field work. I am aware of the ethical issues and dilemma with using exclusive "insider information" to make arguments, yet I think the disclosure of the information may add an interesting twist and different layers that help testify to the complicity of Sinophone queerness.

through the forward march of economic rising.[26] As China continued to "open up," funding from foreign production companies and government ministries from Japan to Europe to America allowed some filmmakers to work entirely outside of the state studio system. Interestingly, these cultural products present the new face of Chinese cinema to the world yet remain undistributed in mainland China.[27] While *jinpian* (banned or underground films 禁片) might more often refer to foreign films with sexually explicit content in the 1990s, in the 2000s, independent and underground banned films became a genre of their own and were celebrated as a viable counterpublic to the official cultural discourse, as they exposed the "raw and unpleasant reality of China."[28] Often shot with a presumed international audience in mind, these films adopt a particular cinematic style recognizable to the taste of international art cinema—if Chinese blockbusters such as Zhang Yimou's *Hero* (2002) tout orientalism and Chinese nationalism for its global success, the independent film productions could be said to be utilizing a different kind of orientalism—and postsocialist realism arose among documentary filmmakers in the early 1990s. Emerging as the epitome of a counterpublic or indigenous minority culture suppressed by the official cultural discourse, these films drew the ire of the authority in China while their "banned status" by the communist state promised a selling point to the global audience. If Richard Florida's "creative class"[29] energizes the economy through their edgy-bohemian-queer cultural capital, the Chinese postsocialist "creative class" represented by the independent and underground cultural producers, also needs to carefully play the cards of socialist repression and to maintain the Cold War self-racialization in order to excel in the neoliberal hegemony of consumption and read to an international audience. Their success in maintaining a larger audience and sponsorship hinged on their artist flexibility and versatility to produce within the rigidity of cultural and political stereotypes.

The spatially mediated "seen" and "unseen," representation and repression, visibility and invisibility generate layered dynamics of capital and culture that cannot be simply described in binary of oppression and liberation, backwardness and progressiveness, and socialist and capitalist. On the one hand, the banned or underground status testifies to the marginalization of the people the cultural productions aim to represent and the precarity of cultural producers themselves who live at the edge of state cultural surveillance and under the

---

26. McGrath, *Postsocialist Modernity*, 18.
27. McGrath, 130.
28. McGrath, 130.
29. Richard L. Florida, *Cities and the Creative Class* (New York: Routledge, 2005).

118   Queer Chimerica

global orientalist gaze; on the other hand, the cultural producers often erase their privileged cultural-class position as they step up and speak for the marginalized and represent "Chinese cinema" on the global stage while having their cultural productions hardly distributed in mainland China and unknown to the general Chinese audience. Therefore, the independent cultural productions reinforce a binary: the general Chinese audience who blindly consumes neoliberal cultural production without being aware of their own exclusion and seclusion versus the liberalized audience who is awoken due to their connections to the global but unable to speak within the state-directed cultural market. On the surface, what appears is an opposition between the enlightened and the blinded, but they are in fact on the same boat of a double erasure: the first one is the erasure of the "raw" and "unpleasant" reality, the second time is that when one enters the "subversive" counter space, one has to enter it through certain pre-routed hegemony.

Viewing it under this light, it is interesting to note that while Kwan's adaption of *Lan Yu* was meant to be anti-Chinese essentialism by mixing diverse Sinophone cast, screenwriters, and words and accents, the "Chineseness" of *Lan Yu* ironically lies in its reiteration of the postsocialist postcolonial logic of capital that instrumentalizes anti-communist sentiment as a cultural capital with a guaranteed return. Often celebrated as the first internationally acclaimed film depicting gay life in the PRC, the submission of Sinophone cultural and political nuances to the movement of capital passes as "innocent" and "queer" as long as "China" is continuously produced in certain stagnant ways. It would be dangerous for a queer critique to turn a blind eye to the economy of well-worn stereotypes of continental "China" when looking from the outside-in and to dismiss the material impacts of these moments of "stuckness" on those who are stuck in China or who stuck precisely because of the stuckness of "China." This is not to suggest, of course, that we should go back to a China-centric view; on the contrary, a queer Sinophone perspective offers a most productive account when it provides thick descriptions of how the "outside" and "periphery" constitute and disrupt how the "center" is conceived, which in turn leads to a material consolidation of the "center," without couching ourselves in the romanticization of "the periphery" as naturally occupying a subversive position.

What if we let go of the "China-cum-Communist oppression" as the always-already taken-for-granted point of departure and instead take the cultural fantasies of "being queer" seriously with a reflective eye? Would we discover different relations between queer and the logic of capital and subjugation?

I guess the overall Hong Kong feel of *Lan Yu* that got on Yang Xiaofei's nerves was a refraction of these elusive asymmetries that is hard to put one's

Beijing Comrades I 119

finger on. At the moment of watching the pirate VCDs recorded in a Hong Kong theater by a cultural smuggler, she perhaps realized a doomed dilemma in her life she was not yet able to articulate: that there was something she was supposed to desire but had no access to. Would the mainland *tongzhi* ever be able to climb onto the global stage of recognition if not "powdered up" as embodying some international queer traits represented by Hong Kong, let's say, a "freer" China? This adolescent confusion, anxiety, and self-denial might come across as defensive, nationalist, and essentialist at first—vice that postcolonial, transnational, and Sinophone queer studies all argue against—but might these improper feelings, in a way, tell more about the hierarchy that one must internalize, the "prerequisites" that one must identify with, in the march to the transnational and Sinophone space, pre-structured by the materiality mediated by capital, affect, and geopolitics?

How one identifies and disidentifies with these conflicting feelings, desires, and confusions in the process of becoming a subject is important, yet the route to articulation has a lot to do with available tools of speaking. The question of "authenticity" that garnered Yang Xiaofei's anger was a *displaced* protest to the material condition of the PRC's political, ideological, and psychic seclusion mixed with a hidden sense of inferiority caused by China's particular route to modernity, its layered othering, its chosen routes to empowerment, aggression, and expansion, as well as the troubled position of speaking, where a queer subject of the PRC anxiously inhabits.

Watching the pirate VCD, Yang Xiaofei had yet to come to terms with her destiny, the one that will lead her to many places: the US, UK, Singapore, and Germany, in the coming years. In her future journeys, she will have to negotiate with different scripts, perform different personages, and labor to purge herself and to pass with many masks, wishing these passes to be as easy as the one in Boss Jiang's Mercedes.

———————

Many scholarly commentaries on *Lan Yu* have bifurcated regarding how to understand the figure of Lan Yu and his death. These accounts tend to perceive Lan Yu as embodying some sort of utopian hope, either as reminiscent of socialist ethos and nostalgia[30] or as anti-neoliberal alternatives[31] in contrast

---

30. Bao, *Queer China*, 79–80.

31. Eng, "Queer Space," 481–83. Here Eng notes that the expressive homosexual desire in *Lan Yu* configures the film as a "melodrama of neoliberalism in relation" to the "economic mandates of capitalist accumulation and the free market," "the tortured political emergence

120 Queer Chimerica

to the Confucian capitalist "new rich" figuratively embodied by Handong. This uncritical equation of the figure of "queer" with revolutionary potential remains a challenge for transnational queer praxis. Not unlike how Yang Xiaofei's individuality was dismissed when passing as the personification of a queer ideal Lan Yu for Boss Jiang, hegemonic expressions of queerness often turn queer life into "stock figures" and spectacles of subaltern resistance and resilience while suppressing the lived complexity of the displaced and dispossessed. Despite myriad scholarship centering on the mundane queer intervention[32] as productive political space, the celebration of queer as "anti-normative" and "transformative" predominantly translates itself into practices that privilege the visibility of dissidents, progressive space, and Western/white queers as the "radical subject" whose political actions are primarily defined through means of political organization and lobbying, demonstration and protest, and/or struggle for rights and recognition. When the privilege of urban cosmopolitan queers is critiqued, a common counterargument is to claim that these queer individuals—activists, scholars, and cultural producers—do not have material capital and they themselves are subjected to precarious conditions. While this claim is often true, it dismisses the fact that there is no knowledge of the "subaltern," the "marginalized," or the "radical" that lies outside of the neoliberal structure that shapes these marginalities and the ways in which they are recognized and validated.

These troubles with recognition undergird Yang Xiaofei's strong dislike of the film's adaption of Lan Yu as a poor college student, a "gold digger," from the Northeast.

"This adaption is all based on stereotypes that associated migrant workers from the Northeast with crimes, unethical trading, and shady business. It is totally xenophobic!" Yang Xiaofei throws the VCDs on the coffee table between the TV and the couch we had just sat on, her voice angry and steady, "And you know why that is? Because the rich can save the poor, the urban gay capitalist can save the countryside, the Cinderella story can be fulfilled! We all love this type of story, don't we?"

She is on point.

---

of socialist modernity and revolution" and so on (481), and therefore reads Lan Yu's death as a disruption to "any simple historical chronology or to any conventional understandings of the 'restarting' of Chinese history through neoliberal progress" (483).

32. See Yau Ching, ed., *As Normal as Possible: Negotiating Sexuality and Gender in Mainland China and Hong Kong* (Hong Kong: Hong Kong University Press, 2010); Elisabeth Engebretsen, *Queer Women in Urban China: An Ethnography* (London: Routledge, 2013); and Hongwei Bao, Queer Comrades: *Gay Identity and* Tongzhi *Activism in Postsocialist China* (Copenhagen: Nordic Institute of Asian Studies, 2018).

Far from being the "country bumpkin" portrayed in the film, Lan Yu is introduced to the reader in the online novel as an architecture major at one of the most prestigious universities in China, *Hua Da* ("Hua University," implying Tsinghua University 华大). Although the young man first appears as a poor college student in desperate need of money at the beginning of the novel, given the background of China's post-1984 urban reform and its soaring demand for urban infrastructure construction and a real estate market (two of China's most profitable industries contributing to the growth of GDP since the 1990s), one can safely speculate that Lan Yu has a lucrative future awaiting him upon his graduation. As the story unfolds, the reader learns, in a conversation between Lan Yu and Handong that occurs two-thirds of the way through the novel, that Lan Yu is from a second-tier city in northwestern China and both of his parents were college teachers. The market reform brought affluence to Lan Yu's family when his father rode the tide of *xiahai* ("jumping into the sea" of the market 下海) by running a small business. Yet the enviable life ended with the tragedy of his mother's suicide as a result of his father's extramarital affair. On the one hand, Lan Yu laments Handong for turning to a capitalist, mirroring his intellectual-turned-opportunist father; on the other hand, he inevitably internalizes the logic of technocratic utilization of knowledge for capital accumulation both promoted by the Chinese state and pursued by the "desiring" neoliberal consumer-citizens. Disguised by a familiar trope of the "sugar daddy and protégé," what *Beijing Gushi* reveals is the link between capital and the political economy of knowledge and ways in which the possession of knowledge by *zhichan jieji* (the intellectual class 知产阶级) shapes redistribution of resources and redemarcation of class differences.

Zhishi fenzi (the intellectuals 知识分子) occupies a unique position in China's dramatically changing socioeconomic and cultural conditions and share an ambivalent relationship with the Communist Party-state. Historically speaking, *keju zhidu* (the scholar-official system 科举制度) developed in imperial China allowed intellectuals to assume important political and governmental roles. Subsequentially, the nationalistic idea of being well-educated and being an intellectual as a significant path to obtaining political and economic power has dominated Chinese public discourses. During the Cultural Revolution, however, the intellectuals were severely repressed by Maoist ideology that favored revolutionary vanguardism of the workers and peasants. In 1977 Deng Xiaoping restored *gao kao* (the National College Entrance Examination 高考) as part of the state-launched "Thought Liberation" campaign that was set to reevaluate the "ten-year chaos" and to repudiate Maoist class struggles. The first generation of college graduates after the restoration came primarily from

122   Queer Chimerica

former intellectual and communist official families. Handong in *Beijing Gushi* is one of them. As the story unfolds, we find out that Handong is the eldest son of a well-placed communist official who gained his first "bucket of gold" through his father's *guanxi* (networks 关系) in the government. Slightly varied from the new Confucian capitalists in the coastal regions who mainly rely on transnational and diasporic/Sinophone networks, the Confucian Communist intellectual-capitalists also have more political power to influence national policies in more substantial ways. They are a powerful "class" that has exclusive access to information, the ability to interpret ideology, and policy-making that are directly linked to capital gain. This well-connected group manipulated their political power and networks to make the best use of the economic reform and built their own wealth from the state. During this period, Chinese society experienced a vast transformation of the property from the state to the private fields and an increasing social inequality. But as Deng stated, these "temporary" social inequalities should be tolerated as a necessary step of a long-term plan toward economic prosperity and the well-being of the majority (which didn't turn to reality).

Lan Yu represents a different kind of intellectual. In contrast to what Handong represents, he appears as "grassroots" due to his presumed lack of material capital. Yet this class of intellectuals are nevertheless crucial to reform as the technocratic governmentality requires a large group of people with both know-how and a taste for progressive liberal culture. In the 1980s, many intellectuals turned to Western humanism and Enlightenment in critiquing Maoist socialism and asserting "independent subjectivity." This period was characterized by massive translations of Western works in the social science and humanities. As most intellectuals prior to the 1990s are employed by state-run research institutes and universities, the "culture fever" was strongly sponsored by state-run institutions. During this period, social sciences such as sociology, demography, and economics were revived as responses to the need of market reform and economic productivity. Witnessing the economic and social changes from the reform policies, some of them with particular knowledge participated in the market and achieved wealthy social status, while others with political and patriotic enthusiasm started to question the direction of reform. The technocratic state met criticism and resistance from the intellectuals who wanted to pursue democratic humanism, resulting in a conflict that largely explains the Tian'anmen upheaval in 1989.[33]

---

33. Feng Xu, "Chinese Feminisms Encounter International Feminisms: Identity, Power and Knowledge Production," *International Feminist Journal of Politics* 11, no. 2 (2009): 198–99.

The triangulation of state, capital, and the economy of knowledge, obscured by the film's binary simplification of the two protagonists as capitalist and socialist, is vividly portrayed in the novel. Before leading up to the scene of the Tian'anmen crackdown in the novel, Lan Yu responds to Handong's warning of not going to the protest with sarcasm, calling out Handong as the "termites of the nation." Enabling a nationalist framework, Lan Yu's comment conveys a mass demand at the time for social equality and justice through embracing revolutionary resistance (either through a socialist or democratic vision). Later in the novel, Handong becomes enraged with a woman after knowing Lan Yu not only does not spend his money but also works at a construction site to gain work and life experience. When Handong calls Lan Yu a *mingong* (a derogative term for rural-urban workers 民工), Lan Yu stands up for himself by defending other "gold diggers" who are deemed as the burden of urbanization. Recognizing their labor as essential to the development of China's megacities, Lan Yu's argument with his lover makes visible what has been rendered unworthy.

Yet we should not solely rely on Lan Yu as a "socialist political agitator"[34] to dominant narrative of neoliberal progress nor as embodying a utopian queer love that serves as a critique to commercialization,[35] even given the dissonance between the lovers. A scene that happened early on in the film version of the story tells us the contradiction of the role of Lan Yu. Before offering himself up in a hotel room at the business center of Beijing, Lan Yu asks Handong, "Sir, have you been to America?" With a TV program introducing Los Angeles in the background, Handong does not answer the question directly but replies, "You come over, I have something for you." In the novel, what is on TV before the protagonists' first sexual encounter is Euro-American heterosexual porn that Handong uses to arouse Lan Yu. This slippage suggests clearly that it is through queer encounters that the fantasy for the US and its phallic-masculinized progressiveness could be realized in China, and the presumed differences between the PRC and the US could be bridged and resolved at the moment of neoliberalism-conditioned queer intimacy.

This particular route out of which queer desire emerges in a strange way refracts an Orientalist expression regarding the complex interconnectedness of the two countries. As the proxy third-world producer and first-world consumer who do not demand and deserve American benefits, the Chinese masses need to be kept in their place through a "crucial optimism"[36] of upward mobility, cos-

---

34. Eng, "Queer Space," 476.
35. Bao, *Queer China*, 76.
36. Lauren Berlant, *Cruel Optimism* (Durham: Duke University Press, 2011).

mopolitan worldliness, and whiteness. The construction of the fantasy through idealizing queer "desiring subjects" in China, like Lan Yu, does just that. In fact, as both the film and novel tell us that, although he prepared for a TOEFL exam, Lan Yu had never been to the US. He used his savings and the money received from Handong to bail out the cosmopolitan well-connected Confucian capitalist before the young lover's death, mirroring the contradiction that Chinese vast saving and overproduction benefited from socialist planned-economy bailing out American/Americanized overconsumption in the 1990s while the actual Chinese labor and their subjectivity must be socially and discursively "killed" at home or trapped at the center with no escape, through continuous construction of "unskilled," "numbness" "struck," and "non-assimilability." The inevitable death of Lan Yu sits at the crossroad of necrobiopolitics and necroeconomy of producing a proper queer subject that fundamentally sustains the symbiosis of various forms of neoliberalism.

This recognition of the economic, labor, and geopolitical interconnections of the PRC and the US and their cultural forms is also important to understanding Chinese globalism and the new empire. Going back to the biography of Lan Yu in the novel, one might notice that the Northwest region where Lan Yu comes from falls on the map of China's twenty-first-century mega-transregional project, the "Belt and Road Initiatives." Although the author would not predict such development at the time when the novel was written, the choice of location conjures up memories of complex histories between Han settlers and ethnic minorities in China. One could speculate that Lan Yu's family belongs to the Han settlers in western China as a result of the historical and ongoing projects of western development, a state-sponsored Han settlement for economic, political, and military reasons across socialist and postsocialist eras. Unlike "troubled frontiers" such as Tibet and the Xinjiang Uyghur region, which are more likely to garner international attention, regions like Lan Yu's hometown are the "quieter" voices and "dimmer lights" on the screen that nonetheless play important roles in restructuring China's domestic racial politics, class relations and economic development—it is not just Uyghur labor camps that feed into the post-millennial transition from coastal industrial zones to inner and wild lands but also the unseen billions whose differences are written off as the homogenous "Chinese." What if we could let go of the fantasy of the oppression/liberation binary and the fetishization of the most marginalized-cum-resistor, and instead trace what has been split over the "belt and road" of racial capitalism and pay more attention to the "proxy" labor that queer subjects, politics, and culture undertake in forming the Sino-US non-frontiers?

Since the first decade of the twenty-first century, as the Chinese economic model shifted from export-based rapid growth to high-technology-oriented steady growth, Sino-US relationship changed significantly. On the surface level, "decoupling" was used by many critics to describe the heightened tensions between the two powers. Yet, a striking similarity between China and US was also evident in China's racial policy on regions such as Xinjiang Uyghur. If the US War on Terror happened in the Middle East, the battlefield of China's military industrial complex was in the domestic land. Although the forced labor issues were lambasted by international society, the United States and other Western liberal states were called upon to curb China's human rights violations. Chinese technology of surveillance, such as facial recognition and big data tracking, was also used by settler colonial states like the United States to further patrol racialized populations and to manage their own racial tensions. As both countries were facing austerity and stagflation, the "war business" and necroeconomics became the two promising sources of economic growth. In this sense, the democratic and authoritarian neoliberalisms worked hand in hand as China and the US were becoming "similar" and "greater" together.

Yang Xiaofei and I had a major fallout in the last year of high school.

"Is the United States better than anywhere else in the world?" She yowled and shriveled, "I will never be able to see you again."

"Stop making a mountain out of a molehill!" I folded my arms, "There are more important things than our puppy love!"

"Come to Europe with me, at least we will only be five hours away!"

"But I want to go to the States. That's where the most cutting-edge queer study is! Plus, I am not abandoning you; I will only be there for two years, and there is something called 'the Internet,' have you not known?"

After the fight, Yang Xiaofei blacked out in a PE class and was sent to the emergency room. Then she cut off communication with me completely and isolated me from our mutual friends, ignoring me as if I was a ghost. The reticence remained so much longer than I expected and could have endured.

Years later, I learned that Yang Xiaofei married a man. After her dramatic "fall from grace," she denounced her homosexuality and lived a happy heteronormative life. In their wedding slideshow that I snooped and discovered online, Yang Xiaofei, dressed in her British-style school uniform and shiny Dr. Martens, sat on a school bus, leaning quietly against her husband's shoulder. It was a scene that felt so familiar. In those long years of adolescent alienation, self-doubt, and dreaming for an unknown future yet to come, it was *me*, and *me alone*, who sat next to her on the school bus, lending her the puny shoulders of mine. She erased me from that timeline. There was no greater betrayal than deleting a history. Must I diminish and die in her world, like Lan Yu's inevitable demise, so that she can grow in her heart the rosy flower of our untainted past? A past of passion, love, and aspiration, only to hide the self-serving egoist coward she has become?

PART IV

The Best Moment of Love

CHAPTER 10

Your China Will Not Work

THIS IS OUTRAGEOUS! *I lived a happy heteronormative life? I denounced my homosexuality? Self-serving and egotistic? Who are you to judge my life and decisions!* With seething anger, I pull myself out of the Nano Pod. Memories of my adolescence break through like tidal waves, crashing against the fragile levees of my mind. The day you abandoned me to pursue what you deemed sublime is now so clear. I sat before the A&W restaurant where we used to hang out and wept for four damned hours. How pathetic I was! Out of desperation, I dialed Boss Jiang's number, confessing our pitiable stunts. And Boss Jiang offered me one hundred *yuan* in exchange for "*Lan Yu* style" make-up sex with him. I texted you in the taxi ride to his hotel, hoping you could get jealous and realize your grievous mistake of letting me go. And what did you reply? "The best moment of love is when the lover leaves in the taxi."[1] What an asshole!

I ache thinking about you. Recollections of our time together cripple my concentration, *yes, there are more important things in the world than our stupid puppy love!* Although the exact details of what occurred may elude me, the feelings won't lie. You were callous, and manipulative, and you used others like wood for fire. Beneath your deceptive friendliness lies an insecure heart yearning for attention and validation. Though you projected an image of bold forthrightness, the slightest hint of criticism would be enough to nurse a grudge. You held yourself in high esteem, a paragon of uniqueness, originality, and ambitious vision, a queer Prometheus who suffers and saves all. Yet, in truth, you were no more than a mere imitator, repurposing the words and ideas of others. At the end of the day, you were nothing but a sad façade.

---

1. A quote from Michel Foucault, *Politics, Philosophy, Culture: Interviews and Other Writings, 1977–1984* (ed. Routledge, 2013)—ISBN: 9781134976294

Oh, you know what is funny? It was *you* who never truly embraced queer theory, despite having a Ph.D. in gender studies. "Gender fluidity" was just a convenient tool for your internalized misogyny. Did you even call yourself a trans gay man at one point? What a pathetic denial of your femaleness that got you taken advantage of in the first place! Knowing the movement of promoting LGBT visibility was gendered and erased women, you chose to exercise power through being a gay man you could never achieve. Socks in your pants will never save you from your smelly hypocrisy. "Anti-normativity" was just the quick way to approve yourself in a normative world that never accepted who you really were. Like so many of the glitterati popular feminists and queers whom I would later come to know, you touted progressiveness for living, and your behaviors transgressed no boundary of heteropatriarchy and dictatorship! It all makes sense now. It is not out of character for you who must be so lost in fame and vanity to steal and trade Beets.

"What leads you to think it is fame and vanity that drives the transporters to carry the Beets of others?"

"The transporters? The thieves now hold official titles? Are they getting pensions too?" Andrei's metallic voice rouses me from the Synchronization, like one's first inhalation on a crisp winter morning. What did just happen? Did I lose control of the process again? How come my thoughts were enmeshed with the Beets? And have I too been monitored?

I clamp out of the Nano Pod, this time for real, that is, if I still have the sanity to discern what reality is. I unleash my anger, frustration, and confusion upon Andrei, "Whatever business you are doing, leave me out! Did I surrender my memories only to have them recalled by another? And I certainly have no interest in being reduced to the building blocks for *your* 'China'!"

"Ah, what a *pleasure* to see you angry again. You have been rather detached these days, since you lack the anchor of memory, perhaps?" The passive-aggressive jabs again! Andrei rests his chin on his fingers, and I can smell the sourness.

"Why are you provoking me, Andrei? You knew from the beginning that *it was Na Na who stole the Beets and didn't even bother to tell me a word*?"

As soon as I spill her name out, I regret.

"Do you not comprehend what you have become, my friend?" Andrei's eyebrows come together in an ugly twist, "You have unplugged yourself from the world, disconnected with friends and foes indifferently since your return. And look at what a life you are living now, devoid of passion, consumed by materialism, and dreadfully boring. You are adrift in triviality, preoccupied with empty pettiness and the mundane: what to eat for breakfast, lunch, and dinner, and the best bargain to be had . . . Where has the Yang Xiaofei with hair like a hedgehog and eyes like stars gone? Your once animated face is now a dull stone mask, your heart no longer trembles at injustice, misfortune, and wrongdoing. You have surrendered to the comfort of ordinary life and forsaken the queer child within you. You believe in agency, resistance, and alternative no more!"

"Enough!" I interject sharply, cutting off Andrei's escalating insults. "For some of us, forgetting is a matter of survival. I disconnected myself from the toxic world to reflect and rejuvenate. I stepped away from my queer past and its drama to find healing and peace. And I have found solace and meaning in ordinary objects, pleasure, and abundance. What could possibly be wrong with that?"

"If nothing were amiss, my friend, you wouldn't have lost control of the Synchronization and allowed the noise to lure you down the rabbit hole of memory that you denied and buried so well," Andrei retorts.

"Excuse me, let me remind you that I didn't choose to be synced with an ex-lover who left me and turned into a Beets thief, did I? And stop 'my friend' me, it's patronizing!" I turn away from Andrei to hide my disgust and hurt. "So you want to save me with your so-called 'radicality'? Like Na Na, who wanted to save the world with her 'queer theory'?"

"You're no better, Andrei." I snap, feeling my anger rise. "You're a narcissistic savior who is so out of touch with reality. You and Na Na would make a great pair. Underneath the facade of your sublime purpose lies your Orientalist romanticization of Chinese history. 'Queer China' is your wishful projection of agency onto people who lived and suffered. You want examples of queer people who survived harshness as if the dark times have some lessons to teach you. You seek to gather knowledge of their resistance, all to evoke some alternatives to the co-opted realm of liberalism. But you don't care about the *people* beyond the abstract symbolism they hold for you. So you tell me, how is your 'China' any different from the Beets we extracted for the Unity, and how is it not a fetish of the queer Left, like yourself?"

"Of course, it's different. It's anti-fetishism," Andrei responds, smugness seeping through his words. I can't help but laugh. His weak defense with the esoteric trick of words always annoys me, but he pays no mind. "Believe or not, the histories of the people speak to me. It is through the stories of the Chinese past that I have uncovered the lost gems of my own, long been repressed by today's neoliberal rebranding of everything. When I visited Beijing, I didn't see the *legacy, monuments, or museums* of socialism; I saw a living, breathing socialism that resonated deeply with my own roots. And when we found the materials in the ruins of your grandfather's workplace that we later used for

132   Queer Chimerica

Chimera Purple, it was a moment when the threads of history wove themselves together, a moment of hope."

"Delusions, Andrei. You may have set foot in China, but you have never truly lived the life of its people. You have only glimpsed its history from afar, cherry-picked stories that prove your point. You make them into data, words, images, arguments . . . . . . but the lives and deaths of real people don't impact you in any meaningful way. You believe you're resurrecting the lost voices of history, evoking alternatives from the dead, like Orpheus seeking to revive Eurydice, but what if you are simply trapping them in the Underworld with your backward glance? In a society that is based on making best use of everything possible, the relation to the past and loss can only be instrumental.[2] Like Na Na, or whomever you call 'transporters,' you are feeding into the stealing, from people like Zhang Shanping, Yang Tao, and Guang Hui; you are appropriating them as tools to build something that ought to be doomed. You make them hollow, you rob them of selfness and autonomy, you bury them in the tomb of voice and representation, your 'China' will not work."

Andrei's response is predictably infuriating. "In what way, precisely, am I stealing from them? Our 'China' is an opportunity for these forgotten stories and lives to be seen in a new light, especially in a time when global memory is manipulated and controlled by the stories, ideas and images of the ruling class.[3] These fringe histories are like seeds in a black box, who carry with them the potentials to cultivate new futures. Although I haven't figured out the algorithm of the 'how' and might never be able to, I am certain that alternatives will happen as long as we keep the preservation and input going. And in this era of advanced capitalism and digitalized precarity, *we*, yes, I said *we*, the privileged intellectuals with social capital, resources and internal networks, have a responsibility to rebuild social, political, and conceptual infrastructures that can facilitate changes."

I roll my eyes at his neo-Marxist nonsense. "Your hypocrisy knows no bounds, Andrei. You and Na Na are cut from the same cloth, believing that your superiority can save the world. What if the lost prefers to remain 'dead,' like Lot's wife who stands still between Sodom and salvation? In the story of Eurydice, it is *him* who turns and leaves *her* behind, like you Marxist and queer

---

2. See Heather Love, *Feeling Backward: Loss and the Politics of Queer History* (Cambridge, MA: Harvard University Press, 2007), 9.

3. This conversation draws loosely from W. J. T. Mitchell's essay "From Robots to iBots: The Iconology of Artificial Intelligence," published on July 22, 2023, in *Los Angles Review of Books*, https://lareviewofbooks.org/article/from-robots-to-ibots-the-iconology-of-artificial -intelligence/

intellectuals whose historical materialism, dialectics and radicality end up trapping those on the ground. But in the story of Lot's wife, it is *her* who looks back and refuses to be severed from the everyday dirt and labor of the Sin City. As a woman whose life is so integrated to the mundane, the trivial, the unnoticed and the forgotten, being alive might mean something very different."

"So are you saying that there is nothing we can do except surrendering to the doomed fate we are inevitably thrown into? That does not sound like something you would say." Andrei rebuttals.

"How could digging out forgotten experiences help people if the medium of being seen is always already the very structure of inequality and exploitation? Yes, representation and visibility might have lifted some queers from the status of so-called oppression but would never lift them from being used as resources. And it is precisely through transforming those that are deemed waste, obsolete, or dead, that queer values of 'self-conscious liberal identity' and 'herculean resistance to oppression' are affirmed and made useful. Mining queer resources, that is exactly what we do and what we do well, isn't it?"

As I speak, a terrifying thought crosses my mind. Is Andrei part of the whole thing that's stealing Beets and erasing memories to build his "China"? Is he complicit in creating these "shrimp dumplings"—muted, whitened, and protected from the pain and burden of memory? I push the thought aside, not wanting to fall into the trap of conspiracy.

Andrei's head hangs low, filled with defeat and helplessness that pained me to watch. Despite the fight, I can't dismiss what an exceptional friend, lover, and mentor he has been to me. He has tried to protect me in his own way, after all. So I stop.

For an uncomfortably long time, silence envelops us until Andrei finally breaks it, "I omitted where the stolen Beets came from because . . . because Na Na is no longer with us."

What does it mean? I frown.

"When found, she was already irreparably damaged, perhaps because of carrying the beets of too many others. Nobody knew why she would take such a risk. She herself was fragmented, shattered, and enmeshed with the Beets, like, you know, the bad breast implant injections people used to use that grew into the body tissues," Andrei's voice gets caught in his throat. "We had to choose the Beets over her since they are the Unity's most valuable property. There might be a reminiscence of her, some murmuring, noise, and broken speech you have noticed, but no, the reality is, Na Na is gone."

I am left rooted to the ground as he speaks. No wonder I couldn't reverse-image her.

134   Queer Chimerica

"What is going to happen if she cannot be restored?"

"Well, the transporters might be kept for some time since their bodies would function as a storage medium for the Beets, but eventually they will become obsolete and get repurposed by the Unity, I suppose. They are of no value once their usefulness is exhausted."

Obsolete and repurposed. I couldn't imagine what that is like. A beat-up Teddy Bear with head and arms and legs being cut off from its body? I am sure that is not what is going to happen to Na Na. But it could be worse.

Wait, that shouldn't be the end of it. I had known Na Na for a long time, and we crossed paths often, even after our initial fallout. What if I could use my own Beets to resurrect her, to bring her back from the brink of oblivion? Combined with the fragments, would there be enough information to restore her through the Dome? It is true that Na Na and I had a complicated history, full of tensions and conflicts, and I still don't think highly of her, but I shouldn't let her be lost to the void, a mere afterthought in the grand scheme of things. I know the task will be monumental, fraught with difficulty and uncertainty. I know there will be a jumbled mess of emotions if I have to relive the pain of recalling. I know there is a risk that I might be disqualified from continuing my work. But how can I let her fate be sealed without at least trying?

Where should I begin then? I close my eyes and focus, trying to draw forth any memories of Na Na that I can. It's no use. My mind is a blank slate. Panic sets in, a cold sweat breaking out on my skin. How could I hope to save her when I couldn't even remember what she looked like?

CHAPTER 11

Ex-Queer

One of my greatest strengths is that I don't give up easily. Rather than wallowing in despair and complaining about shit, I seek out solutions.

Before the advent of Immersive Synchronization, I used to write letters to Andrei. To be accurate, those letters were not intended for him, but for those with whom I struggled to find common ground—Na Na being one of them. It was my own version of the "empty chair" method used in psychotherapy, whereby one invites those with whom they seek reconciliation to sit and engage in an imaginary conversation. Andrei would join me by the bonfire in our backyard, reading aloud the letters that I had composed. This allowed me to see things from the perspective of those who had hurt or wronged me, without demanding redress. Then he would toss the letters into the fire. We watched the words turning to ashes in the silent starry night.

I'm sure that Na Na was a frequent topic of discussion during our rituals. In theory, I could request Andrei to make Beets of what I wrote to him and transfuse them back into my consciousness. With any luck, this may serve to reactivate those vital neural links and unlock the remaining fragments of my memory. Surely, Andrei would have no reason to decline such a small favor, would he?

Still, as I stand on the precipice of making this request, I hesitate. I'm embarrassed, especially right after our fight and me calling him a narcissistic neo-Marxist hypocrite. Though I trust our friendship and love, there is still a lingering fear that Andrei may take advantage of my vulnerability. This, I know, is very unlikely, but the last vestiges of my imposter syndrome cling stubbornly to me. I'd better be my own savior this time.

So, I bestow upon myself the permission to hack into Andrei's Beets. Glad

136 Queer Chimerica

I saved his biodata when we were intimate. I reassure myself that I won't delve into his thought beyond what is necessary. It's not theft—my memories are mine, after all.

My "Empty Chair" with Andrei #1

It was after the Chinese New Year in 2012, I left Berlin for Beijing. Despite my eight years of experience living abroad and having a dual master's degree in neuroscience and psychology, I found myself taking a temporary job selling classes at a high-end foreign language training institute. The company required each and every female employee to wear a business suit, complete with a dress skirt, pantyhose, and heels. I couldn't help but wonder how absurd I would look in such attire with my short, spiky hair and tomboyish appearance, and when I put on the dress suit, Mom happened to walk in on me and burst into a laugh, "Take it off, you look like a pervert *renyao* (ladyboy 人妖).

"See, you're falling behind the era," I replied, reaching to her wig that sat next to the mirror, put it on, and teased her, "It is not *renyao*, it is called *kua xingbie* (transgender跨性别), *xingbie ku'er* (genderqueer 性别酷儿)."

On Valentine's Day, I took Mom to the Qianmen Pedestrian Street. Near Tian'anmen Square and lined with plenty of restaurants and stores, Qianmen is one of the most popular tourist spots in Beijing, attracting locals and out-of-towners alike. I had not relished spending time with Mom. She was aggressive, manipulative, and never ceased to criticize my decisions. One of my early memories was Mom throwing a coffee cup at the wall and yelling at my father during a heated argument. Since I was a little child, I was told that being street smart is more important than reading books, unless I wanted to end up like my "useless" father, who can't even hold a tenured position at the university.

At the age of twelve, I had had enough of her verbal abuse and fled from Shenzhen to live with my grandfather. This protest apparently worked because the next day Mom showed up at the door of Grandpa's condo in Beijing, pleading with me to come back home. She told me that a daughter is the most tender part of a mother's heart, and how could she possibly live without me? Only for her to disappear again with her mahjong friends the next day.

When I graduated from high school, I received two presents: an ASUS laptop from Grandpa and a black leather case from Mom so that I could cover the brand of the computer. Mom mocked, "*Baba*, what kind of Chinese copycat did you buy for her? All laptops are at least above ¥15,000, how much did this one cost? Only ¥8,000? Her German classmates will surely laugh at her."

I had every right to blame Mom for my childhood misfortune and adolescent unhappiness, as well as my compulsory need to cater to others and seek approval. But it was a miracle that I had grown into a healthy, lighthearted, and cheerful person. Thank queer theory!

Let me clarify. The queer theory that was reintroduced to me through queer *lala* activism, not the queer theory Na Na left me for!

Na Na held the activists in disdain, viewing them as opportunists, easily agitated by the hollow rhetoric of tolerance, human rights, and diversity. She regarded their involvement with activism as just a fleeting passion and saw their mindlessness and lack of long-term goals as leading to the reinforcement of social norms. But within me, there was always a curiosity that went beyond the high theory she was so fond of, and a desire to meet people beyond the small circle of her "Foucauldian gay pals."

From 2007 on, I already began spending most of my school breaks back in Beijing volunteering for a *lala* organization. The first expression I gave to people was cheerful and humorous with an approachable cool vibe (I hide my trauma deep), so I was always surrounded by well-educated yet beautiful young women. Obviously, my openness to sex made me a great facilitator for activities like discussion sessions and role-play. I still remember how excited I was the first time I went on the streets on Valentine's Day sending free roses to passers-by in 2008, or when I was part of the organizing team of the "*tongzhi* wedding photo" event in Qianmen in 2009. "Sending free roses" and "*tongzhi* wedding photo" were part of our annual Valentine's Day outreach activities co-organized by several lesbian and gay activists in Beijing from 2007 to 2011. The volunteers gave out free roses with flyers about supporting same-sex couples attached. Branded as a *commercial* activity of celebration, this method of activist outreach effectively avoided the risk of police harassment. Similarly, activists also took advantage of the "gray area" between the public and private space when they staged the same-sex couple's photoshoot in 2009. Framed as an "individual business" in public, it successfully attracted large domestic and foreign media attention while protecting the activists being arrested. Public demonstrations and protests without governmental permission were not allowed in China, but the "behavioral art type" of activities that were adapted by many later activities struck a perfect balance between awareness raising and abiding by the law. The annual event was developed over time to include various activities, such as inviting passers-by to take photographs in a life-size wedding gown-shaped display board, which allowed them to send well wishes to same-sex couples. Additionally, in 2011, a "kissing contest" was introduced as part of the festivities. Although the official kissing contest was called off by the police, we, the

138 Queer Chimerica

organizers, were still able to stage the kissing among the audience. At the time, lesbian and gay organizations in Beijing grew together, supporting one another, and sharing funding resources, meeting places, and personnel. The volunteers used to proudly call these strategies *Beijing moshi* (the Beijing Model 北京模式) to distinguish themselves from organizations that would fight for resources. I might be romanticizing the "Beijing Model" since the cooperation between lesbian and gay activists was made possible by the fact that a big city like Beijing was among the top-tier receivers of transnational funding, and both lesbian and gay men had relatively sufficient money for organizing events, a privilege that would soon be revoked.

A few months after my "honeymoon" with *lala* organizing, I noticed some structural issues. What I thought of as the cause of LGBT liberation turned out to be a competition for fundraising. My primary job was to write funding proposals and raise money from organizing parties and securing sponsors. Despite my fluent English, I failed the task most of the time since I was not versed in the language that would appeal to the international donors. The organization personnel were required to assume laborious tasks that didn't match their salaries. In addition to working overtime, they often took the blame for not accomplishing the work on time or the failure to secure more funding. At first, I didn't treat the volunteer work as professional work, so I made no attempt to flatter the leaders of the organizations and cared very little about my failures. Like many volunteers, what drove me to work there was the pure desire to meet more friends and perhaps "fuck buddies," not being used as a piece on a chessboard to balance the power struggles within the organization. If I had known that the organizing work operated like a company, I could have built up myself a good reputation early on and made good use of my social skills and charms. There was a fleeting moment I thought about how Na Na must be gloating at me somewhere, sipping her Frappuccino with a book by Derrida in hand while I was busing my ass around and begging for a one-hundred-yuan donation at a lesbian bar. But the thought would vanish immediately when my name was announced, followed by my newly earned title "the director of (/////) LGBT center" at the fundraising party, or when younger activists offered their eyes of admiration and themselves to me.

When Mom and I arrived at Qianmen, a trio of young women clad in wedding gowns stained with fake blood caught our attention. Amid all the street noise, the traffic, and the bustle, the young women held aloft posters, chanting in unison slogans like *Da bushi qin, ma bushi ai* ("Hitting is not intimacy;

scolding is not love" "打不是亲,骂不是爱"). They distributed anti-domestic violence pamphlets and cards to anyone who would take them. Mom wanted to get closer to take some pictures, but I pulled back.

"Aren't they your friends?" Mom tried to be supportive, something she started to learn after falling ill.

"Well, there is no 'friends forever' on the road of LGBT liberation." I faked my composure, masking the tremor in my voice, "You know, I am not really involved in that kind of stuff anymore."

Was the statement true? I asked myself when we exited the crowds. Knowing there would probably be some activist events today and the chance of running into some old friends and nemeses was high, why had I brought Mom here and "accidentally" stumbled upon the old colleagues who despised me so badly? Was it another attestation? What was I trying to prove, and to whom?

Like the "free roses" V-day event, *shoushang de xinniang, daixue de hunsha* (The "Blood Wedding Gown and the Wounded Brides" "受伤的新娘,带血的婚纱") was a series of "anti–domestic violence against women and sexual minorities" stunt outreach activities on streets initiated by who would later be named *qingnian nüquan xingdongpai* (young grassroots feminist activists青年女权行动派). From 2012 to 2015, grassroots feminists—some of whom were queer feminists who had been involved with activism for some years, others came out of training programs led by *lala* activists—as well as newly emerged Chinese feminists mainly influenced by social media, organized a number of attention-grabbing events in public space, such as *zhanling nan cesuo* ("Occupy Men's Toilet" 占领男厕所) inspired by Occupy Wall Street, *wo keyi sao, ni bukeshi rao* ("I can be 'Slutty' by You should not Harass" 我可以骚你不可以扰) inspired by Slut Walk, *tiguangtou liangxia jiaoyubu* ("Shave Head to Blind the Bureau of National Education" 剃光头亮瞎教育部), and *fandui bihun mingxinpian* ("Anti-forced Marriage Postcards" 反对逼婚明信片) in major cities, including Beijing, Hangzhou, Guangzhou, Dongguan, Zhengzhou, and Shenzhen. Complementary to conventional feminist advocacy and education, the young grassroots feminists made waves and increased the visibility of gender inequality and gender/sex-based discrimination in China and raised public awareness of new forms of feminism. Together with other feminist activists, these women worked to replicate their success in other areas of women's rights, including employment and education discrimination, gender-based violence, and the rights of sex workers.

The grassroots feminist activism emerged at a time when the popularization of the new media economy met the uptick of governmental surveillance of pub-

140 Queer Chimerica

lic space. The prevalence of personal digital devices gave rise to new forms of activism for the "digital natives,"[1] while the ability to attract wider international attention and the increasing exposure also evoked concerns from the Chinese state authorities. Initially, the new form of the feminist movement was not only socially successful but also praised by the authorities. More than a dozen newspapers and online media outlets reported on the activities. Attempting to seize the opportunity, young feminists sent letters to representatives in the National People's Congress, advising them to propose legislation to improve restroom gender ratios. As a result, congressional delegates raised the issue during legislative sessions in March 2012, and several cities made plans to improve the gender ratios of public restrooms. But as the movement spread and became more connected across regions, the authority began to worry and censor their protests and online posts.

At the beginning of the second decade of the twenty-first century, China gradually shifted from an export-oriented labor-intensive economy to a high technology-oriented one. New social media platforms and technologies such as Sina Weibo, WeChat, and later short-video sharing flatform such as Douyin offered unprecedented public space for feminist and queer visibility and networks. Meanwhile, the government started to further scrutinize civil societies, leading to stricter oversight over foreign-sponsored NGOs since late 2013. Feminist and LGBT activists found themselves more frequently *bei qinghecha* ("being invited for a cup of tea" 被请喝茶), being called upon and questioned by the National Security authority or local police. The tensions among the government, transnational sponsors, and grassroots feminist activism mounted to a tipping point in early 2015.

On March 7th, 2015, the eve of International Women's Day, a group of young feminist activists in Beijing, Hangzhou, and Guangzhou were taken into custody by local policemen. After the initial arrest and interrogation, several were released, leaving five of them who were sent to detention centers. Later the state security broadened its investigation to many more feminist and human rights activists, leading to the shutdown of several influential women's rights NGOs. The five women were later released after thirty-seven days of detention without formal charges but remained criminal suspects and under surveillance since then.

This incident generated unprecedented publicity of feminist activism in China and strengthened coalitions among feminists across borders. Images of the five women and the activist activities they had previously engaged in went

---

1. Borrowing sociologist Manuel Castells's words.

viral on both Chinese and global social media networks. Influential Chinese feminist scholar Wang Zheng at the University of Michigan sent out a petition link through academic listservs calling for transnational feminist support and solidarity. Many foreign political and governmental officials, including Hillary Clinton and Samantha Power also stood up and announced their condemnation of the violent act.

I, too, was summoned for a "friendly chat" over a cup of tea following the March 2015 incident. It was a stark reminder of the extensive reach of National Security and the impressive thoroughness of their information-gathering capabilities, a far cry from the days when I was actively doing activism just a few short years ago. Despite my relative inactivity in organizing queer *lala* events for years, the police had managed to unearth the minutest details of my previous activities, including those fleeting sexual liaisons that had long since slipped my memory.

Walking out of that ghastly but, thank Chairman Mao, short interrogation, I found myself compelled to offer a middle finger in the direction of the police station. I snapped a photo of myself in the act and shared it on my WeChat moments. Almost immediately after I posted my trophy, a new friend request arrived:

"Hey, you are in Beijing too?! Add me, it's Na Na."

CHAPTER 12

Queer-Ex

<u>My "Empty Chair" with Andrei #2</u>

People say that time heals. No, it does not. It is not the passage of time itself that heals us, but the work we do to confront and engage our experience. We must learn from the love, pain, and regret that have anchored and shaped us. We must resist the temptation to fill the voids within us with others. For it is only when we find strength and beauty within ourselves that the baby bird will finally spread her wings and soar to great heights.

I wouldn't claim to have transcended the past that anchored me in joy and pain, aspiration and disappointment, but I am certainly curious about what lessons *she* has learned over the years (or what punishments she may have faced for abandoning me in my time of need).

So here we were, Na Na and I met at a tea house near the Chongwenmen subway station, a spot she used for interviewing her informants during her fieldwork. The first sight of her stirred something within me. She almost looked unrecognizable from the person I once knew in our shared days. Adorned with on-fire-red lipstick, she was like a typical Asian online influencer of the time. Her eyes were shadowed by a fan of thick faux lashes, sleek hair split in the middle, framing her face and accentuating her sharp features. It was all so fake, a facade to hide her inner insecurities. Eh, what had the years living in the States done to her?

"What do you think about the 'Feminist Five' arrest?" asked Na Na as we sat across each end of the small coffee table.

That's the first thing you want to know from me? Caught off guard, I was taken aback by how quickly she jumped into the "research stuff."

142

Queer-Ex 143

#FreeTheFive. Digital political cartoon by Badiucao 巴丢草.

Seeing my hesitation, she began to fill me in,

"Have you seen these Andy Warhol–style cartoon avatars of the five detainees online lately?[1] After the arrest, many of the young feminists circulated the digital posters on social media, and a lot of them also posted photos of themselves wearing masks printed with the faces of the five women, demonstrating in public spaces."

Na Na pulled out her cellphone as she spoke and showed me the screenshots. They were supposed to send the message that feminists cannot be taken down altogether by state authorities. A photo of five masked women walking across a pedestrian crosswalk, styled after the Beatles' *Abbey Road* album cover, caught my eyes.[2]

Referencing the Beatles, a white, hippie, global icon of the 1960s counterculture, the cyberspace "performance art," sort of speak, certainly indicated how the young feminists regarded themselves as part of a larger protest cul-

---
1. The art piece is created by political cartoonist Badiucao 巴丢草. See https://chinadigitaltimes.net/wp-content/uploads/2015/04/自由五人-free-the-five-1007x1024-295x300.jpg
2. The poster is created by an anonymous author. See https://asiasociety.org/blog/asia/interview-masked-chinese-activists-show-solidarity-detained-feminists for the image.

144   Queer Chimerica

ture across borders as opposed to a localized movement in China. The hashtag #FreeTheFive, the headshot posters of the five women, and retweeting activities the arrested women previously engaged in, all bore similarities with other icons of dissidence, such as the Cuban Five, Pussy Riot, and FEMEN. Explicitly or implicitly drawing connection with these identifiable cultural symbols, these activities used the tactics not unlike commercial branding, when trying to draw attention to their cause and garner support.

"Does it seem a little opportunistic? Recognizable 'trademarks,' reproducible eye-catching, hands-on, and creative activities," Na Na added. "I mean, why are feminists becoming like entrepreneurs?"

She paused and waited for me to chime in. Long have I been privy to Na Na's reservations about activism, and yet I cannot discount her questionings. Are the flashy tactics we see proliferating on social media platforms truly groundbreaking methods for raising consciousness and building solidarity? Or are they, in fact, nothing more than another neoliberal ploy, preying upon the global "selfie" economy and making grassroots organizing more vulnerable to the watchful eyes of both state and capitalist surveillance?

Despite the tightening governmental disciplining and adversary political environment, feminist agency and resistance these days are too often reduced to economic activities, boiled down to a tally of clicks, tweets, and signatures gathered. Rather than seeking genuine structural changes, the focus has shifted from "political correctness" toward "commercial correctness,"[3] whereby feminist "prosumers" become fixated on measurable outcomes, sacrificing depth of strategy and long-term planning. The result? Attention-worthy conflicts within the community or eye-catching "hot" incidents are inevitable, and ah, the power of conflicts. . . . who knows all the better than I do?

My mind started to meander. Before I allowed myself to get lost in the personal anecdotes, I tried to steer the conversation back toward the big picture. "There are numerous ways to approach your inquiries. One could be to examine the origin of 'gender feminism' and its rise in popularity, in the larger historical and political context of NGOization, or perhaps the Cold War geopolitics that shaped Chinese feminist embrace of the global stage."

"'Gender feminism'? Educate me on that!" Na Na's humility surprised me. I always found it interesting that talking about these political and academic things was how Na Na and I used to bond. The difference, *she* used to be the

---

3. Li Sipan 李思磐, "Weibo Nüquan de Qianshi Jinsheng: cong 'Zhengzhi Zhengque' dao 'Shangye Zhengque'" 微博女权的前世今生:从 '政治正确' 到 '商业正确' [The Past and Present of Weibo Feminism: From 'Political Correctness' to 'Commercial Correctness'], *The Paper* 澎湃, June 16, 2020, https://www.thepaper.cn/newsDetail_forward_7854160

eloquent one, the one who educated others. And should it be her job to learn about history if she was the one conducting the research?

So I briefly mentioned what I knew about how Marxist *funü gongzuo* (women's studies 妇女工作) had given way to "gender feminism" to her, while she jotted down some cursory notes in her tiny field journal.

A Brief Transitional History of "Gender Feminism" and its Implications on China

In 1992, historian and philosopher Li Xiaojiang, who pioneered the discipline of women's studies in China in the 1980s, was invited to a conference on Chinese feminism at Harvard University. At the conference, Li disputed the Western feminist assumptions of Chinese women by pointing out two myths created by American women's studies scholars: the myth of the idealized "women's liberation in the 1950s" and the myth of "double oppression" by both patriarchal family traditions and the undemocratic socialist state. Li's critique of both myths simultaneously addresses a unique form of sexism sponsored by the socialist state patriarchy and the "othering" process of socialist women under Western ideology. However, as Shuh-mei Shih notes, most of Li's writings in the 1990s turned to interrogate the first and consequently ended up reinforcing the second. In the early 1990s, Li, as well as a group of emerging Chinese feminist writers and scholars, made it clear that the state-led gender equality campaign inherits a male-dominant logic, in which women's equality is framed in terms of women's sameness to men; therefore, degendering women and depriving them of their gender difference and femininity. To break free from the dictate of the socialist state, Li and others further advocated for self-discovery and self-consciousness in order to search for *funü zhutixing* (women's subjectivity 妇女主体性). Although Li admitted the potential problems of regendering women, such as the commodification of women and capitalist exploitation, she insisted that women are liberated from patriarchy and reconnected to their gender by being given more choices and subjectivity than under state-sponsored liberation.

Li's writings reflect a pivot point of Chinese women's study and feminism, when the paradigm of *funü* gave way to the paradigm of "gender." "Gender" was first introduced to China in the early 1990s during the preparation process of the United Nations Fourth World Conference on Women in 1995. The translation and dissemination of the concept into Chinese *shehui xingbie* (社会性别) had been a collective effort by individuals, grassroots organizations, and official institutes such as the All China Women's Federation; but most prominently, the

146   Queer Chimerica

Chinese Society for Women's Studies (CSWS) comprised of promising Chinese scholars in the United States. Feminist historian Wang Zheng, a key member of the CSWS and professor at the University of Michigan, regards the Fourth Conference as a "turning point" of Chinese feminism as it makes the expertise of "gender" accessible to women worldwide and empowers them to speak about their subordination to patriarchy.

Although the category of "gender" has been used as one of the most important tools of analyzing power and structural inequality in Western-based feminisms, the very formation of "gender" as part of the larger Cold War economy that informs a specific working of racial capitalism and imperialism remains underexplored.

Feminist political theorist Jemima Repo provides a genealogical analysis of the concept of "gender" and its entanglement with the biopolitics of postwar capitalism in Western industrialized countries. According to Repo, since the 1950s, "gender" went from being a nominator of types to the sexual order of things as a result of psychiatrists' efforts (such as John Money) to discipline and normalize the minds, bodies, and selves of intersex children in the US. The origins of the idea of gender are grounded in postwar projects of social and sexual engineering that targeted not only the ambiguously sexed body but also the psychosexual development of the white, middle-class individual against racialized others.[4] In the 1970s, the concept of "gender" as an apparatus of biopower was instrumentalized to cement Western postwar capitalism through many newly developed "gender equality" policies in Western industrialized societies. For example, in Europe, as the shortage of human capital and taxpayers threatened welfare systems and economic productivity, neoliberal governmentality advanced the discourse of "gender equality" to encourage men and women to share domestic tasks in order to increase flexibility in the labor market. As a result, women are induced to reproduce the organic bodies that constitute the labor force, and therefore work and family life can be reconciled as a solution to economic slowdown. Through the rhetoric of "gender equality," the "two-income family" has become the social norm, thus producing a larger pool of labor power, accompanied by lower wages, poorer job security, and lower living standards.[5]

When second wave Anglo-American feminists took up the discourse of gender in the 1970s to challenge biological determinism, the biopolitical apparatus of "gender" failed to be recognized and challenged. The failure could be

---

4. Jemima Repo, *The Biopolitics of Gender* (Oxford: Oxford University Press, 2015), 1–24.

5. Repo, *Biopolitics*, 75–104.

said to speak to the geopolitical apparatus of gender, which has also remained underexamined in the dominant US feminist realm. Scholars of second-world feminism such as Karen Garner and Kristen Ghodsee have provided thorough historicization of how "gender" and "gender mainstreaming" are direct results of the shifting power struggles of the postwar geopolitics and global economy mediated by the ascendance of US imperialism and the fall of international communism. Due to Cold War anti-communism, US feminists began to deradicalize since the 1960s. As women's concerns started to mainstream, cultural and liberal feminists have shifted to work within the dominant capitalist structures in order to make the system more favorable to the unique needs and requirements of women. These "unique" needs and requirements could be applied to all women against patriarchy. Therefore, class and race were subsumed under gender oppression.[6] This US feminists' agenda of seeing gender and women's issues as separate from the geopolitical, paved the road for further racialization via gender at the UN conferences internationally. The three United Nations World Conferences on Women and the process of "gender mainstreaming" after the Fourth conference are examples.

In 1975 the UN declared the years 1975–1985 as The Decade for Women. Three international women's conferences, in Mexico City (1975), Copenhagen (1980), and Nairobi (1985), were held with the aim to advance women's equal opportunities in economic, cultural, religious, political, and judicial fields among its members. At the UN conferences, as Karen Garner and Kristen Ghodsee note, women's issues took center stage for the Cold War competition between United States and the Soviet Union.

In reflecting on the tensions that informed the conferences, Ghodsee points out the complexity between US Cold War imaginary and rising domination of Western feminism. During the conferences, American feminists believed that their leadership of the international women's movement was challenged by the anti-imperialist rhetoric of the socialist feminists of the Soviet Union and its allies. American politicians, otherwise reticent, in fear of socialist women hijacking the international conference and mobilizing women in the developing world with their anti-capitalist "peace" agenda, was forced to take the emerging international conferences seriously. US congressmen were actively involved in constructing an "appropriate" agenda for women's issues for the American delegates, which laid the foundation for what would later become the

---

6. Kristen Ghodsee, "Feminism-by-Design: Emerging Capitalisms, Cultural Feminism, and Women's Nongovernmental Organizations in Postsocialist Eastern Europe," *Signs: Journal of Women in Culture and Society*, 29, no. 3 (2004): 732.

148   Queer Chimerica

hegemonic internalized form of Western feminism after the collapse of communism in 1989.[7]

The collapse of the Soviet Union four years after the Nairobi conference in 1985 reoriented the international women's movement toward the American feminist perspective by the 1995 conference in Beijing, reinforcing the link between women's issues and political economy.[8] In 1995, women from the Eastern Bloc, seen as "free" from their communist governmental control, started to accept Western liberal feminism instead of an anti-capitalist agenda. The "gender first" paradigm allowed US/Western feminists to imagine themselves as representing democracy through a universalizing value system of women's oppression and their solution at the cost of racializing others who did not share the same values. The formation of "gender" and its global circulation and acceptance through US- and UN-sponsored projects and institutions, like racial liberalism, functions as a technology that marks the differences between the free and unfree, the liberal and illiberal, and the democratic and the tyrannical. This universalization was epitomized in Hillary Clinton's famous "Women's Rights are Human Rights" speech in 1995.

What is important about these geopolitical struggles is that the racialization through ideological differences has yielded economic consequences that advanced the US global neoliberal hegemony. The post-1995 era witnessed a groundswell of gender and development (GAD) aid in the former Eastern Bloc and countries, such as China, that had voluntarily undergone a socialist to post-socialist transition. As the successor of previous women in development (WID) programs implanted in the third world by the UN and other powerful nations in the early 1970s, these programs, as part of the neoliberal agenda, helped to incorporate women into economic growth and to prevent the spread of world communism.[9] Although GAD projects were supposed to rectify the capitalist and first world feminist values of WID, its modifications did not fundamentally challenge the capitalist model of development nor seriously consider a class-based analysis of women's oppression.[10]

---

7. Ghodsee, "Revisiting the United Nations Decade for Women: Brief Reflections on Feminism, Capitalism and Cold War Politics in the Early Years of the International Women's Movement," *Women's Studies International Forum* 33 (2010): 3.

8. Ghodsee, "Revisiting the United Nations," 9.

9. See Arturo Escobar, *Encountering Development: The Making and Unmaking of the Third World* (New Jersey: Princeton University Press, 1995) for further discussion on Cold War and development programs.

10. Ghodsee, "And If the Shoe Doesn't Fit? (Wear It Anyway): Economic Transformation and Western Paradigms of Women in Development Programs in Post-communist Central and Eastern Europe," *Women's Studies Quarterly* 31, no. 3/4 (2003): 27.

These WID/GAD programs defined and popularized the very notion of "basic needs" for women, approaches and means to "equality," and framed women and their programs in a capitalist measurement of productivity while maintaining liberal ideology such as "rights" and "citizenship." As billions of dollars rushed into former socialist countries through development projects and international aid to develop "democratic institutions" and "free markets," Western scholars and activists rode a tidal wave of grants available for research and projects in those countries undergoing transition. These Western feminists imported the paradigm of "gender first" without fully understanding the significance of the historical struggle of women over class issues.[11] Western feminists and gender NGOs' emphasis on gendered difference transcending class, race, ethnicity, and other identity markers were understood as uniting women across regions and creating "women" as a single category. But what is behind this category of "women" is the Western "whitening" through liberal ideas of womanhood, female subjectivity, and the Westernized model of gender roles. Those who do not fit this definition are said to be less liberal, less democratic, and less "woman" in the Western sense.

These projects and resources constructed women as a group of victims and "losers" in the economic transitional period, needing to be saved by Western democracy and capitalist economic structures. Under this political and economic structure, the strategy for women to assume the position of "victim" of the state and economy is proven working. These projects also distinguished women in the postsocialist and transitioning counties as those who identify with and those who do not identify with the discourse of empowerment through political and economic "whitening." The "honorary white" liberal feminist in former socialist countries would have more access to capital and visibility compared to their sisters who resisted and adhered to older socialist models. That is why the "gender first" paradigm and its mainstreaming functioned as a technology that assisted the replacement of socialist radical gender politics and movement by neoliberal ones that rest on identity, "basic needs," and rights, which are said to be lacking under communism/socialism.

It is not difficult to notice that the emergence of "gender feminism" in China was coeval with Chandra Mohanty's foundational piece "Under Western Eyes."[12] While challenging global liberal feminism through third-world and transnational feminism started to dominate the field of North women's and

---

11. Ghodsee, "Feminism-by-Design," 733.

12. Chandra Talpade Mohanty, "Under Western Eyes: Feminist Scholarship and Colonial Discourses," *Boundary 2*, 12, no. 3 (1984): 333–58.

150   Queer Chimerica

gender studies in the late 1980s, Chinese feminists steered away from solidarity with third-world women to disrupt imperialism and placed its priority in the 1990s to connect to the globalized world.

Situating the post–Cold War emergence of Chinese "gender feminism" within the larger motif of the biopolitics and geopolitics of postwar capitalism, we can trace the ways in which Chinese routes to women's issues and the adaption of transnational gender politics are conditioned by a particular double-bind where Chinese women are "othered" as both the "third world" and "communist" anomalies. Rather than merely being the passive recipients of global trends of "gender" or "gender NGOization," Chinese feminist activists' and scholars' embrace of the "international" through affinity to Western liberal feminism can be seen as a response to the double-bind through negotiation of their positions with both state patriarchy and neoliberalization.

The emergence of "Chinese women" as a subject of Western scholarly inquiry can be traced back to the nineteenth century following China's defeat by European colonialism. Largely influenced by Euro-US political interests in Asia, early missionaries and ethnologists documented Chinese women's subordination to Confucian patriarchy and sought to civilize them from perceived cultural backwardness. As a mixture of Christian humanism and orientalist fascination with China, this type of knowledge production emphasized the weakness and victimhood of Chinese women and used their subordination to validate Western superiority and thus justify their imperialist agenda.

The Western study of "Chinese women" took a socialist turn starting in the early twentieth century when women's liberation movements in the West started to focus on women's rights to work, education, and political participation. Supplemental to the victimhood representation, Chinese women in the communist revolution who enjoyed rights in the labor force and public space were taken as "role models" for the Western (both white liberal and black radical) feminist political agenda. Socialist feminists in the West used the status of Chinese women as litmus to test the viability of socialism for women's liberalism in their own locations. Prominent examples are socialist feminist Judith Stacey and poststructuralist feminist Julia Kristeva who to some degree, shared the savior's sentiments with early missionary Westerners.[13] Ironically, both Stacey and Kristeva's utopian imagination of socialist China were compromised by disillusionment with communism/socialism and followed by a retreat

---

13. See Judith Stacey, *Patriarchy and Socialist Revolution in China* (Oakland: University of California Press, 1984); and Julia Kristeva, *About Chinese Women* (London: Marion Boyars Publishers, 1977).

to Western superiority after visiting China and witnessing Chinese women's oppression by both traditional society and the economic underdevelopment of China. These works, as many Chinese-critical socialist feminists have argued, show how North-based feminists replicated McCarthyism and Cold War anti-communism in their theorization by reducing Chinese communist revolution to patriarchy and simplifying the relations between women's liberation, anti-colonialism, and the nation-state.[14]

The orientalist and idealist knowledge production of Chinese women as both victims "needing to be saved" (from patriarchy, communism, poverty, and so on) and as radical revolutionary resisters as a supplement to Western radical politics and US women's studies, was both reinscribed and disrupted in the late and post–Cold War enterprise of "the global woman."

At the first three UN conferences on women, China sent delegates but due to domestic political and economic reasons[15] did not assume pivotal roles within the Cold War power struggle at the conferences. Even as an official socialist and namely third world country, China was not explicitly taking sides with the "Second World/Third World" women's coalition against Western feminists through the anti-capitalist "peace agenda" during the UN Decade. Yet, against the backdrop of the 1989 Tian'anmen upheaval and Western economic sanctions, China was motivated to move past its political and economic impasses and reassert an international reputation and global status. Like the 1990 Asian Games, the Fourth Conference provided prolific opportunities to polish China's tarnished international image through showcasing Chinese women's advanced social positions. These series of national projects in the cultural spheres enabled China to regain connections, networks, and international investments and capital, as showing "good government policies" consolidated China's commitment to and confidence in advancing a more open international market where goods, capital, ideas, and people flow with ease. While WID and GAD paradigms had great difficulties taking root in the former Eastern Bloc as addressed in the previous section, Chinese feminists in the late 1980s predominantly gave up the

---

14. See Wang Zhenling 王珍玲, "Zhongguo Shehuizhuyi Nüquan Shijian Zaisikao" 中国社会主义女性主义实践再思考 [Rethinking Chinese Socialist Feminist Praxis], *Funü Yanjue Luncong* 妇女研究论丛 [Collection of Women's Studies] no. 3 (2015): 8, https://doi.org/10.3969/j.issn.1004-2563.2015.03.001; and Song Shaopeng 宋少鹏, "Shehuizhuyi Funüjuefang yu Xifang Nüquanzhuyi de Qübie: Lilun yu Shijian" 社会主义妇女解放与西方女权主义的区别: 理论与实践 [Differences between Chinese Socialist Women's Liberation and Western Feminism: Theory and Practice], *Shanxi Shida Xuebao* 山西师大学报 [Journal of Shanxi Normal University] 38, no. 4 (July 2011): 147, https://www.docin.com/p-1449500826.html

15. Due to many economic and political reasons, including the Cultural Revolution (1966–1976), China was not actively participating in the UN Decade.

152   Queer Chimerica

long-standing anti-imperialist, anti-feudalist tradition of Marxist-based *funü* women's liberation and turned to identifying with the globalizing concept of "gender." Under the zeitgeist of *zhuanxing* (transition 转型) and *yu shijie jiegui* (connecting the tracks with the world 与世界接轨), embracing "gender feminism" was instrumental for both the state and women's work at the time to forge dialogue and to be recognized by the world internationally. Domestically, "female subjectivity," as well as the framing of the gender issues in terms of "women in relation to men," rather than "women and men" in relation to "the state" in the previous socialist era, allowed the state to shrug off responsibilities for providing social security and welfare, economic stability, and opportunities for re-employment. The individualist approach to gender inequality would soon lead to the commodification of femininity, further feminization of labor, and revival of traditional gender roles.

Despite its anti-essentialist nature, fresh perspective of accounting women's experience, and unquestionable impact on Chinese feminist movements and women's studies since the 1990s, the translation of "gender" from its inception was met with many troubles. Some of the major debates were on the term's adoption of universalism as an analytical norm in both women's studies and NGO work and its implication of a break from the Chinese socialist past.[16] Critics of "gender" have pointed out that the category of gender subsumes Chinese feminism and the experience of Chinese women into a global formula marked by its "differences within commonality."[17] Severing socialist women's liberation from both patriarchy and imperialism, the concept of "gender" promotes the idealization of freedom, the individual, the body, and subjectivity as opposed to justice, collectivism, and the economy as the central object of feminist critique.

Dong Limin, one of the major opponents of gender feminists, also criticizes local feminist scholars' willingness to accept "gender" and sees it as reflecting the Chinese inability to produce theory independently, a prism of the Chinese colonial aphasia vis-à-vis the West. "Gender," Dong further argues, alienates Chinese feminism from its own socialist history of liberation and turns it into

---

16. For a detailed discussion of the gender "trouble," traveling theory, and localization, see Nicola Spakowski, "'Gender' Trouble: Feminism in China under the Impact of Western Theory and the Spatialization of Identity," *Positions* 19, no. 1 (2011): 31–54. For a critical socialist feminist critique of gender feminism and a reclamation of socialist Funü and women's liberation, see Nicola Spakowski, "Socialist Feminism in Postsocialist China," *Positions* 26, no. 4 (November 2018): 561–92; and Xin Huang, "Funü in the Gender Legacy of the Mao Era and Contemporary Feminist Struggle in China," in *Gender Dynamics, Feminist Activism and Social Transformation in China*, eds. Guoguang Wu, Yuan Feng, and Helen Lansdowne (Abingdon, UK: Routledge, 2019).

17. Spakowski, "'Gender' Trouble," 42–44.

Queer-Ex 153

the "other."[18] This colonial anxiety and the othering of the self is also echoed by the works of Song Shaopeng.[19] But these critiques were largely suppressed in the 1990s both domestically and transnationally due to the waning of postcolonial critique and the winning globalization of "gender." The following anecdote serves as a good example of these complications:

At the "Socialist Women's Liberation and Western Feminism" workshop held at the People's University of China in 2011, Du Jie, a researcher of All-China Women's Federation, recalled her experience of attending the World Asian Pacific Women's Conference in 1993.[20] As the representative from the Federation, an organization perceived in liberal and democratic thoughts as an apparatus of the socialist state and the official voice of the Communist party, her speech was frequently disrupted by the booing audience. Du observes the predicament of Chinese socialist feminism, where the Federation is marginalized in both the domestic official discourse of the state and on the international stage of feminist and women's movements that adopted an uncritical view of communist authoritarianism and romanticization of transnational NGOs and civil societies. One may wonder where the anti-colonial and anti-racist feminist voices were at such a troubling moment. It is important to remember that colonial studies had retreated from Marxist nationalism and turned to postcolonial literary and cultural critiques in the 1980s. The global anti-communist fad for postsocialist transition and esoteric academicism all came together to render colonial critiques insignificant to Chinese women in the late 1980s. Du's marginalization was also magnified through both language and theoretical barriers, yet another indicator of China's seclusion from the transnational world and the punishment of its chosen "wrong-side."

"Given the history of 'gender' and how it has been impacted by the bio- and geo-power of postwar capitalism and neoliberalism since the 1970s," Na Na sat the teacup on the table, "I would say that the neoliberal entrepreneur-like ways of doing feminism come from the incomplete and ongoing effort to integrate Chinese feminism into the family of global feminism, a result of a complex

---

18. Dong Limin 董丽敏, "Nüxingzhuyi: Bentuhua yu qi weidu" 女性主义：本土化及其维度 [Feminism: Indigenization and Its Dimensions], *Nankai Xuebao* 南开学报 [Nankai Journal] no. 2 (2005): 11, https://www.docin.com/p-1430365368.html

19. See Song, "Lizu Wenti, Wuguan Zhong Xi: zai Lishi de Neizai Mailuo zhong Jiangou de Xueke: dui Zhongguo 'Funü/Xingbie Yanjiu' de Sixiangshi Kaocha" 立足问题，无关中西：在历史的内在脉络中建构的学科—对中国 '妇女／性别研究'的思想史考察 [Questions of Positionality: The Genealogy of Chinese Women's Studies in the History of Disciplinary Development], *Funü Yanjue Luncong* 妇女研究论丛 [Collections of Women's Studies] no. 5 (2018): 37.

20. Song, "Qübie," 148.

colonial and imperial doubling through which Chinese women are othered as both the 'communist' and the 'third world' victim-resistor."

I flicked a cigarette and finished the claim for her as I used to, "Yet, the desire to shake off this double-hat and the labor to navigate through the two-layered 'othering' simultaneously reformulates previous colonial formations and reproduces new forms of struggles and agency."

"And this persistent battle has gained new expressions in the age of digital capitalism, especially with incidents like the 'Feminist Five' arrest," Na Na added.

"I was talking with the activists since the detention, and it struck me to see how easily the complexity of the incident and differently positioned feminist politics around it were reduced to a simplified opposition that replicates a too-common Cold War trope of the repressive communist party-state vis-à-vis its oppressed yet heroic resistors. In the early stage, one of the debates among the activists was whether this incident was a routine round-up before *lianghui*, and whether feminists should rely on international media and resources to pressure the Chinese government for the release of the five women. Some folks expressed concern, for example, that international pressure would escalate the tension between the government and civil society and portray feminist and LGBT activists as political dissidents. Not only might it worsen the situation of the arrested young women, leading to harsher treatment at the detention center, but also making 'feminism' a sensitive subject, breaking the 'unhappy but still working marriage' between feminism and the state. This type of concern was severely criticized by others. For them, the state is the ultimate embodiment of patriarchal power, and the detention is an example *par excellence* of patriarchal oppression executed by the state. To dismantle patriarchy, feminists must dismantle the state. A critique without targeting the state is seen as being complicit, feeding into the continuous expansion of state violence under the name of national security and social stability.

"Now I see the longer history behind the tensions, but help me understand, why can't the movement allow these differences without pulling people into opposing camps and attacking one another? Why were different voices homogenized and the people whose opinions were not considered the most radical were labeled anti-feminists? Is it inevitable that cyberspace activism encourages people to invest in the pursuit of potential 'enemies' and (re)producing 'others within,' an extension to existing conflicts within the communities?"

I gave her a smirk, inwardly mocking her naïve ignorance, "A successful movement needs clear targets, bad guys and good guys, and black-and-white politics," I add, "Ambiguity allows for no action."

As I engaged in more conversations with Na Na, I surprisingly found how much I actually enjoyed them. I began to miss my days with her as well as the friendships and heartbreaks when I was part of the queer *lala* activism. But I should have known better to prepare for the worst in the time of happiness.

Days later, I woke up to a barrage of cellphone notifications and saw myself being tagged in an inundation of *Sina Weibo* tweets. I hadn't used the platform for some time, so what could it be? A traitor, a government spy, a rumormonger, a detractor . . . . . . I skimmed the messages, what had I done to bring about the wrath of God?

An anonymous article titled "A Rictus of 'War of Words'" went viral online, and apparently, I was suspected to be the author. The article was regarded as "attacking feminism," "undermining global solidarity," and written by a spy "serving the interests of the surveillant state and the CCP." Who else could possess such internal information about feminist organizing and simultaneously harbor such strong disdain for the activists as I did? I took a quick look at the anonymous article and of course, its content was unmistakably based on my chat with Na Na. Ah, how surprising. No sooner had I given you a tale to cite then I see you trash me once again in despair.

That's how Na Na betrayed me once again! Now I recall. But why? Why would she do that, and why would I hate the activists so much to denigrate them?

As I sit here in the Nano Pod, trying to decipher Na Na's behaviors in my search for more of my Empty Chair writings, I am suddenly blocked out by some brainwave interference. The images that were once clear in my head now blur together, leaving me buzzed. It is then that I am met with the piercing gaze of Andrei, his lake-colored eyes locking onto mine, his lips moving fiercely, "Stop your probing unless you're ready to confront what you hide deep from yourself."

Taken aback by his sudden aggression, I recoil instinctively. "That's ridiculous! What do you mean? What else could I possibly be hiding from myself that I don't already know? I have faced my past. What else about myself couldn't I face?" I demand, my voice rising in pitch as I struggle to keep my emotions in check.

"Perhaps you seek comfort in being a victim yourself, you certainly know the power of being a subject of trauma well. The trauma narrative allows you to bury painful memory and guilt deep inside. It legitimizes your crave for the care and attentions from others. Involving in the Beijing Dome Project has

156 Queer Chimerica

provided you with a convenient escape from facing these difficult experiences. But it's time for things to change."

Andrei then seizes my wrists, "I dare you to take off your glove, my friend."

I quickly pull away from his grip and tuck my hands into my pockets, hiding the translucent whiteness spreading from my fingertips and seeping through underneath my skin.

The next day Andrei hands me a mint green binder.

"I must confess that I had some reservations regarding your attempt to restore Na Na," Andrei says, "But I know what is happening to you." He gestures toward the binder, "Take this as my apology. It's the last piece of Na Na that I could muster for you."

I take the binder from him. The pages inside are falling into pieces. The color-coded tabs are warped and bent, sticking out from the sides like crooked teeth. But the handwriting on the plastic cover is still clear:

Fieldnotes

Ye Shana

ADDRESS: 323 7th SE, Apt 307,
Minneapolis, MN 55414

PLEASE RETURN IF FOUND, thanks :)

PART V

The Transporters

CHAPTER 13

Inequality Must be Created

With great curiosity, I unfurl Na Na's field notes. If I were to restore her, I must put aside my negative feelings about her and gather as much information as I can. I must understand what drove her down the path of a Beets theft and a "shrimp dumpling." What she learned in her search must tell, and her words must illuminate.

There are some selfish reasons beyond altruism too. I look at the pallor of my skin that I can no longer hide. Why, after all these years, had she re-entered my life only to exact a painful revenge? What did I do to deserve such a betrayal?

Contents
To-Do-List ——————— Green
Interview Schedule ——— Yellow
Forms ——————— Blue
Historical Background —— Red
Journal Entries ——————— Orange
Research Questions ——— Indigo
Lit Review ——————— Pink
Correspondences——————— White
Reflections ——————— Purple
Miscellaneous ——————— Clear

Journal Entries

JUNE 19, 2014

I met Guang Hui today when I visited an LGBT organization in Beijing. He made a cup of tea for me and showed me around when I was waiting for the interview with the director. My first impression of Guang Hui was that, unlike other employees, he seemed a little out of place. He was of medium build, hunched over a bit, deep wrinkles between his giant double-lidded brown eyes. He wore a pink floral shirt, and dark-skinned with a metrosexual vibe. But his cigarette-stained fingers and Northeast accent betrayed his "NGO professional" shell. I was also a little surprised by the fact that, as a person with masculine expressions, he was the one doing most of the feminized work of a receptionist around the office.

Guang Hui was a core member of the organization in the early 2000s when it started as an HIV/AIDS intervention group. He believed in social progress and thought any society should advance from backwardness to western-style civilization. As a pioneer, it was his obligation to spread the progressive ideas of Western democracy. This devotion was to uproot any lingering barriers from feudalist and socialist old thoughts.

When he came back to the organization in 2011 as a cameraman for some "crumbs of bread," the leadership of the organization had long changed, and it had successfully transformed from an AIDS community group to a well-funded leading LGBT advocacy NGO.

To my surprise, Guang Hui WAS very upfront about his unhappiness at his current job as he confessed to me:

> I guess it is because of my own pettiness though. When I was an HIV/AIDS volunteer a decade ago, I was the representative of 'advanced' Western thoughts. At the current organization, there are many more 'advanced Westernized representatives', and I have become one of those who need to be 'educated'. When I talk about 'sexual liberation', what I had in mind is the *gongle* (shared pleasure 共乐) culture of places like cruising parks, but they would teach me some fancy new concepts of *duoyuan xingbie* (diverse gender/sex 多元性别) and *duoyuan qingyu* (diverse desire 多元情趣) or drop the same-sex marriage, adoption, and surrogacy card.

If you look at the ordinary LGBT people in China, how many of them really care about marriage before job security, filial responsibilities, or access to medical care and housing? At an LGBT conference I attended some years ago when almost every gay activist was talking about human rights, equality and social acceptance, a lesbian woman from Yunnan stood up and told the audience that her problem was that her workplace asked female workers to wear a skirt or they would be fired. This struck me a lot. Did the rights-based advocacy help to solve her issue? No. Did they care to solve her issue? Probably not. In my opinion, that's perhaps why LGBT advocacy is so dislodged from the real needs of the communities.

At first, I actively participated in roundtable meetings, offering strategic ideas for the movement, fundraising, possible activities, and so on. Soon I found out that compared to the younger, well-travelled, and abroad-educated advocates, my opinion did not matter much. So I learned to retreat to the break room.

Correspondences

Dear Mr. Guang Hui,

I would like to express my gratitude for the opportunity to meet with you earlier today. I regret that our conversation was brief, as I would have appreciated the chance to delve more deeply into the topics we discussed.

During our meeting, you mentioned the gap between advocacy-oriented activism and community needs. I am curious to know your thoughts on the reasons behind the apparent failure of LGBT activism. Could it be attributed to the utilization of Western advocacy models by NGOs that do not align with the local contexts? Please educate me on this matter.

Sincerely,

Ye Shana

June 19, 2014

162 Queer Chimerica

Dr. Ye,

Is this gap caused by the Western advocacy model? Yes and No.

Long story short, you will have to look at the history of the Western NGO industry and how international funds have impacted Chinese activism. You probably already know this, the discourse of developmentalism started in the 1960s is the precursor to the nonprofit industrial complex in the 1990s. Instead of looking at broader social issues and the well-being of homosexuals as a whole, the NGO industry has encouraged local organizations to focus on "projects" that could yield quick and measurable results. This trajectory has several consequences:

Firstly, because international NGOs promote projects for LGBT communities, the subject of LGBT needs to be constructed. Local sexual practices, such as men who have sex with men but do not consider themselves "homosexuals," were reoriented into more "enlightened" ideas of westernized sexuality through the concepts of "rights" and "liberation." Those previously stigmatized people—*tuzi* (rabbit 兔子), *liumang* (hooligan 流氓), *eryizi* (effeminate man 二刈子)—are now LGBT and *tongzhi*. An interesting paradox you need to pay attention to here is that the "enlightened" subject is also the "violated" subject by state oppression, societal ignorance, or family pressure. This might explain your question about why the mainstream discourse of LGBT focuses so much on oppression that we talked about at our first meeting. Oppression and violence are real, we all admit, but what the discourse about oppression does is another issue. It is apparent, though, that only when you have a group of "helpless," "violated" subjects can expert interventions and solutions be justified and implemented.

Secondly, I don't know if you have been in the field long enough to notice that current mainstream activism emphasizes "community service" a lot. For example, my organization is paired up with several multinational companies to promote *duoyuan xing/bie* (diversity of gender/sexuality 多元性/别) training for their employees. Each year, the organization holds LGBT leadership workshops and training camps for LGBT-related creative projects. Professional counseling and therapy services are also underway. I also remember seeing advertisements for immigration services for gay and lesbian couples. When I first joined the group a decade ago, community service meant very different things: organizing dating opportunities, hiking, dancing, cooking, sports clubs, or sharing advice on love, break ups, and family relationships. Oh, this reminds me, I was a member of a swimming club. Back in the northeast, there were many *yangge* dance troops organized by volunteers. These activities, however, were usually regarded as "low-brow," "fooling around," and "lack of organization." They didn't meet the vision of the funding agencies and donors because they were not thought of as raising the consciousness of LGBT identities. But I must caution you here, Dr. Ye, when I said that these activities were "low-brow," I didn't mean they were lower-class activities. Well-educated and well-off people used to go to cruising sites. Back then, the gap between the rich and poor was not as large as it is now. The problem, in my opinion, is that the LGBT model categorized different activities into hierarchies and divided the participants into each of their proper slots.

At first, in order to get money, an organizer would have to play very smart and write these activities under "office supplies." But you could only go so far faking it before you had to grow an entrepreneurial mind of your own and come up with eye-catching projects. Gradually you learned how to utilize new concepts and new trends to write successful proposals, how to remold your projects to fit each donor's special taste, and how to cultivate a group of participants who are willing to and capable of buying into these new projects. You turn a blind eye to the needs of those who do not fall in your "clientele." The less you invest in them, the further they drift away from your "targeted community." The more they become the low-brow waiting to be enlightened, the more money and more projects could be justified to be brought in. So, Dr. Ye, you tell me, does the uneven distribution of funding create class differences? *Inequality must be created* to move capital. Since the processes of fund applications were very much formulated, volunteers were encouraged to be specialized in a certain part of the projects, and the supposedly advanced, democratic, and innovative means of activism also ended up creating the bureaucratization of the organization. If Karl Marx were still awake today, I am sure he would write a book on labor division and the alienation of gay capital.

Returning to your questions, in my opinion, international donors are not to blame. When Western LGBT activism and theories (social construction, poststructuralism, and queer theory) came to China in the 1990s, queer culture and advocacy in the West were already very diversified. It is not that there was a hegemonic Western theory to draw from. In fact, it was the indigenous NGO workers and activists who chose what was the best for China and constructed the "most correct" practice so that the homosexuals could be *xibai* (white-washed 洗白) as "pure" to be accepted by the society. This leads to my third point, that mainstream LGBT politics wanted to construct homosexuals as respectable people who can be tolerated by society and deny the "dirty secret" of gay culture, which is the fact that sex could lead to disease. But so what? Gay sex leads to AIDS? If it is the case, then build a healthcare system that treats it, instead of prohibiting sex!

Some people say that being LGBT is like competing for the "model worker'" in the old socialist system (*pinxuan laomo* 评选劳模). Those who advocate for same-sex marriage, pure love, and coming out are the first-tier models; those who stayed in the closet are the ordinary people; and those who married the opposite sex are the "bad elements" who poisoned the liberation movement. But don't get me wrong, this hierarchy has for sure changed lately. After 2010, many activists have been advocating for destigmatizing sex and the diversity of sexual desires. There have been lots of workshops like the BDSM one you went to, targeting middle-class, urban, young people like yourself. They started to teach people how to explore unconventional relationships, such as non-monogamous and polyamorous relationships, as if these were something drastically new. You might have also noticed that many LGBT websites advocate for the more Western advanced, monogamous and coming out models while also advertising for pornography and gray-zone sex work. There is an economic link between these two if I am not making up conspiracy theories. The flip side is that non-monogamous, multipartner sexual practices have been the norm among men at the cruising park, which are fiercely assailed as dirty, dangerous, and uncivilized. The behaviors of *lanjiao* (promiscuity 滥交), as the business of the lower half of the body, is never brought up on the LGBT agenda, except when being blamed for causing the spread of AIDS. Have you thought about what caused this differentiated construction of promiscuous sex?

It is late. Although I like writing, chatting in person sounds more enticing. Plus, please don't be so formal with me.

Guang Hui

June 21, 2014

Dear Guang Hui,

Thank you so much for your sharing! It feels like you are doing the research for me and I could be finishing my fieldwork next week :) Have you ever considered writing a book about the history of the Chinese LGBT movement? Although some work has been done on this subject, I am sure that your unique perspective, straddling two worlds, would offer a fresh and fascinating take.

Also, as per your request to not be so formal, call me Na Na, as my friends do:)

Na Na

June 22, 2014

Morning Na Na,

I haven't slept for twenty-six hours! Conversations with you have kept my brain hypervigilant. I am happy that I am useful for your research, but I am not interested in writing about activism and social movements myself. There have been many "internal" materials of community experiences shared among the activists. Who would be my audience? And who am I to write a book? A loser and outcast of the movement? I don't have the right identity to write about LGBT activism. And most important of all, I am not going to set myself up for personal attacks.

But I *am* writing a book! One on the lives of older gay men, which interests me more than the debates within the activist groups and scholarly rumination of normativity. If you want to understand how people manage to live, you gotta have your foot on the muddy ground. Care to tag along?

Hui

June 23, 2014

CHAPTER 14

Zhang Shanping the Hooligan III

Journal Entries

JUNE 30, 2014

Today Guang Hui introduced me to Lao Zhang at Dongdan park. They had crossed paths many times. When Guang Hui was a volunteer, Lao Zhang was his subject to mobilize, now, he is a treasure to mine and study.

For the past several years, Guang Hui has spent his days at cruising parks talking to elders like Lao Zhang and his nights in front of his desk reading books and articles, in Chinese and English, purchased or pirated. Without a stable source of income, he has exhausted his mom's savings account. He moves to the outside of the sixth ring suburb and takes advantage of the daily three to four-hour commute mapping out his book chapters and filling in holes. Besides the six hundred yuan rent for his single room, most of his salary goes to cigarettes and the English books he orders from Amazon. He is interested in my research. He had not heard of affect theory prior to knowing me, so he is very delighted to be my "sidekick" and exchange ideas with me. Lao Zhang was perfect for both of us. But since Guang Hui and I had very different research agendas, our conversations often went multidirectional, which frustrated, if not irritated me.

Lao Zhang is still doing some sort of HIV/AIDS-related work. Nowadays, as both the HIV/AIDS and LGBT movements have moved toward a professionalization that prioritizes civil rights–based advocacy, the everyday tedious work has been left to retired, low-income, and migrant *tongzhi* men. At the parks, a volunteer usually works a four-hour shift for most of the year, conducting HIV rapid tests, delivering educational material, and providing basic information on condom use, medical care, and mental health assistance. Oftentimes they also escort positive individuals to the hospitals, picking up medicine for them and providing care for sick patients. Depending on the "quota" of intervention the volunteer group receives each season, the volunteers are given different amounts of money for compensation, ranging from a few hundred yuan for the volunteers to about two thousand yuan for the person who is in charge of the group (the average income in Beijing at the time of the research conducted was ¥6900).

It was quite difficult for me to call Lao Zhang's work "work" at first since he just seemed to be hanging out at the park. As a result of the uneven neoliberal reform and globalization in China that created a strong bourgeois and cosmopolitan middle urban class, the rural-to-urban and laid-off workers have lost their privileged status as the working class under Maoism and become underprivileged outcasts of the society.[1] In other words, the old and unemployed are the worthless litter and baggage of the labor migration–orientated economy. They are, in the words of health and administrative officials, idling at the park and would not have gotten a job to start with. A CDC official told me that the few hundred yuan they gave the volunteers was much more than they deserved since they were too old to be really "productive," and their "only" job was to hang out in the park and distribute condoms along the way. The official saw no explanation other than that the CDC was doing a favor to people like them. Certainly, I do not doubt the kindness and good intention of this official, but the irony here is that the idea of Chinese traditional and socialist virtues of "doing good" and "serving the people"—both from the CDC official who believes in "helping the helpless" and from *tongzhi* volunteers who internalize their responsibility to "sacrifice"—disguises the unacknowledged truth of "slow death" left by structural inequality: precarious *tongzhi* people are not only stigmatized because of their nonnormative sexuality but also as the nonnormative surplus of China's growing economy, while their labor is in fact central to the social reproduction of the economy. At the moment of the economic transition and "rise of China," the state not only fails to account

---

1. Travis Kong, "Transnational Queer Labor: The 'Circuits of Desire' of Money Boys in China," *English Language Notes* 49, no. 1 (2011): 141.

168 Queer Chimerica

for people's life at the juncture of homophobia, sexual normality, and labor restructuring but also further exploits them as forfeitable subjects for producing capital under the name of assistance and job opportunities. The social security system also takes advantage of the "charity" of transnational donations to deal with the made-invisible litter of the market economy. Given the normative and normalizing power on queer life, HIV/AIDS intervention as a business of physical, material, and social death, ironically engines up the billion dollars transnational NGO industry that is crucial to China's economic development.

Lao Zhang's work unit has long gone. Even if the factory were still standing today, there would have been no way for the hooligan to return. After tricking a doctor by marrying a woman, Lao Zhang left Nanjing, where he was being treated as a patient for sexual inversion and schizophrenia. He hopped on a train to Beijing without paying the fare because he wanted to see Tian'anmen Square. There he started selling counterfeits under the watchful eye of Chairman Mao. He was caught several times by the city patrols, but luckily enough, his fortune was turned around. He finally found a temporary job at a bicycle shed belonging to a *zhaodaisuo* (state-owned hostel) in the Qianmen area. He would not be given that job since "watching the bicycle shed" was reserved for "retired" socialist workers who needed reemployment at that time, and he certainly did not qualify given his record. But the owner of the *zhaodaisuo* had a heart of gold.

Lao Zhang told Guang Hui and I at the cruising park:

I used to hang around in the area and noticed many young migrant workers coming and going. Sometimes I initiated conversations with them and asked if they were looking for jobs. These youngsters were often poorly educated and had no credentials or qualifications, and they were like headless flies having no idea where to look for jobs.

I told them about a governmental office in Xuanwu District, just a couple blocks from Qianman. They were the first labor market (*renli shichang* 人力市场) in Beijing, not a human resource market (*rencai shichang* 人才市场), and they didn't charge agency fees.

Both Guang Hui and I were waiting for Lao Zhang's story to reveal some unexpected romantic encounter that finally led him to the realiza-

Zhang Shanping the Hooligan III   169

tion of his gay identity, but he did not go in the direction we hoped. He continued,

> About a year later, I heard from a hostel acquaintance that a young rural migrant worker at a construction company had been denied salary for no reason for three months and couldn't afford living in Beijing. I gathered some legal documents and went to his workplace, arguing with the managers and telling them I could file a legal case against them. They saw me as an elder who knew about laws and compromised and gave him his salary in the next few days. "Selling oldness" (*yilao mailao* 倚老卖老) apparently worked.

I did not want Lao Zhang to go astray from the topic of how he realized his *tongzhi* identity and then interrupted hastily, "So were you attracted to the young worker? Is it why you did a favor for him?"

"No," he responded quickly, "he was not a *tongzhi* and I never saw him again after he went back home with his salary." Both Guang Hui and I were confused then. Why did Lao Zhang tell us this story if it was not related to his *tongzhi* awareness?

Lao Zhang explained, "It was only because of the social responsibility. For my generation, the official education was that as a member of the society, each of us should contribute to it." He went on,

> One day a neighbor in my hostel came to me, "Hey Lao Zhang, I heard that you are a *rexin ren* (hot-hearted person or kind-hearted person 热心人,). I happen to know a *gongyi* (welfare 公益,) program that you might be interested in." This program he mentioned is *Aizhixing* (爱知行).[2] That's how I started my volunteer work, and it was at the same time that I realized that I am a *tongzhi* as well.

It took me by surprise that Lao Zhang understands his *tongzhi* identification first and foremost in terms of his political awareness of assum-

---

2. Beijing *Aizhixing* Institute was an influential nongovernmental organization for HIV/AIDS intervention, founded in 2002 by Dr. Wan Yanhai. It was developed from Beijing Aizhi Action Project established in 1994. Wan was one of China's most prominent AIDS activists who set up the first AIDS hotline, conducted the first AIDS-related surveys among gay men, and formed a health promotion group and AIDS education campaigns within the gay community. His projects were often shut down by the authorities, and he was detained many times. Eventually Wan was pushed out of his position and now lives in the United States.

170   Queer Chimerica

ing social responsibility and helping underprivileged people rather than through an awakening of a repressed sexual desire that has so powerfully characterized modern gay identity. During our conversation, both Guang Hui and I impatiently waited for Lao Zhang to cut to the "theme," and we intentionally asked questions that could lead to the sexual aspect of his *tongzhi* identity, but, Lao Zhang challenged our scopophilia by making a temporal, not a causal, connection between his volunteer work and his realization of *tongzhi* identity. Unlike many stories of the origin of one's gayness, Lao Zhang resisted seeing his *tongzhi* identity as a hidden essence that was woken by an event. Frustrating our desires to mine the utility of sexual knowledge, Lao Zhang led us to confront our own epistemological stuckness and to recognize the subjective formation of *tongzhi* as a process practiced on a daily basis through affective labor in sustaining mutually constructed sociality. This form of political participation and intervention has been crucial to the collective survival of those whose lives are impoverished by state-based social services and transnationally sponsored LGBT charities.

In a different conversation, Lao Zhang told another story of how helping homeless young rural migrants at the cruising sites consolidated his sense of being *tongzhi*,

> It was probably the year 2007. I met a homeless teenager, Xiao Hai, at Dongdan Park. This kid was in dirty clothes and had not had a full meal for days. He ran away from home and ended up sleeping on the bench at the park.

Lao Zhang paused for a little bit and looked at us.

> You must have a strong sense of security or trust to be able to sleep on the bench at a park. During wartime, people only slept when they were surrounded by their trusted comrades.

Noticing the confusion on Guang Hui's and my faces, Lao Zhang went back to his story about Xiao Hai,

> Sometimes he went to Babaoshan Cemetery to steal tributes to get by. He came here and wanted to sell himself for money, but who is going to want such a dirty bum? A few of the elders in the park and I chipped in some money for Xiao Hai, brought him to wash up at a bathhouse, got him a haircut, and bought him several meals. We started to educate him that being *tongzhi* is not

a mental illness and encouraged him to get a job if he wants to survive in Beijing. I learned later Xiao Hai became a HIV/AIDS volunteer like me. This is what *tongzhi* means to me.

The abundance and "ordinariness" of these examples from Lao Zhang remind me that mutual aid, self-knowledge, and care are not some new phenomena evoked in the wake of "exceptional" events; but since these forms of labor are primarily recognized and called upon during exceptional times such as epidemics, disasters, and protest and war, they easily fall prey to capitalism's lasting strategy for optimizing economic gain and reducing risks through mobilizing invisible labor.

Correspondences

Brother Hui,

I NEED YOUR HELP! I was at the Parents and Friends of Lesbians and Gays (PFLAG) annual conference, and something puzzled me.

As you know, PFLAG is notorious for its promotion of biological determinism to persuade parents, and society in general, to accept gay and lesbian people. I even heard of it when I was in Minneapolis. I hate to admit it, before I arrived, I was planning to kick open their door, document the absurdity, and make a good case for gay conformity and assimilation in my dissertation. But at one of the after-conference evening parties, a mother of a gay man came to me, holding my hands, and asked, "I heard that you are a doctor from the United States, specializing in homosexuality (I think she misinterpreted me as a medical doctor treating homosexuality). So you tell me, is it true that my son is really born this way?" The heartbreaking, struggling, but also loving mother was desperate to hear what she wanted to hear from another so-called authority, as if the advanced knowledge I brought from the States could be the Holy Grail to her family's happiness. "If he is born this way," she spoke with a voice barely audible, "I guess I could stop my worries and resentments and just let him be."

There was a short silence following her question. Many other parents stopped their chats, hoping to hear what the "authority" would say. Several students of queer studies who were doing fieldwork there just like me also stopped and waited to see how I would handle this situation. It was one of the most embarrassing moments of my life, where I found myself speechless under the spotlight. I wish I had more training before going to the field: am I gonna tell her about Judith Butler and Michel Foucault and that all sexualities are historically and culturally constructed? Wait a moment, I don't even know how to properly translate "sexuality" into Mandarin. Am I gonna tell her that she is trapped in a "heterosexual matrix" otherwise she wouldn't even ask the wrong question? If I gave her the "wrong" answer, would it undermine my credibility among my colleagues and make a fool of myself? I felt like an imposter, and I could sense my face on fire. Something I have dearly believed, something I have so eloquently spoken of, something I have been invested in for so many years of my precious youth, shamed me, embarrassed me, and disempowered me at that moment. I am confused, I am caught between all kinds of different positions, conflicts, "right" and "wrong," the fieldwork and what I learned do not match up, my original research questions are no longer valid, have I done this all wrong? Or am I not doing good here? When facing the helpless others, I realize my own helplessness.

Na Na

Sep 20, 2014

First off, how *did* you answer? I am curious. Did you just do your regular "scholar's thing" to detour the question and gracefully exit the conversation? Or did you pass the spotlight to another poor graduate student? Hahaha.

Secondly, what made you think the mother was helpless? Maybe she is just using whatever tools she has at the moment to make sense of her relationship with her son. Whatever answer you give her is probably only going to be *one* of the tools in the toolbox she is building and carrying with her. Quit thinking of yourself as someone so important as to save or destroy her life, hahaha.

And I see your scholarly existential crisis. Life is too complicated, kiddo. Your research, your dissertation, your publications are like light beams that could only illuminate particular areas of the messiness.

It would be so much easier to say that the desperate mother you met in Guangzhou happened to stand on the "wrong side" of history and fail to embrace the "radical queer theory." But why does the discourse of biological determinism held up by PFLAG have any appeal to many queer people living in China if it is so wrong? If you as a scholar are obligated to take Chinese materials seriously as intellectual resources rather than treating them as local illustrations of theoretical paradigms developed by the Western canons, should you be better trained to face the messiness with more honesty, courage and . . . skill?

Unlike medical authorities and sexologists whose disciplinary power is fiercely disrupted by Foucauldian queer theorization, the studies of gender and sexuality in the PRC shared a complex relationship with the medical authority within the discourse of socialist modernization and postsocialist technocracy for economic development. Since the May 4th movement in 1919, elite Chinese intellectuals have promoted learning Western-scientific knowledge as a crucial method for Chinese national restoration. This emphasis on science and technology has also been picked up by the communist party since 1949 as part of the anti-colonial nationalist agenda. Constrained by funding, political surveillance, and public hostility, many professionals and experts in the 1990s and early 2000s believed that if homosexuality could be proven by science as being inherent at birth, it would help the activists make the argument of scientific normalcy, thus pushing the legalization of homosexuality. Although not all gay activists are convinced by this agenda, many of them saw its merits and accepted the idea that "scientific proof" could be strategically deployed for political and activist purposes.

Instead of blindly upholding state-centered views, early gay activists, were well aware of losses and gains in appropriating the dominant narrative to meet their activist goals. Rather than simply supporting the authority of experts and being responsible for the state interests, they saw themselves as active agents who could take advantage of the culture of respecting authority and experts in order to train medical professionals, state experts, and local police to serve the community. Their "queer fluidity" and "queer bending" are expressed through their flexible labor and willingness to be "fragmented" and contradictory in practice, not through terms of poststructuralist and postmodernist subjectivities. Simply adopting a Foucauldian critique of biopolitics without considering the specificity of the scientific discourse in the PRC would not only dislodge a queer critique from grounded materiality, but also forfeit a possible coalition among the laboring queer people who are differently positioned.

By the way, I think it could be helpful for you to learn about the story

174   Queer Chimerica

from the other side, from the antagonist. It will help you unlearn what you have learned, unhouse who you are.[3] And maybe, to truly understand other people's stories and become a better ethnographer, you have to be the antagonist yourself.

Hui

Sep 20, 2014

Thanks for the insight, Brother Hui. Who are these antagonists and how to find one?

Na Na

Sep 20, 2014

I think you have met plenty, myself included. But I have a good one for you—a once die-hard queer hero, now a *hei wulei,* a "bad element," ostracized by the activist community. A protagonist turned antagonist of the queer drama. Yang Xiaofei is her name.

---

3. I thank Richa Nagar and the "Bodies, Stories and Movements" class in the fall and spring 2017 at the University of Minnesota for their inspirations. For a more detailed discussion on the antagonist, see Richa Nagar, "Part Four: Stories, Bodies, Movements: A Syllabus in Fifteen Acts," in *Hungry Translations: Relearning the World through Radical Vulnerability* (Urbana: University of Illinois Press, 2019).

CHAPTER 15

Battle for the Queer

Me? A *hei wulei*? A "bad element"? My heart jolts when I see my own name mentioned in Na Na's field notes. How does the antagonist have anything to do with me? *Ostracized* by the community? Didn't I quit willingly because I couldn't stand the drama, the personal attacks, and the Red Guard-style mobilization? Could this be the very thing that Andrei had warned me about?

A looming sense of worry begins to grip me. See, this is why I have been wary of letting the harsh lines of the past etch the tenderness of the present.

I look over my shoulder, making sure that the door to my work bay is shut. Alone with my thoughts, I continue to read.

Journal Entries

SEP 21, 2014

What a small world! I couldn't believe my eyes when the name Yang Xiaofei popped up on my screen.

The last time I got a hold of her was when I was writing my Master's thesis on *Lan Yu* in 2009. By then, four years of living in a Midwestern city in the United States had stripped off some of my edges and bold confidence in queer studies. My shaved hair had grown to waist length; comfy gray hoodies replaced my black leathers; the punk kid found her refuge in the drag of a Miss Butterfly. Facing the bizarre racialization of Asian women that I still struggled to wrap my head around, it was queer theory that once again provided me with a sense of belonging.

175

Don't get me wrong though, I don't mean the deconstruction of identity or the performativity of gender themselves, but rather my positionality with queer theorization. The 2010s was a moment when transnational sexuality was hot. Experiences in China (as well as other locations in Global South and Asia) piqued academic interest, while works done by scholars of PRC origin remained minimal. So *I,* an "authentic speaker," happily assumed the role of a cultural transporter, interpreting Chinese queer culture to my curious American colleagues. My inadequate English often prevented me from telling the "fuller story," but that didn't matter much as long as I, as Yang Xiaofei once said, "deliver the fantasy right."

Traversing in two worlds that were both structured by postcolonial and postsocialist mandates, I quickly learned to utilize the positions of a marginalized subaltern and an anti-communist dissident, mixing the spice of postmodern counterculture chic with my cultural and class privilege to gain visibility, acceptance, comradeship, and other social capitals. To identify with and attach to "what is trendy" and to follow certain lines of inquiry that are "safe" while maintaining the status of being an anomaly was a necessary survival skill. At the same time, there was a general disinterest in and disengagement with people, communities, and histories that were neither considered the most politically correct nor as embodying the most radical queer "alternatives." This carefully played identification and disidentification rewarded me a queer "green card," one I wouldn't obtain otherwise through Homeland Security, to stay and thrive in the US academia.

As a doctoral student now five years later, am I safe enough to listen to the antagonist and maybe to be one, as Guang Hui suggested? Perhaps not, perhaps never. Knowing how to play my cards has become so much more important these days, if you don't want to be "canceled."

And what about the more personal stuff?

"I only enjoyed queer theory because of those conversations we shared! They were the fire that ignited my soul! It was not the theory itself that I cherished, but the precious moments we dearly spent together."

"That's precisely why we are not meant to be. Going to the States is my choice and the purpose of my life is not to be your Muse!"

The dramatic breakup with Yang Xiaofei echoes in my ears as I am writing now. And am I ready to meet her whom I left behind for something that I thought was sublime?

Journal Entries

SEP 29, 2014

So my decision was to take a detour and gather information about her from my other informants. Without much difficulty, I found that Yang Xiaofei was a "domestic violence abuser" and an "informer" who reported NGOs to the police and busted the queer feminist solidarity.

What? Those could be severe allegations that certainly could get one canceled in activism. I wanted to know more. I had to. Pulling the thread, I was led to the *meishaonü zhanshi lala* (beautiful young women fighter lesbians 美少女战士拉拉) incident and the biological determinism versus queer theory war that it triggered.

The Meishaonü Zhanshi Lala Incident

Arguably, LGBT activism in the PRC began with the HIV/AIDS intervention in the late 1980s. The early activists were mainly (male) medical doctors, (straight) scholars of sexuality at universities and state research institutes, and *tongzhi* network leaders. Since transnational and state funding was channeled to HIV/AIDS-related research and intervention, gay men, not lesbian women, were the priority of the movements during the early years. Although lesbians played crucial roles in the early organization and community building (such as through leading entertainment activities, salon discussions, and organizing services and events), the disadvantages in securing resources further marginalized lesbians from gaining public attention.[1] After the 1995 UN's Conference on Women in Beijing, women's rights and development projects mushroomed in major cities and received a handful of national and transnational resources for organizing. Yet these women's and feminist NGOs in the 1990s and early 2000s were unaware of lesbian issues at best and homophobic at worst, pushing lesbian organizing to the corner of both feminist and LGBT movements.

The uneven distribution of resources predicted the flexible nature of lesbian organizing from the get-go when it came to strategies and tactics. For example, around the late 2000s, some groups were able to take advantage of petty cash from HIV testing and breast cancer–related projects to raise lesbian consciousness. But this channel was never suf-

---

1. Lucetta Yip Lo Kam, *Shanghai Lalas: Female* Tongzhi *Communities and Politics in Urban China* (Hong Kong: Hong Kong University Press, 2013), 5.

ficient nor sustainable. Other groups at the same time established transnational networks across Sinophone communities from the mainland, Hong Kong, Taiwan, and the US and were supported by international lesbian-focused foundations (this would later make them "foreign forces" in the eyes of the Chinese authorities and lead to the strict surveillance of and crackdown on local groups). In the late 2000s, however, lesbian groups started to enhance their solidarity with women's and feminist groups, both domestically and transnationally, and to break their troubled liaison with gay organizations. What made this change possible was partly because the transnational HIV/AIDS money began to dry out and to be replaced by Chinese governmental funds, and because an increasing number of scholar-activists educated in women's and gender studies–related fields or influenced by Western intersectional feminism joined the groups as volunteers, fund interlocutors, and researchers. As the uneven distribution of sources further normalized the unchecked misogyny and the erasure of women and lesbian experiences in LGBT activism became more pronounced, tensions between gay and lesbian organizations mounted to a tipping point in 2011.

In early 2011, gay activist and columnist Damien Lu published an article on the website *Aibai* titled "What is Queer Theory and How Does It Relate to the Gay Movement."[2] Lu contended that "queer theory is the product of the imagination of those living in an ivory tower," and as "propagated by Western and Western-educated critics and scholars," it misled people to believe that sexual orientation is socially constructed and fluid, and therefore subjugated to change. In other articles that followed, Lu further pointed out the danger of queer theory as it could be used to justify the harmful public discourse of converting homosexuality. Instead, Lu advocated for scientific research on the "naturalness of homosexuality" so that LGBT people could free themselves from discrimination and self-loathing and convince society and the authorities to normalize nonnormative sexualities.

Lu's advocacy for *tiansheng lun* (theory of biological determinism 天生论) triggered heated debates on and off the Internet. An anonymous user named *meishaonü zhanshi lala* (*meishaonü* for short) on *Sina Weibo*, a Chinese equivalent of Twitter, posted a series of tweets tagging Lu and the NGO *Aibai* where he worked as a consultant and refuting

---

2. Damien Lu, "What is Queer Theory and How Does It Relate to the Gay Movement" [in Chinese], *aibai*, May 30, 2011, https://www.aibai.cn/read/31(什么是"酷儿理论"?它与同志运动有什么关系?)

their stance and claims. *Meishaonü* translated several articles of canonical queer theory to denounce biological determinist accounts of homosexuality, and soon the debate turned into calling out gay male privilege within the LGBT movement and the uneven distribution of resources in activist organizing.

This event was considered one of the biggest queer *lala* victories against patriarchy and gay privilege for several reasons:

A common way to historicize the genealogy of *ku'er lilun* in the PRC is to follow the translation of "queer" into *ku'er* by Taiwanese scholars Chi Ta-wei, Hong Ling and Tan Tang Mo in 1994 across the strait. The word was initially introduced into the mainland at *dajuesi huiyi* (dajuedi LGBT Conference 大觉寺会议) in 1997. Unlike the waves that *ku'er* made in Taiwan, however, queer theory was predominantly confined to Chinese academia because of its connection to poststructuralism and Chinese academics' interests in Foucault and Derrida at the time. It was later picked up by cosmopolitan artist-activist communities (such as Cui Zi'en) in the early 2000s, who adopted the word in their discussion of international queer cinema and art. Although the purpose of Taiwanese queer theorists was to challenge gay male domination and consumerism in the 1990s, queer theory potential as an anti-normative critique was sort of lost in its particular travel in the PRC and hued by its "male" and "high culture" properties. The "reintroduction" of queer theory by *meishaonü* through social media allowed it to become the "theory of the oppressed," reviving the radical potential of queer as a theory leading the masses. Concepts such as sex/gender system, gender fluidity, nonbinary gender, and anti-normativity became commonplace terms, at least among young feminist and queer *lala* activists. Around late 2011, offline queer theory reading groups, workshops, and training sessions also popped up in major Chinese cities where transnational queer *lala* feminists gathered and exchanged insights. If queer theory in the US were critiqued for dislodging from materialism and grounded experiences, the revival and popularization of *ku'er lilun* in the PRC is, in fact, the very product of transnational activist praxis. Yang Xiaofei was one of the folks who led these activities during her tenure as the director of a feminist queer NGO, and the weaponization of queer theory also sowed the seeds of her later downfall.

Another reason that the reintroduction of queer theory was regarded with great significance is perhaps the medium through which the knowledge was able to spread. Lu's articles were first published on

Aibai, a gay website that has run for almost two decades, a space most lesbian and queer feminists had no access to or refused to participate in. This echoes queer women's lack of access to print media (with rare exceptions such as sociologist Li Yinhe who, in a sense, also benefited from the fame of her deceased husband Wang Xiaobo), compared to gay male scholars who at least found limited channels for disseminating their work. The emergence of social media as a decentered space fits well with the idealized organizational form of the feminist movement, namely, a structureless and leaderless space, as opposed to the "over-structuredness" and elitism[3] of gay and homosexual social movements. Through tagging, Lu and *Aibai* were pulled into the vortex and could not sustain their images as the authority of public knowledge producers by shunning away from criticism or deleting the comments.

Like all social movements, the activism and movement of *ku'er lilun* through social media and the anonymous, informal, and structureless collaboratives of feminist, lesbian, and queer alliances were not freed from its inclusions and exclusions, visibility and erasure, and normality and otherness. At first, *wangluo lunzhan* (online debate 网络论战) was an excellent means to meet the end of blowing the whistle, consciousness-raising, and spreading new ideas. Yet, when the organizing grew beyond this stage, problems occurred.

As Jo Freeman (2013) points out, contrary to what feminists would like to believe, there is no such thing as a structureless group. Because the idea of structurelessness does not prevent the formation of informal structures, it becomes a smokescreen for the strong ones to establish unquestioned hegemony over others; in other words, structurelessness turns into a way of masking power.[4] Although the context of Freeman's work is the women's movement in the US, her observations bare striking similarities to the Chinese transnational queer *lala* feminists in the social media era. Given the precarity of queer feminists facing both governmental surveillance and gay male domination, the hegemony and power dynamics within the group were initially masked, even though dissonances and differences were immediately recognized. Since successful organizations such as *meishaonü* require anonymity, the information and rules are only known to certain people and not others, which causes

---

3. Jo Freeman, "The Tyranny of Structurelessness," *Women's Studies Quarterly* 41, no. 3–4 (2013): 231.

4. Freeman, "Tyranny," 232.

confusion, complaint, and even resentment. Because of the limitation of resources and the realistic concerns of being infiltrated by agents of government and state security, it is necessary for queer feminists to carefully pick and maintain their trusted circles. Activists who want to join and scholars who want to do research on the group usually need to show a great degree of allegiance: for example, identifying the values, doing work as volunteers, proving why the study will contribute to the community, providing sources of funding, etc. Although these measures are unquestionable given the material condition of queer feminist organizing, one of the results of this chosen exclusivity is the "friend groups" and "locker room mentality." One listens to the other often because of their personal relations and likes, not whether or not the opinions are significant. Those within the "friend group" share exclusive networks as their means of communication and repeat each other's points, ignoring the opinions of those who are "outs." Criticisms are considered as undermining solidarity, and people who voice out concern are often attacked and pushed to the circle of the "dislikes" or "enemies." A significant amount of labor is spent on tagging, tweeting, and commenting—these are political actions that function to carefully maintain and manage the "ins" and "outs," even though the lines are not sharp and rescripted and subject to change frequently. The silent audiences who "lurk" and watch debates on social media can easily detect these dynamics and also carefully manage what to repost and comment on.

Through several rounds of online debates, certain "leaders" and "stars" emerge. Either those who are already "seniors" in organizing, who are eloquent, well-versed and have certain personality traits and charisma or the "flag wavers" who bang the drum when debates happen. They rarely claim themselves as the "leaders." Yet whether they like it or not, they are labeled and perceived as the "leaders" and followed by others, becoming the "political influencers." Similar to what Freeman points out, because many of them do not see themselves as leaders and are strong advocates for decentering, they don't assume responsibility for the movement and often underestimate the public consequence of what they say as "individual voices." This "individualist nonresponsibility"[5] sometimes gets them into trouble and other times exonerates them from being responsible for what they do. Since the movement does not select the leaders, they cannot

---

5. Freeman, "Tyranny," 239.

182   Queer Chimerica

be removed.[6] Yet, a leader and star can be brought down from a pedestal and canceled if it serves the need of the movement.

Correspondences

One day when Yang Xiaofei woke up and checked her cellphone, she was surprised to see her *Sina Weibo* account bombarded by over a hundred notifications. *Am I that popular?* She must have thought. What she found out was not what she expected, of course. An ex-girlfriend tagged her on *Weibo* and accused her of being an abuser in their relationship. With the tag, the girlfriend listed the "seven sins" of Yang Xiaofei: verbal abuse, physical abuse, bipolarity, and unstable emotions . . . and the worst among all, being a prosecutor of NGO workers and reporting activists to the police.

This shouldn't surprise Yang Xiaofei. Not too long ago, she had had a fight with her girlfriend. Fights were common between the couple those days, but this was the last time, she must have sworn to herself. She had been fed up with the drama and gaslighting, and distorted communications. She stormed out of the apartment they shared and called their landlord. She told the landlord that her girlfriend was a sex worker from Taiwan and got her evicted. As a feminist queer sex work activist who came to Beijing by herself, the girlfriend was left with nowhere to go. Other activists offered her a couch in their apartment, yet the assistance was far from being enough to quench the fire of this sexual and geopolitical episode. At the time when feminist and *lala* organizing turned to consciousness-raising around sexual harassment and gender-based violence as its major goals, the *ku'er lilun* veteran turned out to be a violent perpetrator. At the time when the government tightened its surveillance on civil societies and started to arrest activists, the *ku'er lilun* veteran turned out to be a traitor within. Since then, Yang Xiaofei gained her title of *weixian renwu* (the most harmful person 危险人物) for activists to watch out for.

Dear Brother Hui, I followed your suggestion and opened Pandora's box. I had looked into the battle for queer theory and found Yang Xiaofei again in other people's words. She might be the last person I expected to find committing these things, but why am I so generous to the villain when the crime was so easily identified? I do not know how to confront

---

6. Freeman, "Tyranny," 238.

her and ask her about what happened. Are the rumors based on misunderstandings? Or things she actually committed? It would be unfair if I could only hear her side but not that of the girlfriend and many others who convicted her. But how can I ask the victims only to have them hurt again?

At the same time, there are some tiny voices in my head telling me that's not the whole story. What about other forms of violence, the violence of cyberspace, the violence that is based on stereotypical assumptions of lesbian masculinity, the violence under the name of "greater good," the violence that cannot easily speak its name? Must we tell the story of violence at the cost of other things? Am I entitled to tell this story? Do I have the ability to unpack the complexity of things and narrate what is often eluded by language? And why do I even want to hear the accounts of the *heiwulei*? Why do I empathize with the bad guys? Because we were friends? Or because . . . . . . I am one of them?

Na Na

Oct 30, 2014

CHAPTER 16

The Love That Dares Not to Speak Its Name

Na Na's words sear me with a scorching glare. Could it be that I really committed such heinous acts? Banishing an ex-girlfriend and having NGOs reported to the police? Me, the victim is, in fact, the perpetrator? But why would she paint a damning portrait of me if it were not rooted in true events? Why would she concoct such a falsehood about me if I didn't indeed do these things?

I leaf through her fieldnotes, frantically searching for any semblance of evidence and clues of alleged misdeeds, but the pages offer little. The next journal entry in the binder is dated almost a year later. That couldn't be it. Our conversations about the "Feminist Five" at the tea house in Chongwenmen I saw in Andrei's Beets should not be the extent of our interaction. Even if what she wrote about me were true, it shouldn't define me nor diminish the value of my contribution to the community and to her. There was so much more we shared during her fieldwork, I am certain. Where are the missing pages about the good things? Or could it be that her disappointment in me was so great that she chose to erase me altogether from her stories? *There is no greater betrayal than deleting a history.*

The remainder of her fieldnotes seem to have veered in an entirely different direction. The writing becomes scattered and the intervals between each entry enlarge. And the once analytical reflections of the complexity that roiled within the LGBT and feminist movements become more intimate, unfolding a raw and vulnerable landscape of emotion, her innermost world in front of me.

The Love That Dares Not to Speak Its Name   185

Journal Entries

AUGUST 08, 2015

Two national events in 2008 marked the collective memory of the PRC.

In May, about seventy thousand people lost their lives in the Wenchuan earthquake, and in August, six million foreigners came to China to watch the Olympic Games. This was the first time a Communist country had hosted the Games since 1980 when the Moscow Games were boycotted to protest the Soviet invasion of Afghanistan.

In early 2008, Yang Tao's father fell while taking a walk in a park and had a hemorrhage. Half of his body was paralyzed, and he drooled with hoarseness when he tried to talk. When the old man saw the news of the earthquake and the Party's call for donations, he insisted on going to the donation center. The idea seemed ridiculous to Yang Tao. He made up some excuses, "I am too busy recently" or "I am traveling abroad" as usual, to avoid bringing his father to the donation center. Unconsciously, or maybe consciously, he wanted to punish his father for what he believed, just like his father once punished him for what he believed. It was a petty but necessary revenge.

Without the help of Yang Tao, the old man managed to climb out of his bed and inched his way to the donation center in his neighborhood. The distance from his home to the center is about a five-minute walk for an average person. But because of his missing leg and half-paralyzed body, it took the old man about an hour. He donated ¥5000. Most donations on the list were ten and twenty yuan.

Yang Tao's story reminds me a lot of my relationship with my father.

The sky had not turned red yet. The balmy air was delighted by the chorus of birds and cicadas. Willows sang in harmony. I was too busy licking the ice cream dripping along the tiny waffle cone on the bumpy road and ignored the grumpy complaint from the canvas case on my back, jostling in the rear rack of dad's bike seat.

"You stinky hooligan!" A sudden cry broke the lazy summer evening. A man bolted out of the public toilet, struggling to hold his pants. Another two followed.

I was frightened and urged father to pedal faster. We managed to cross the park quickly, and made a stop at a shish kabob street vendor. This was a special one, besides chicken and lamb, there was fish on the grill. It was my first-time seeing barbequed fish stuffed with herbs and

186   Queer Chimerica

vegetables. Fish was costly, but the mixture of charcoal, cumin, and drizzling fat was persuasive enough for the duo to indulge themselves, especially after the unexpected incident.

Since then, Dad and I visited the vendor for fish kabobs every week. Not too far from the grill, a young man was begging for food from the patrons. They called him *shazi*, the "retarded." Some people bought the kabobs, ate the lean meat and gave the fatty leftovers to *shazi*. Others teased him, waving the kabob in front of him only to drop it on purpose when he reached to get the stick with naïve excitement. But *shazi* did not understand, he went down and licked the fatty meat off the ground, surrounded by wicked laughter.

It is one of the very earlier memories I share with my dad, about the brutality of the world.

Dad did not want to challenge these mean guys. After they left, he bought two kabobs for *shazi*, and told me that if I could not finish my fish, I should share it with *shazi*. Next time before we went to the vendor, I made sure to fill my stomach with soda so I could leave half of the fish to the poor man. "Showing kindness to the helpless" is the grace of the unacknowledged vanity running through my family.

A few years later, riding the tide of *xiahai* (going to the sea 下海), Dad and his buddies started selling used motorcycles. I moved up from the backseat of his bicycle to the backseat of his Kawasaki.

In the 1990s, China started its healthcare reform. Benefiting from his medical doctor's day job, Dad started trading medicines. The price of Penicillin, fifty cents to make, after the hands of several medicine companies and medical representatives, could increase a hundred times by the time it reached the patient. From the backseat of the Kawasaki, I moved up to the backseat of a Mercedes.

But I never saw my dad as an "evil" capitalist opportunist. Deep down, I knew that he was the same sensitive guy with endless knowledge and practical skills, talented at writing poems, blushed in the slightest arguments, but accountable on any occasion of decision making. He was a dreamer, and he had edges.

There was an unspeakable promise my dad and I kept. We used to "accidentally" leave books and news articles we wanted the other person to read on the back of our family toilet and spent hours enjoying our most "private yet opening" time. Our "smelly pleasure" led my outraged mom to put a sign on the door of our bathroom, "In case of causing a loose anus, one shall not spend more than thirty mins here."

The Love That Dares Not to Speak Its Name   187

It was on the shelf of our "toilet library," I first read *The Subculture of Homosexuality* by Li Yinhe and *East Palace, West Palace* by Wang Xiaobo, Sigmund Freud's *Three Essays on the Theory of Sexuality*, and *Kinsey Reports* and *The Hite Report*. Queer Theory was a late arrival.

One day when I was organizing notes during my field work, I found a case study in a book. The gay man in the interview told the researcher that when he was sitting on the back of his father's bicycle cutting through a local park, he saw a man being chased by the police, and it was his first memory of homosexuality, of his unspeakable desire and identity.

Was the bicycle story a coincidence that is so common for Chinese queer individuals? Or was it a collective memory fabricated into my own that became so real? To know the truth, I could simply ask my dad, but I did not. I wanted to remember my childhood the way I did. Stories about the bike, the park, kabobs, and *shazi*, and the secret queer encounter are about the love that cannot speak its name between him and I.

Today the man who stands in front of me is this typical *chouloude zhongnian youninan* (ugly greasy middle-aged man 丑陋的中年油腻男). He does not know how to smile; he treats the family with loud nonsense; he refuses to learn but dominates all conversations among friends with his BS . . . After knowing I had been hanging out with positive gay men at the park, he warned me "Don't be around those people! You don't know what disease they have!" I could not believe this was coming from my medical doctor father who supported me in studying sexuality thousands of miles away; yet the next day, he brought free medicine from his company for the low-income *tongzhi* I met at the parks.

Queer memory/fiction is the link between me and this (un)familiar father. Queer memory/fiction is the link between me and this lost home/homeland I could no longer return to.

In May, my whole family came to Minneapolis for my wedding. It was a disaster. My dad picked a fight with my mom at a grocery store, as if there was nobody around. After the fight, he wandered to a park nearby, and soon after, I received a phone call from the police. The policeman told me with "Minnesota Nice" that somebody reported seeing an Asian man smoking around the kindergarten and they were worried that he

188   Queer Chimerica

was dangerous to the kids. Then the police asked to see my dad's passport, but my dad did not understand English.

I was irritated but had to put on a "nice Asian girl's face" to explain, apologize and assure the police that I would "watch over" him. At this time, I had grown my hair long, put on cheerful orange-red lip colors and passed as an exotic, sweet Chinese woman, not the androgynous punk queer kid anymore, so that definitely helped a lot. Without any clue of how dangerous this incident could turn, my dad asked me to pick up a couch he had just seen on the street on our way back so he could sit on it and read Chinese news on his iPad. A fucking couch!

After my wedding, I went on a road trip with my family, without my husband. At the Grand Canyon, Dad took pictures of other people's license plates because he wanted to make a collection of the US plates. In Hollywood, he was stopped by a guy asking him to delete pictures from his camera. My "honeymoon trip" turned out to be my endless apologies for being the "rude Chinese tourists" and constantly blaming and disciplining Dad like a bad parent does to their child. I thought about the conversation between Yang Tao and his father. Am I now the doors and windows for my dad to a new world, a world where a privileged Chinese man must confront his racial inferiority and impotence? For years, the queer façade has protected me, giving me a green card in the "ivory tower," an illusion of my liberation and freedom. I lose this superpower when my racialization becomes so blatant in the presence of the family of whom I am proud and ashamed. To many people, leaving China, the confining "home," is how they confront their queerness; but for me, "China" is my queer home, one that I left behind only to be confronted with conformity.

In front of the Big Bean in Chicago, Dad finally snapped. "I can't even be free in the freest country in the world? Why do you always constrain what I do and cater to the Americans!"

"Unlike you, I didn't come here for sightseeing or buying cheap Nike sneakers and Coach handbags. I came here for a cause, and now you know the cost of pursuing that cause!" I yelled back.

Then Dad swore never to come to the States again and refused to sit with us for lunch. He snatched a sandwich my mom prepared and went along to feed the pigeons in the middle of the square under the blazing sun. He sat next to a fountain, head dangled, belly sticked out, like the number 6. I took out my cellphone and secretly snapped a shot. I didn't tell him about the picture, nor did I show it to anyone else. In fact, I have never looked at the picture again. My heart is too fragile to be broken again.

Too many words unsaid . . . so we can protect one another in our own silent ways.

———————

At the end of 2008, the health of Yang Tao's father deteriorated, and he was sent to hospice care. According to the nursing workers, when awake and conscious, the father often pointed at a tin box that housed many certificates of the Honorary Communist Party Member he had received over the years, including the one for the earthquake donation. Knowing this, Yang Tao became furious, "Fucking Certificates of Honorary Communist! How stupid!" Following his anger, there was guilt, "How did I become so crucial to the old man?"

Soon Yang Tao's father was sent to the intensive care unit. Pipes went through his body. The old man looked like an unanimated cyborg. His lungs were connected to an accordion-like machine. The song of his life was hanging on between the compression and expansion of the bellows. Because of the combination of kidney failure, heart failure, and lung failure, the once skinny man now bloated like a balloon. He seemed strangely youthful with no wrinkles. Yang Tao was struck by the strange affinity between death and life.

Yang Zhongguo passed away on the New Year's Eve of 2009. Yang Tao surprised himself and kept his father's tin box, along with his certificates.

"Here, why don't you keep it?" Yang Tao handed me what his father left, "Since you are doing the research . . . . . ."

I took over the box, touching the smooth surface of it and trying to feel the last breath of the old man. Under the certificates, I found a brown paper bag. "One is not Enough." A piece of note sat on a handful of confession files.

Like the picture of my dad in Chicago that I secretly took, some of the most important parts of the old man's life remain forever unknown to his beloved son.

CHAPTER 17

Till Death Do Us Part

Correspondences

Dear Brother Hui,

I have a favor to ask. After my return to Minneapolis, I couldn't stop thinking about what Lao Zhang had said to me. I wanted him to tell me more about how he survived the Cultural Revolution, the *Yanda yuandong*, and all other dark times; but instead of telling me more stories, he just put a slice of mooncake I brought him into his toothless mouth and said, "I am too old to even stick my ass up, how am I gonna remember things well?" And then I remember his lips making ripples across his liver-spotted face, "If there is any life lesson I can give you, kid, that is, don't live for too long!"

Help me understand it, Brother Hui. I want to argue in my dissertation that Lao Zhang and folks like him are anti-neoliberal queer alternatives because their "idling" in the park—the non-productivity and non-participation in a capitalist economy is the key to imagining the otherwise. But it does not look like they are consciously "resisting." They don't have an *agenda* to organize and stand up against oppression. Am I speaking for them and robbing them of their own voices? If you happen to go back to Dongdan, can you help me ask if they also think that they are resisting the norms and creating different life possibilities?

Na Na

August 10, 2015

Till Death Do Us Part   191

If they say so, would you feel more assured citing them and putting their example of resistance in your dissertation?

The Master said, "At thirty, I planted my feet upon the ground. At forty, I no longer suffered from perplexities. At fifty, I knew what the biddings of heaven were. At sixty, I heard them with docile ears. At seventy, I could follow the dictates of my own heart; for what I desired no longer overstepped the boundaries of right." Lao Zhang has been "knowing the biddings of heaven" for thirty years, do you think that these questions are meaningful to him? Resisting the norm, do you really think that is what people like him think about daily? That's what the discourse tells you, that's what the media tells you, that's what scholars like you tell yourself. Even if they say so, don't believe them. They are just doing you a favor so you can complete *your* story. Life is too complicated to be captured by a dissertation.

Hui

August 12, 2015

Correspondences

Brother Hui,

Hope this email finds you well. I have been busy, please forgive my slow response. I purchased the books you wanted from Amazon. I will bring them to you when I go back to Beijing next month. On a side note, I am curious why you are buying these books, how are they helpful for the book you are writing?

Na Na

June 16, 2016

Na Na,

Thanks for the books. I glanced at some of them online, the books on boy-wives and female husbands, two-spirit people and down-low cul-

192   Queer Chimerica

tures all seem to suggest that there are preexisting queer cultures before Western influences. I started to understand why you are interested in colonialism and sexuality. I think this could be helpful for my own book.

June 17, 2016

I see. They are all great reads. But I would be very cautious about cherry-picking the examples as they are just the tip of the iceberg in a vast literature on this topic.

P.S. I really think you should write a book on the history of Chinese LGBT activism. The more I talk with you, the more I am convinced that the questions you have answered for me are already an invaluable book itself on the tensions and disputes of current LGBT activism. Maybe write a memoir and get it published? It probably has better market.

June 17, 2016

I am just not interested in writing about activism. I have said that. Plus, I do not have a position to write about it. Who am I? And who would want to read a book about activism written by a gay loser?

Journal Entries

JULY 21, 2016

The night had fallen. Guang Hui and I waited in line for the Ferris Wheel at the Happy Valley Park. "What do you think about my book?" He asked.

Over the past year, Guang Hui and I have exchanged ideas for our book projects over numerous tea times. He shared with me his manuscript, hoping I could translate his book into English. I encouraged him to keep writing, but I could never have the courage to tell him my honest opinions.

His book will not be published. At each and every crossroads, he made the "wrong" turn. He was not properly trained in either the academy in China or the US and the UK. He does not have connections with established scholars and editors in the field of queer studies. He does not know what the trendy topics are and how to pitch his writing in both fields. He is not at the forefront of the most radical queer movement nor queer Sinophone studies. Although he is extremely perceptive, he simply does not have what it takes to become who he thinks he wants to be. The barriers in information, theories, and identity politics make his book an impossible "freak." But unlike the freaks whom we proudly call "queer," the queerness of Guang Hui's impossible book, like many others in the boxes under his adolescent bedroom mattress, speaks silently about queer fluidity's own stuckness.

Watching the flow of the cheerful people at the amusement park, Guang Hui sucked his cigarette in the cold air and said to me out of the blue, "Queer is like a revolving Ferris wheel at a carnival; each of the capsules is a 'highlighted moment' of identity reduced from the complexity of life. As some are elevated, so are others being let down. Unlike a pyramid, its stability lies in its fluidity. It will not be toppled by those who wait in line for their turn because their hope for being brought to the top cannot be wasted."

Inspired by such a philosophical statement, I raised my head. Yea, the Ferris Wheel against the indigo night sky did look like a panopticon, erected.

Journal Entries

JULY 21, 2017

The night before I left the field and returned to Minneapolis a year ago, Guang Hui accompanied me to Dongdan Park. I planned to treat some of the old friends I met at the park for dinner. We arrived early and Guang Hui came up with an idea, "What about we go and get tested at the rapid testing van?" While we were waiting for the results, a volunteer in the van stuck his head out and said to Guang Hui, "You, come inside, alone."

The volunteer took Guang Hui's ID card and put down his information in the record book. He handed him some booklets and comforted him with a soft but confident voice, "Don't worry, don't be scared. AIDS is a treatable disease now; in this country, we have good policies." He went on to elaborate the "Four Free and One Care" policy and urged Guang Hui to book an appointment for a comprehensive confirmation test immediately at the local CDC. Guang Hui interrupted the volunteer with a smile and said calmly, "I know, I have been doing AIDS education for over a decade; I know about everything."

I didn't know how to react to the news. The only thing I knew was that my heartbeat was fast. A huge stone pressed tightly against my chest. I pinched my hands hard while trying to fake my composure.

Our whole walk to the dinner turned into a laborious lecture, where Guang Hui educated me about AIDS, from the CD4 counts to anti-viral drugs, from side effects to the corruptions within activist groups. He said that he knew it was coming, given how much unprotected sex he had. He was a talkative guy, but I had never seen him talking that much, as if it was his responsibility to make sure I was not sad and didn't feel bad for him. At the dinner, he made improper jokes and bored everybody with his outdated theories of social construction as usual.

Our dinner ended before the last subway train. Guang Hui and I shared our walk to the station and a couple of cigarettes. I must have looked exhausted, and he could sense it. On the train, he asked me why I was so quiet.

"I am having a bad cramp from my period. Walking around the park for so long did not help." I explained with a murmur.

"Where is the cramp? Is it in the lower abdominal area, under your belly button?" He added, "It is so strange. I am feeling a cramp around my lower belly too."

I did not know what to make of his words, I did not know how to respond, so I just leaned still against the subway window and did not say anything. Then the door of the train opened, I hopped off. I stood on the platform, looking at Guang Hui looking at me. Then as the door shut, he smiled and said, "Hey, next time you come back, I will probably have already started taking medicine. I will make sure to tell you about the side effects, so you will have some first-hand material."

I couldn't tell him that my fieldwork had ended. I won't be able to return to China as often as I had in the past two years. I couldn't tell him that I was married to an American guy, and that I will get my green card and become an American too. I will stay in the States, write my dissertation, obtain my Ph.D., and get a job. Eventually I will become a professor and continue my academic journey, giving lectures to students and curious audiences about the lives of Chinese LGBTQ folks like Guang Hui.

"Till Death Do Us Part."

And Guang Hui himself, my loyal informant, my generous teacher, and my best sidekick in the field, will stay in his ten-square-meter basement in suburban Beijing, writing his unpublishable book. Our lives are set in different directions as if our paths had never crossed. The future has yet to happen, but I already know where it is leading to.

I often think about the moment when Guang Hui stood on the train, asking me about my cramps. How scared he was, and how eagerly he wanted my comforts, my validation. I could have given him a hug, brought his hands to my belly, or at least said something funny and smart. But why didn't I say anything when he reached out to me? At the moment on the subway, it was the "bad blood" running through our doomed social bodies—as women and positive gay men—that connected us intimately.

But I didn't do anything.

I imagined the people who died from AIDS in the 1980s and 1990s like those I saw in documentaries about ACT-UP. Even though I know that nowadays before AIDS kills you, there are going to be cancers, Alzheimer's, and other misfortunes in life. But I couldn't stop thinking about Guang Hui lying on his deathbed in a hospital, dark red spots silently climbing up his tanned back. On the side of his face, yellow pus oozes out from the never-healed wounds. His body diminishes and sinks into the white sheet of his tiny hospital bed. Nobody is by his side. No me, certainly. When we stood in the cold Harbin night looking at the pink, snowy sky, when we stood in the cold Minneapolis night looking at the pink, snowy sky, and when we stood in the cold Toronto night looking at the pink, snowy sky, how lonely we were and how much we longed for each other's warm arms.

Solitude was the only courage we had for each other.

The night at the Beijing subway station two years ago was the last time I saw Guang Hui. But what did part us was certainly *not* Death.

CHAPTER 18

Beijing Comrades II

Holding Na Na's binder in my hands, a fragmented memory surges into my mind's eyes. I see Na Na in her plaid jeans and Dr. Martens, a punky jacket draped over her shoulders, leaning against the grimy wall of the subway station. She pulled out two cigarettes as I approached and lit both. Her ruby-red lips glimmered like the flickering flames from the lighter. She proffered one of the cigarettes toward me, her voice teasing, "All-natural and rolled by real human hands!"

I took the cigarette and had a few quick drags, "Organic cigarettes give you organic cancer!" I joked as though time and conflicts had never erected an ice sheet between us.

Smoking in public had become an "uncivilized" act, especially among middle-class urbanites. But for Na Na and I, it was a time machine that whisked us back to the good time of our adolescence. Na Na claimed that it was also a useful tactic for getting access to conversations of gay men and lesbians at the cruising parks.

She brought me on a train, and we traveled to the southeastern suburbs of Beijing. There, her informant Xiao Hai was waiting for us. Xiao Hai invited Na Na to visit his home in Majuqiao. Located in the Tongzhou District near the South 6th Ring Road, Majuqiao had a bad reputation among Beijingers. The area had many *chengzhongcun* (villages-in-the-city 城中村) with low-income migrants, sex workers, and illegal business owners, who provided indispensable yet unrecognizable labor for the Yizhuang Development District, the largest economic and development satellite town in Beijing with high-technology research centers and transnational joint ventures. Majuqiao was only separated from Yizhuang by an inner-city river twenty meters wide.

198 Queer Chimerica

At the subway station, what greeted us was Xiao Hai's embarrassing apology, "Sorry, sis, I have to bring Xili here, this lazy ass is off work today and insists on tagging along. What a pain!" Xili talked back, "Me, a pain? I can't go to work because I have diarrhea. And I cannot bend over and move the heavy bricks while having a bleeding butthole." Xili crossed his arms and pouted, "if you want me to make the hundred yuan, then I am not going to bottom next time!" He suddenly turned his attention to Na Na, "Sis, are you a Thai ladyboy? You look like one."

"She is not a Thai ladyboy, silly, Xili! She is here to do research on *tongzhi yundong* (*tongzhi* movement 同志运动)!" Xiao Hai explained.

"*Tongzhi yundong*? Like *tongzhi* sports?" Xili put up his hands and made a runner pose. "By the way, she must be a ladyboy; look at her feet. Those are huuuuuuge!"

After Na Na and I finally managed to stop laughing, we all got into a *heiche* ("black car" meaning an illegally run taxi 黑车) Xiao Hai had already arranged for us, heading to his home.

"There is a saying that '*shi nan jiu ji*' (there are nine gay men out of ten 十男九基) in our village. It is true, you will see yourself on the street later." Xiao Hai prepared us in the *heiche* with some pride, "I think lots of us became *tongzhi* after we arrived here. *Tongzhi* is like *xiongdi*, or *gemen* (brothers or buddies 哥们儿), we look after and help one another survive the city."

The Majuqiao area seemed nothing special other than an average Beijing suburb at first—residential buildings with small business stores on the ground floor standing close to one another, buses and delivery bikers running around the loud streets, and retired local couples strolling on the sidewalk. But the *heiche* could only bring us so far, we got off in front of a building. Xiao Hai led Na Na to a hidden gate to an alleyway. The path was slicked with small puddles and mud, Xili and I followed in a single file. Quickly the repugnant smell of a public toilet signaled our arrival to an unfamiliar dimension folded within the familiar Beijing. Subconsciously I lowered my head and tried to bury my chin in my collar only to realize that my collarless tank top failed to hide my discomfort.

The fastest route to Xiao Hai's place was through a row of shanties and shacked stores. Young women in bright-colored bras and miniskirts sat in front of the doors trimming their nails. Cheap cupboard signs advertising temporary jobs stood next to men giggling over their secret cellphone chats. Dogs barked at visitors with friendly curiosity. After several turns, we finally arrived at Xiao Hai's place. It was a small room at the end of a crowded two-level temporary housing building. We took the staircase and when Xiao Hai opened the door,

Beijing Comrades II 199

three men, a full-size bed, and a hot pot welcomed us. Seeing us, the man who was sitting on the edge of the bed stood up and moved to sit on the floor with the other two. Xiao Hai directed Na Na, Xili, and I to take over the bed, and he joined the three men on the floor. All the men were his "fledglings." When they first came to the "village," Xiao Hai helped them find temporary jobs at the construction sites, shared his bed with them, and protected them from the discriminatory urbanites.

Dumplings were boiling in the hot pot. Xiao Hai grabbed a few pork and shrimp dumplings with his chopsticks and put them into Na Na's bowl and then mine, leaving the egg and chive ones to himself and his other brothers. Na Na gave me an embarrassing smile and I took the dumplings from her bowl without a word. She had been a vegetarian since high school, and I used to joke about her dying from anemia. Then Na Na silently watched Xiao Hai interacting with online fans, and taking mental notes with a growling stomach that I could hear clearly. Most of Xiao Hai's fans were also gay men in the "village" who knew him as the "contact person" to get jobs and condoms.

"The dwellers in the 'village' are young and do not usually hang out in public like those in Dongdan." Xiao Hai introduced,

"If we only set up a table to distribute condoms and pamphlets, we are not going to reach out to many people. *Tongzhi* also don't go to events organized by LGBT activists, not only because they are afraid of being looked down upon but also because they will miss their hours and don't get paid. But as HIV volunteers, if we can't finish the 'task' and meet the 'goal,' our group won't receive the 'quota' for next season, which means we won't get money. Thanks to Xili, who introduced me to this short video-sharing platform *Kuaishou*, we are reaching a great number of men nearby."

During our reunion in Beijing, Na Na had a way of making me believe that our reconnection was destinated. It was love, not just any love, but a shared love for knowledge and the maniacal curiosity to dig deeper into things that reunited us. It was as if we shared the same frequency, finishing each other's sentences effortlessly, as we did before. We visited old haunts and explored new ones where Na Na conducted her research; she introduced me to fascinating people I would never have met otherwise. My tomboyish appearance and butch demeanor made it easier for her to blend in with the queer communities while she refreshed my knowledge of the latest developments in queer studies and feminism. It was a rekindling of respect and admiration, and I began to imagine

200 Queer Chimerica

the possibilities of the great duo we once were and could still be, roaming freely in the dazzling queer world that had always been ours.

One evening, after leaving the Pony Garden, a renowned cruising spot, we stopped by a 24-hour McDonald's. The restaurant had a spacious basement where migrant workers could find temporary shelter. Among the slumbering homeless people, we settled down with our Filet-O-Fish and syrupy pancakes, and it was then when I noticed a faint shadow of sadness on Na Na's narrow face.

"Do you remember you used to ask me why I wanted to learn about queer theory and save homosexuals when there are so many people living in poverty in China? I used to get so mad at you, defending myself with whatever reasons I could think of, or not talking to you for days," Na Na spoke softly, almost to herself. "Lately, I've been questioning that myself."

Now as I let Na Na's introspection echo in my ears again, her words seem to take on a new light. I hear her confusion, her qualm, her hesitation, all intermingled in her attempt to make sense of things that perplexed her search. The once eloquent Cool Child, with her aspirations of saving the world, found herself adrift in a sea of moral ambiguity, struggling with decisions of right and wrong, proper and improper. Now I realize that she probably had a lot to say to me; instead of vocalizing them, she let them dissolve into the thick air, heavy with the creamy savor of French fries and apple pies.

CHAPTER 19

Unqueer the Cool Child

Journal Entries[1]

MARCH 15, 2019

After the Feminist Five Incident in 2015, Chinese feminist movement underwent significant changes. The spread of feminist thoughts through digital platforms led to a surge of "feminist immigration." Many young students, visiting scholars, and activists of Chinese origin relocated abroad to pursue gender and queer studies, as well as employment at law firms, journalism, and NGO work. While not all of them may be considered middle- or upper-middle class according to conventional Marxist standards, they benefited from the One Child policy and the expansion of the educational system since the 1980s, as the state invested a great deal in cultivating a cohort of healthy, well-educated, metropolitan young people for China's prosperity and global power.[2] They gained feminist consciousness from international collaboration programs at Chinese universities[3] and transnational activist organizations, as well as through social media and digital space animated by new technologies. If Chinese feminism in the early 1990s anchored their politics on "connecting to the world" through identifying with liberal feminism and

---

1. A significant chunk of this section is based on an unpublished work co-authored with Weiling Deng. I thank Weiling's generosity for giving me permission to use it in the book.

2. Susan Greenhalgh and Xiying Wang, "China's Feminist Fight: #MeToo in the Middle Kingdom," *Foreign Affairs* 98, no. 4 (July/August 2019): 174.

3. Such as the Shanghai Fudan-Michigan Gender Studies program pioneered by Professor Wang Zheng.

building global sisterhood, the twenty-first-century Chinese feminists no longer debated on local-global differences but rather grounded their activism and scholarship in the pursuit of the question of how Chinese feminism could contribute to the global.

This affective shift could be captured in several high-profile examples in the late 2010s: from Chinese diasporic feminists' participation in the Women's March against the inauguration of President Donald Trump in 2017 to young grassroots feminist Liang Xiaowen being featured in Hasan Minhaj's Netflix show *Patriot Act* in 2019, from a touring series of lectures on Chinese feminism at US universities to reporting the sexual assault case of Liu Qiangdong, founder of JD.com, and so on. The cultural and political message of this shift was that despite China's tightening authoritarian and patriarchal politics under president Xi Jinping, Chinese feminists still managed to succeed in making themselves known to the world. As feminists from China who were equipped with the rich experience of fighting for gender equality under authoritarian patriarchy, Chinese feminists' unique experience of radical politics had a lot to offer for the American left in the era of Trump. Instead of being followers of the global feminist movements, Chinese feminists in the United States started to find a way as pioneering leaders.

The transnational desire to reclaim radicality also found its expression in domestic feminist politics as the theoretical and practical distance between diasporic and local Chinese feminists was significantly shortened by digitalization and strengthened by increasing transnational mobility. One prominent example was the grassroots movement of reclaiming the stigmatized concept *funü* through the rejection of the March 7 *nüsheng jie* (Girls' Day 女生节) and the recelebration of March 8th *funü jie* (Women's Day 妇女节). The mainstream society in recent years has been celebrating *nüsheng jie* as a consumerist strategy. In contrast to the old socialist concept *funü*, *nüsheng* embodied the juvenile female subjectivity. If the primary articulation of Chinese feminism in the early 1990s departed from socialist Marxist *funü* in favor of the concept of "gender," feminist reclaiming of *funü* in the late 2010s was meant to be a critique of the deepening neoliberalization of Chinese society, even though the young generations had little ties with Marxist feminist conventions and in fact emerged against it. This new trend was in tandem with a globalized return to class-focused critiques of political economy and leftist politics in the recent North academy. Forging a cultural front of a transnational socialist feminist coalition was quite enticing as both an intellectual intervention and an achievable political agenda.

Although I have long finished my dissertation and secured a job, I continued to struggle with making sense of my positionality and finding my proper voice. And my relationship with queerness and feminism became more troubled. It drained me.

While the increasing number of gender and feminist professionals of Chinese origin brings hope, "feminist immigration," to a large degree, remains structured by the same dynamics that perpetuate asymmetrical power relations and an uneven distribution of resources. On a transnational level, as young feminists promoted gender equality and feminism across borders, they were often utilized as political tokens when the liberal discourse demanded supporters for corporatized democracy and global dominance. As the "new settlers" in America and the "free world," they were both vulnerable and volatile; yet their intellectual, cultural, and monetary capitals made it possible for them to be assimilated as the redefined "model minority" carefully walking the line between being politically edgy and embracing multicultural liberalism.

Different from previous Asian immigrants such as indentured and high-tech laborers, their specific ways of "settling" informed their unique experiences with and understanding of both US and Chinese racism and imperialism. They needed to de-Asian themselves while simultaneously claiming their Asianness, visible and not visible at the same time. Despite that, the framework of intersectionality was taken as an analytical norm among transnational and diasporic feminist activists-scholars, issues of class, racial capitalism, and imperialism remained hardly tackled in substantial ways. When claiming the position of the radicals became a political and professional need, the revival of Marxism in feminism rarely went beyond "roll calls" that could decorate the participant with a feminist queer punk edge.

In early 2019, an episode of *Patriot Act* finally pushed me over the edge. The show invited Chinese feminist activist Liang Xiaowen as a special guest for its episode on Chinese and Saudi Arabian authoritarianism. As a political comedy, the episode's major laughter relied on racist and orientalist stereotypes of Asian culture and out-of-context comparisons between different dictatorships. I sat on my couch jaw-dropped as Minhaj, the host, interrupted Liang Xiaowen with his joking comments about "Asian parents crush dreams" when asking her about feminist ac-

204 Queer Chimerica

tivism in China. Liang was caught off guard and responded hesitantly with a confusing "yeah," to which Minhaj added the remark "You hear that? That's the sigh of thousands of A minuses." His sexist misogynistic manner in the guise of humor left me appalled.

To no surprise, the episode went on to tell a familiar narrative, one that reduced the complexity of geopolitics to the well-worn claim of the Chinese government and the Chinese family as oppressors of young feminists who are forced to flee to the US for freedom. When Liang Xiaowen introduced the Chinese #MeToo movement, *mitu* (米兔), and its symbol, the "rice bunny," Minhaj made a face, revealing that he may have associated it with the racial slur "snow bunny."

This show was a miniature of many miss-matched agendas of young diasporic feminists and consumer-orientated multicultural liberal media in the US. Being featured in a Netflix show was enthusiastically celebrated in the North American Feminist WeChat group, as it was believed that the show would increase the visibility of Chinese grassroots feminism against state oppression. Liang Xiaowen was also highly praised for "being brave," "speaking very good English," and "doing a great job of representing Chinese women." The possibility of the Chinese women being deployed as the "raw material" and the "actors" for the show and its predetermined narrative was barely addressed.

When the racist and sexist connotations of the episode were called out in the group, Minhaj's manner was trivialized by most of the group members as "just being sarcastic" and "doing self-mocking for the show" because of his own Asian background. Many feminists in the group did not recognize the racialized and sexualized "snow bunny" association, and I interpreted that as a sign of the gaps in knowledge about histories of racial and sexual oppression in the US, even when they self-claim as supporters of intersectional analytics.

And to voice my frustration and avoid a personal attack, I wrote an anonymous critique that was circulated in the chat group. Immediately somebody influential in the community "recognized" the writing style and "confirmed" that it must be written by Yang Xiaofei, the dangerous *heiwulei*. Her past sins and misconducts, confirmed and unconfirmed, were once again brought up and denounced in public like déjà vu; the indicted was convicted without being present, the absent "bad egg" was "canceled" over and over among those who cheerfully swore allegiance to feminism. What kind of structural fragility and precarity was there, and has that made defending solidarity and internal homogeneity a primary goal of Chinese feminism? Yang Xiaofei has become the symbol of anti-feminism, the "bad elements" who "undermined solidarity," the collateral damage that the battle of "saving the world from patriarchy" cannot live without.

So, I rode the downward spiral and passed as her. Under the bulletproof armor of "Yang Xiaofei," I wrote a couple of articles whose contents nobody really cared about. It was the oppositional position itself that raised ire. I no longer beat around the bush, shying away from confrontations. I excelled at biting remarks. I met my adversaries head-on. Like Guang Hui suggested years ago, I finally became the villain, the *heiwulei*, the antagonist, on the stage of the Cool Child, where I thought I ought to be the hero, the righteous, and the protagonist.

In a "queer" way, Yang Xiaofei and I became "partners in crime" once again, pulling off stunts together as we did two decades ago. The way we defend the world created a world that may not be worth defending.

PART VI

Beijing Dome

CHAPTER 20

Homecoming No More

That's it. This is the last page of Na Na's notebook. The last words she concluded her research with. The last words she had about me. *The way we defend the world created a world that may not be worth defending.* Is that the lesson you learned after all these years of studying abroad and struggling with the people you met?

Now my memory is crystal clear. Na Na's fieldwork was the catalyst for my transformation, an opportunity to confront what I was not proud of. We shared letters with each other, exchanging our pain and joy, being each other's "empty chair" therapists. It was a journey of self-discovery, a coming-of-age that I thought was long behind me. Yet just as I thought we were on the path to healing and inner peace, Na Na vanished from my world altogether. A familiar betrayal I had known fifteen years ago. The difference this time was that she didn't leave to fight for the cause, but to denounce it.

I searched for her relentlessly, scouring gay bars and cruising parks, combing through social media, and reaching out to everyone she had interviewed. She was nowhere to be seen. I flew to the address listed in her notebook only to be met with an unforgiving Minnesotan blizzard. I sat at the airport, lamenting her irresponsibility. I detested her for the childhood promises she chose not to keep.

A man sat next to me with a can of root beer in his hand. I hadn't seen a root beer since A&W's closure in China in 2003.

"You look a bit sad. Parting anxiety?" asked the man.

"More like uncertainty about the future," I answered.

"Well, one thing certain about the future is that we are going to be stuck on this airplane together for the next twelve hours, smelling each other's farts and bad odors." He laughed, pointing to my boarding pass, "By the way, my name is Andrei Lenkov,[1] and you are . . . ?"

---

1. The last name "Lenkov" means "the defender of humanity."

"History is what hurts, my friend."

I buried my face in Andrei's arms. Tears darkened his white shirt.

Soon Andrei offered me a strange job: to spearhead a neural interface he called "QueerFi," a platform designed for LGBT-identified participants to trade their biodata for NFTs and cryptocurrencies. I couldn't care less about the financial aspect of it, but I accepted the job so that I could take advantage of the infrastructure for a cause close to my heart.

I created a blockchain of brains, a synaptic web of electro-emotional exchange, a Commons of somatic experiences, so to speak, so in one another's arms of pain and joy, we could feel how others feel, see and understand the world beyond the pigeonhole we arrogantly call "self." I named it "Beijing Dome," in homage to the observatory where Na Na and I once gazed upon the "two suns" in the velvety blue-red dawn sky when we were teenagers. A home that is no more.

I encoded Na Na's fieldnotes, her documentation and fabrication of the lively people she met along the way, their happiness, regret, conflict, drama, hatred, aspiration, pettiness, retaliation, and reconciliation into the content of the Dome. I tested it on myself. I relived the many lives and stories as she did. On the verge of success, I was hacked, for Beijing Dome would put out of business those who thrive on our separation and demise. The life experiences of others I carried collapsed my neural system, cluttering access to my memory, my past.

In the thick darkness of my dreams, I saw Andrei holding my hands that light penetrated with ease, my colorless face reflected in his tear-filled eyes; he whispered, "'History is what hurts,' my friend."

CHAPTER 21

Here Comes the Cool Child

My name is Yang Xiaofei, the *fei* of "flying," soaring above all constraints of convention. Long ago, my invention transformed the world in a way one never imagined. It gave a chance for the marginalized to be at the center stage of revolution. The cost? I was turned into a translucent vessel, a matrix, an interface, a selfless "Mother" who nurtured the experience of others. Is the world better now?

I part the heavy drapes that shield the work bay and walk up to the terrace. Below the hill where the observatory is mounted lays the quiet city in the thick morning fog. In a matter of moments, as the fog disappears, the Dome will fold out its gigantic arms to emit particles of photon-convertors into the air, like an eagle, or an owl, enveloping the hard-working citizens under its magnificent wings. The crystal-like material will turn to clouds, filtering out the harsh blue light, casting only a crimson hue in the sky, harmless to the clear body of the Chimericans. By the way, the derogatory term "shrimp dumpling" was outlawed in 2039 at the tenth anniversary of the Confederation.

I remove my gloves and dark hood, letting the sunlight burn my face. I stretch out my arms and legs, observing the dark spots that creep up my luminous skin. In the end, I couldn't restore Na Na. But it is the echoes of her presence that have protected me from the fate of turning white and unremembering. I am one of the lucky ones who can still walk under the blue sky these days.

It has been some time since I last saw Andrei, but I heard that you can still find good Beets in "China," and the transporters are still around.

I lie down in the Nano Pod and let my eyelids meet, seeing myself in front of the A&W restaurant. So far, I have managed to cry for four hours. Out of desperation, I dial Boss Jiang's number, offering myself to him. I want to text

Here Comes the Cool Child   213

Na Na and make her jealous. Soon I will receive her cold-hearted message, and I will laugh about it. I have become too familiar with this bittersweet drill.

But today, something is different.

A woman comes to me. Her red lips are on fire; her eyes are shadowed by thick fan-like lashes; her sleek hair is a dark waterfall, split in the middle, making her face sharper. As she lowers her body to sit beside me, the industrial bar that juts out of her undercut reveals a tasteful of her humble rebelliousness beneath the façade of a soft Miss Butterfly.

"You look sad." She frowns.

"My best friend left me. I fear I may never see her again."

"'Never' is a long time," she cracks up and her large eyes bend like crescents. "When I was at your age, I too had a falling out with my best friend. She was one of the most important people who made me who I am today. We had some great time together, shared a lot of dreams, happiness, pains, struggles, and disappointments, but after all we had different prospects for life."

"Then how did you move past the desire and get healed from the loss?"

"I don't. I still love her, long for her, but longing is different from desiring. Desire requires an object to be fulfilled; longing is an act, a process, an orientation, that doesn't need closure." The woman turns her head to me and her face beams with a beatific smile, "As years passed, I realized that she has become part of me. It was the time with her that drew out the best of me, gave me the strength to pursue what I always wanted. It was with her that I found true love in myself. And it was precisely the strength, the inspiration, and the freedom she gave me that drove me to leave her, many times, to become who I meant to be."

My eyes widen as she speaks, "It was you. This woman I met forty years ago in front of the A&W when you first left me. I knew it was you from the future. Did you come back to mourn the kids we once were or to deliver the message that took you so long to form?"

"I went back to say 'thank you.'" Her tenderness radiates outward, her icy gaze softens, her brown eyes glimmer, "Thanks for all the path-crossings."

"But I should be the one to say thank *you*. I would have never found myself without what you have left and bestowed on me."

"You know all of these are in your mind, right? Me, this, and everything you are seeing right now, are the materialization of your inner world. Memory is not like data stored in a computer that we faithfully access at will. Every time we recall it, we are recreating a past, a new reality. It is through the reflective work you have done that you not only found yourself, but also others who were just like you, longing for another intercourse, another handshake, another heartfelt hugging and holding. Isn't that why you made Beijing Dome in the first place? So that people can do the labor of longing over and over and be surprised by the bonding they never expected before?"

Na Na's luminous face becomes the faces of Yang Tao, Zhang Shanping, Guang Hui, and many others I know and don't know. Then this fifteen-year-old schoolgirl in a British-style suit and Dr. Martens picks up my hands; with a warm timbre of voice, she says, "Our departure was destinated. Like Lot's wife, it is the dirt of our own Sodom and Gomorrah that roots and anchors us, even at the cost of us turning into a salt pillar."

She gestures toward the people over the city who are meant to be used as new sources for the Beets, "There, what matters now and here is those who stand next to you in the Sin City, who share *this* life with you."

Her tiny hand slips away from my rough callouses, leaving a vial of purple liquid on my palm. Her figure becomes blurry in tears, but I am not sure if the tears are hers or mine. She turns her head before she vanishes, "By the way, the best moment of love is *not* when the lover leaves in the taxi. So, suck it up."

I pop the lid of the antidote. The liquid coats my lips, mouth, and throat, and the cooling sensation floods my heart,

"Farewell, my dearest friend; farewell, the Cool Child we once were."

Coda

In lieu of a formal conclusion, I'd like to end the book with a brief reflection on the literary and plotting devices I used that helped me better unpack theories and my research materials.

Through Yang Xiaofei's journey, the book traces three sets of conflicts that I see characterize current studies of queer representation and experience: a universalized queer theorization rooted in a particular political economy of Western poststructuralism and global colonial practices versus embodied queer lives that resist to be simplified by abstract scholarship, calls for visibility and rights-based activism; a queer desire for self-articulation, gender/sexual fluidity and anti-normativity versus capital's demand for labor flexibility and empire's constant transgression of boundaries that hinge on the normalization of certain affect, emotions, and cultural and political idea(l)s; and a queer politics that equates visibility, voice, individual autonomy with agency versus the mutual reliance of the self and the others that frequently go unrepresented. These interdependent contradictions are conditioned by the histories and politics of "Chimerica" but by no means are unique to it. Similar tensions can be found in the studies of "queer India," "queer Iran," "queer Africa," just to name a few. This book stands on the shoulders of previous works and provides a different itinerary to illuminate the ways in which the "area-based" queer studies are inseparable parts of the US "queer institutional complex" that has informed and dominated the studies of sexuality and politics of queer emancipation. Without the "suicide bombers from the Middle East," the "HIV positive gay men desperate for help in Ghana," "the poor *ketoy* in Bankok," "the *hijra* in Kolkata," and the "fallen angels of Russia," would the queer as we know it today look, feel, and speak the same?

216   Queer Chimerica

Making visible this mutuality, I use the Beijing Dome, the fictional empire's techno-statecraft device, to illustrate the dynamism of queer Chimerica. At first, the Dome appears as an infrastructure through which the authoritarian-neoliberalist apparatus manages precarity and mines queer potentials for profit. Similar to real-life representations of queer experiences such as on social media, news, and films, the Dome relies on the production of a timeless "China" where violence and oppression could get recycled for the purpose of making liberal subjects. Secondly, the Dome speaks to an Orientalist and romanticized presumption of "socialist China" held by (Western) queer Marxist leftists, mostly represented by the character Andrei Lenkov. Without much experience in the PRC, they often flatten Chinese history and the people who lived it into stock figures of resistance in the hope of evoking "alternatives" to capitalism. I use this setting to engage current debates within queer Marxism and to urge the leftist queers to reflect on their positionality, privilege, and epistemological blindness. Finally, the Dome signals the possibility of a space where people could build connections across time and place. This, however, requires the "empty chair method," through which one must step out of what they take for granted and get into the materiality of others that could dangerously undermine oneself. In fact, the entire book embodies this type of struggled yet rewarding connection as a politics of queer future, as opposed to the politics of seeing, speaking, and representing, by having most of the stories unfold in the form of the protagonist's "immersive synchronization" episodes with others.

The plot of Chimericans turning translucently white is a metaphor for the dilemmatic experience of the Chinese, transnational, and diasporic queer subjects who must navigate the tension between being visible and invisible. Confessing pain and trauma, speaking oppression and violence, announcing radicality and political allegiance, and denouncing the enemies and outsiders (from the Cultural Revolution to the LGBT and queer activism and to the fictional future) are ways in which one could survive and make into a legible subject; but the means of "becoming" is not unfettered. It requires the subject to stick to flattened narratives and to "de-particularize," "de-area," and "de-Chinese" themselves so that their knowledge and experience can be accepted as more "representational" and themselves as "honorary whites." This setting also indirectly engages with current queer Sinophone studies, whose focus on "decentering" and the "subjects at the margin," to me, might appear to romanticize the queer sojourners who trudge the unevenness of geopolitics, and to underestimate the everyday labor of in/voluntary "passing."

The designs of Life Beets, Immersive Synchronization and the Empty Chair Theory all play with the concept of fungibility and its potential (and its failure) to chart new modes of being and living. In *Scenes of Subjection*, Saidiya Hartman points out that fungibility can slide and be easily attached to a range of concepts and categories within the syntax of liberal sentimentality. One of these sentimentalities is empathy. In her reading of John Rankin's texts, Hartman argues that it is the "thingly character" of the black body that allows the white man to interchange his own body with the body-as-commodity and fulfills the fantasy of experiencing the enslaved body-in-pain. As Hartman writes, this narcissistic identification makes the captive body an abstract and empty vessel vulnerable to the project of others' feelings, ideas, desires, and values.[1] I draw from this powerful critique to engage the questions of whether we can be the empathic embedded ethnographer, researcher, scholar and activist in the hope of capturing the dilemma of knowing about others, sharing experiences and seeking solidarity, especially in an era when technology has provided more tools and sites for research and social movements while reducing concrete and in-depth interactions among individuals and communities. As the end of the story hints, knowing and solidarity can be formed through shared labor embedded in localized struggles, rather than from the romanticized space of the unlimited and the unbounded.

A hidden thread that undercuts the book is family relations and inter- and trans-generational trauma—the blackhole we inherit prenatally that cannot be filled through seeking redress. When it comes to writing about queerness in East Asian cultures, one recurring theme is the father-son/mother-daughter conflict. This persistence can be observed in cultural productions from, for example, Pai Hsien-yung's queer classic *Crystal Boys* (1983) to Michelle Yeoh's recent big-screen hit *Everything Everywhere All at Once* (2022). This book provides a subtle way to upend the stereotype of Chinese traditional families as homophobic and East Asian/Chinese queers as outcasts. Although the respective queer worlds of Yang Xiaofei, Yang Tao, and Yang Zhongguo are made known to the reader, they remain secret in the Yang family, either due to trans-generational reluctance or deliberate "unremembering." Nevertheless, a sense of queer kinship emerges through the characters' shared struggle with being the Uncool in their own ways, enabled by the transporters and through the Synchronization. I use this setting as a means to nudge the study of Global Queer Asia beyond its normal/normative object of study and narrative conventions.

Lastly, readers might find it challenging to see how exactly Yang Xiaofei becomes a *heiwulei* of queer *lala* feminism. As I am completing the manuscript,

---

1. Saidiya Hartman, *Scenes of Subjection: Terror, Slavery, and Self-Making in Nineteenth-Century America* (Oxford: Oxford University Press, 1997), 21.

218 Queer Chimerica

I still find myself struggling with the stake of telling or not telling the stories of Chinese transnational feminism. From those whom I write about, I have learned great lessons of courage, compassion, and community, yet I also need to process and make sense of the hurt, damage, and violence that come with the journey. The narrative unclarity and inability to articulate shield me from my vulnerability, confusion, blindness, and ignorance at this moment. This is precisely when the temptation of speculation becomes stronger and irresistible. I must write from a future, from the point of view of a future me, who has gained the power and strength to revisit and open the past with greater insights. I know this future will come because I have already received her message.

In late 2018, while attending a conference in Washington, D.C., I unexpectedly ran into a longtime nemesis. As we found ourselves two lonely souls on the outskirts of the U.S. Capital city, surrounded by suited-up politicians and businesspersons, we decided to share a quick lunch of camaraderie at a small restaurant. Over a trayful of overpriced shrimp dumplings, we traded gossip about activists we both knew, old debates and disputes in Chinese politics, and complaints about living and dating in the States as queer and Chinese women. As we parted ways and headed to the airport, we exchanged a hug. Although our mutual dislike persisted after the conditional reunion, that hug remained significant to me.

It was to honor the hug and the hope of more to come that I wrote this book.

Appendix

THE MISSING PAGES: EMPTY CHAIR THERAPY

A Letter to Someone Who Might Not Receive It

The strident siren of fire trucks breaks the silent early spring night and wakes you up from a shallow sleep. Your heart beats like a war drum and you have a moment of confusion, asking yourself, Where am I? Another siren flaring from a police car startles you again before you remember that a not-so-close friend kindly offered up a small pull-out couch in her humble New York City flat.

You came to the city for an important meeting hosted by the United Nations. Despite your clumsy English, your speech on the resistance of Chinese grassroots feminism moved the audience from all over the world. You know the magic words to make their neck hair stand up and send shivers down their spine. They, just like your host, admire your aspirations for standing up to patriarchy and empathize with your agony in battling with the repressive regime.

Soon after the conference, you learned that your friends, comrades, and followers in China were detained by state security for handing out anti-sexual harassment stickers on the subway the day before International Women's Day. Feminists arrested before International Women's Day? What a world! You are enraged, but you could see it coming. Since 2014 state surveillance of transnational-sponsored NGOs has tightened, and feminist advocacy has become harder and harder. What is going to happen to you if you go back to China? you wonder. You know very well that you are the "most wanted" in the eyes of the authority. Many of the recent public feminist outreaches, flash mobs, and public performance art were organized by you behind the curtain. You know that your ability to organize mass network and to connect to the international civil society is threatening to the "harmonious society" in the eyes of the authorities, especially when your source of funding is considered the "most sensitive" one, and you know what they would do out of that fear, because for years, you have yourself mastered the skill of thinking and being like a politician. Two decades of activist work have rewarded your virtuosity in playing fire with power: your organizations are often shut down, but you manage to secure networks and resources; you have gained popularity and become the leader, the core figure of the feminist grassroots movement, despite the leaderless claims often made by the younger generations. You are used to living on the edge.

So you tear up the return tickets and decide to embrace the journey of exile, of no return. Life has surely given you some unfair blows, but you are certain that you will always find people who will lend you a hand; and if you try hard, you will probably get a student visa or immigration status. You believe when women are willing to ask for more than what they are given, they will get it; even though the cost is high.

You sit in the darkness. Orange streetlights cast long shadows of the window frame on your narrow sofa bed. Everything is transient. You peek through the gap in the window blinds. It starts to snow. New York City is still chilly in early March. In this room where nothing belongs to you, you begin to recall things at home. The cat litter is not cleaned—you can almost smell the foul smell from afar; dishes are piling up in the sink—you left in a rush that morning and thought that you could clean the mess after your return; and you realize that you even forgot to unplug the dildo from the wall charger in your bedroom and how embarrassing it is going to be when you ask somebody to take care of your apartment in Beijing.

But you understand well what it takes to be a fighter, a dreamer, a resistor, an opportunist, an outlier.

People come and people go. You will never know when the last time it would be to see somebody and to call somewhere home. "Women have no country" is your motto.

Jet lag keeps you up. You lie down on the bed, trying to figure out the relief pattern of the high ceiling. It reminds you of the first time you went to the village in northwest China by yourself to become a "women's issue expert" twenty-five years ago. You were assigned a room with a hardboard cot, and from the bed, you used to stare at the strange pattern of mold and mildew on the ceiling wall. It was the best room they could offer. When you were a young journalist, you had seen too many cases of female infanticide, domestic violence, girls not allowed to go to school . . . so you decided to leave your promising job, the stable life offered by your established family, and to become a "loser" in your

Appendix 221

colleagues' eyes. You rose up as a social outlaw and fought for women's rights without even knowing the word "feminism." You did not even need the label.

The label is important now. To survive in the unfamiliar city that you would eventually call home, you need more allies than enemies. Back in China, you were thrown up as the leader, the star, and the spokesperson by the burgeoning online feminist movements, as well as criticized and hated as the "feminist hegemon." You were argumentative and dismissive of others; you often spoke with an insolent tone; you picked up a fight with people who disagreed with you and isolated them with your marvelous skill of manipulation; you came across as harsh; and sometimes you even threw hands with your nemeses. But in the new country, you learn to play soft. You tone down and use your feminine energy to solicit help from strangers. Young folks gravitate toward you for your eloquence and sharp tongue. You build a new circle of feminists in the alien land. You pull together online discussions, offline gatherings, and tours at universities. To be a "Chinese feminist" of the diaspora is not only a political position but also a need for survival. In this new city, the lively faces of the young feminists represent the home that has been lost and a hopeful new kinship that has yet to come. You welcome everybody who is in the same transient position but carefully manage your "core group."

You have made yourself elastic. Stretchable and resilient. When pulled, you jump high and far. You shoot like an arrow.

You meet a guy. A typical Joe, middle aged, dad bod, white, from an East coast small town. You do not date Chinese men, you never did, for you don't allow yourself to be trapped in the patriarchal family that comes with the BOGO deal. He does not mind your English, your nationality. He is patient in teaching you the new language, new culture. He takes you out for sushi, drives you around and shows you the sparkling city night. How humiliating it is when he treats you like an innocent child.

He does not know much about China, but he is intrigued by you and wants to learn. His ignorance irritates you a lot of the time. But he is the only person who sees you as "you," not as the social position you inhabit. In his eyes, you are the most beautiful woman he has ever met.

You would not consider yourself a pretty woman. For being a long-time hardcore feminist leader, why would you ever consider your looks and objectify yourself for the white male gaze? You tell yourself that being with him is just an experiment in living an everyday feminist life and observing the cultural differences in patriarchy. But isn't it bad when the winter slush and snow soak your cold feet, the only thing you desire is his warm arms?

You like how you look with red lipstick on. The reflection of yourself in the

222   *Appendix*

mirror puts a big smile on your face. You debate between Maybelline and MAC, and finally decide on indulging yourself with the more expensive one. A33. Ruby Woo. Your favorite shade.

Sometimes, you walk past the bakery aisle at Costco, and think he would not mind putting on a few extra pounds if you made some Pillsbury's cookies. Other times, you want to tell him how frustrating it is when you are attacked again and again online by somebody who holds old grudges against you, but he has nothing to respond. His cold, indifferent "I see" enrages you.

And the "somebody" was me. I am very honored to be your nemesis.

Yang Xiaofei

Acknowledgments

As the book's protagonist Yang Xiaofei reminds us, our truest brilliance often arises from reflecting the radiance of others. The book would be impossible without the illuminating love, care, and insights from family and friends, colleagues and comrades, and mentors and students.

My heartfelt gratitude first goes out to my family, to whom I owe the power behind my words. Thanks to Dad who gifted me Alfred Kinsey's book when I was twelve years old and then shared many articles and literary works on homosexuality along my way to pursue my study in the United States. Thanks to Mom and Auntie who attentively listened to stories from my fieldwork and offered invaluable feedback during the formative stages of this book. Thanks to *laolao* who shared personal accounts of what lesbian life was like in her childhood. In memory of *laoye*, who imparted to me a profound understanding of the history of socialism, the Korean War, and the gay life in the Chinese military. Thanks to Qianqian and Xiao Yu, for sharing the growing pains and for being the most exceptional sisters.

I was truly blessed to have been welcomed with open arms by many people who extended their unwavering support throughout my fieldwork. They are: CUI Zi'en, Tong Ge, WAN Yanhai, ZHANG Beichuan, LI Yinhe, PAN Suiming, FANG Gang, SONG Shaopeng, Wenqing Kang, GUO Yaqi, Joan Kaufman, Ga Ga, Zhen Li, Ah Shan, FAN Popo, An Ke, XU Bin, XIN Ying, WEI Tingting, HE Xiaopei, LI Maizi, WEI Jiangang, Damien Lu, JIANG Hui, Darrel Cummings, DU Hui, Ah Ping, Musk Ming, MENG Lin, GENG Le, Ah Qiang, Stephen Leonelli, LI Dan, LI Sipan, Mu Cao; and numerous others whose names I cannot disclose.

Thanks to Shuxuan Zhou for spearheading the Chinese Students and Scholars writing group, without which the completion of the book wouldn't be imag-

224   *Acknowledgments*

inable. Thanks to Wenjie Liao, Qian Liu, Rong Zhao, Yuhan Huang, and Dian Dian, whose company was a guiding light throughout the arduous writing process. Thanks to Anna Ziyi Zhao, Laura Joelle Bell, Mark Reese, WEI Mingzhao, ZHENG Yue, Stephanie Yingyi Wang, Grace Chiyu Lin, Jo Fangzhou Xu, Helen Wenmeng Gong, Nan Hu, and Joan Han for lending me their ears and hands during my years of living with depression. The solace and strength they offered in my moments of need led me to the journey of healing. Thanks to my bandmates and the vibrant Parkour community in Toronto, for infusing my life with immeasurable joy and happiness.

I owe a special debt to the guest editors of the University of Michigan Press *Global Queer Asias Series*, Howard Chiang and James Welker. I had the privilege of getting to know Howard during my years as a graduate student. Through numerous inspirational conversations and timely feedbacks, Howard has nurtured me through the challenges of early-career publication and academic growth. I admire Howard's scholarship, knowledge, and his generosity, especially in his sincere support and endorsement of other people's work, even when he might hold differing opinions. He exemplifies the kind of scholar and teacher I aspire to become.

I also got to know James more than a decade ago and our connections deepened as we both served as board members of the Society for Queer Asian Studies. James has shown me what it is like to be an accountable scholar while enjoying unexpected delights that life brings us. His "one new neighborhood each month" advice helped me survive my early years in Toronto. His work on Japanese feminism and Boys' Love opened up new avenues of thought and exploration for me. I deeply appreciate his dedication to fostering queer networks, lifting others up and fostering non-competing scholarly environments.

Central to this project was also the intellectual labor and steadfast support of Bogdan Popa, Tatiana Klepikova, and Weiling Deng. Bogdan and I are what I fondly refer to as "queer socialist siblings." He brought me to new terrains of queer theorization, histories and political thoughts, aspects without which my project would not be fully fledged. Our conversations on Marxism, Jameson, air draft, postsocialist zombies and vampires, psychoanalysis and generative AIs have been both enriching and enjoyable.

From the very inception of the book, Weiling assumed the role of an encouraging critic, offering thought-provoking feedback that significantly enhanced the clarity of my conceptualization, arguments, and the overall flow of my writing. Her innovative work, expansive knowledge, and diverse interests have opened many doors for me to see the world differently. Thanks for the friendship, book recommendations, and the long walks in the Minnesotan snow and along the Toronto lakeshore.

Tatiana was the first to read my nascent draft in full. She printed off the whole manuscript and diligently underlined the pages, giving thoughtful and punctual comments. Her generosity and patience, alongside the lovely moments shared over BBQ dinners, spaghettis, wines and hiking trips, made it possible for me to foresee the finish line of the project.

I want to extend my deep appreciation to Lisa Rofel and Rahul Rao, whose careful perusal of each chapter of my first draft, along with their contribution of the phrase "antagonist interdependence," helped me greatly in refining many of the book's core arguments. I am also indebted to a group of beta readers who generously aided. They are: Timothy Bult, Kanika Lawton, Yi Gu, Yvon Yiwen Wang, Husseina Dinani and Ian Liujia Tian. Two anonymous readers provided astute reading and invaluable perspectives that generated pivotal revisions. One of them bestowed upon me the word "speculative autoethnography," which eventually found its place in the book's title.

My gratitude extends to Christopher Dreyer at the University of Michigan Press for having faith in my work, as well as to Katie LaPlant, Danielle Coty-Fattal, Delilah McCrea, Marcia LaBrenz, and the rest of the staff for their indispensable editorial guidance and support. I must also acknowledge the substantial and timely editing on my manuscript by Alyea Canada, as well as the meticulous efforts by the indexer Doug Easton and proofreaders Shuxuan Zhou, Wenjie Liao, Tingting Liu, and Tara King.

It is beyond quantification to enumerate the support and guidance I received from my doctoral co-advisers Jigna Desai and Richa Nagar, and dissertation committee members Jason McGrath, Naomi Scheman, and Aren Aizura, at the University of Minnesota. Thank you, Jigna, for the queer Asian sci-fi, supernova and Arizona. Thank you, Richa, for "radical vulnerability," the bus stop chats, and the time shared in the St. Paul gym. Thank you, Jason, for Zhang Yimou, the socialist iPad, and the Savages concert. Thank you, Naomi, for the Ailanthus trees, Wiegenstein, and the Beijing trip. Thank you, Aren, for close reading my sodomy chapter and for the advice on being trans.

Many of the ideas in this book can be traced back to my undergraduate and Master's years. I thank Amy Lind, Deb Meem, Michelle Gibson, Anne Sisson Runyan, and Olga Sanmiguel-Valderrama, at the University of Cincinnati who served as loving and dedicated mentors in my very early years in the United States. Thank you, Amy, for introducing me to the study of empires, your exemplary mentorship, and shared moments over sushi in Shibuya. Thank you, Deb,

226 *Acknowledgments*

for all the chats on Ancient Greek heroes, Oscar Wilde and *Fun Home*. Thank you, Michelle, for the enriching discussions on global sexuality. Thank you, Anne, for the insights into China's One-Child policy and international gender politics. Thanks, Olga, for the decolonial scholarship.

There are many other interlocutors, new and old, to whom I owe a great deal. Thank you, Xin Huang, for numerous conference panels, shared rooms, and food and wine. Thank you, Charlie Yi Zhang, for many overnight discussions, debates, and chit-chats. Thank you, Terry Wong and Shuzhen Huang, for the queer Chinese women project, the bubble wand, and the freebies. I was fortunate to have other colleagues and mentors who gave of their moral and intellectual support: Sasha Welland, Matthew Sommer, Chandan Reddy, Gayatri Gopinath, Petrus Liu, Amy Brainer, Ari Larissa Heinrich, Thomas Baudinette, Christopher Fan, Redi Koobak, Madina Tlostanova, Yevgeniy Fiks, Erin McElroy, Hongwei Bao, Jamie Zhao, Elisabeth Lund Engebretsen, Will Schroeder, Alvy Wong, Wei Wei, Jian Tan, Fan Yang, and Zheng Wang. The following friends and interlocutors also helped sustain my intellectual passions: Ai Wang, Jingzhu Zhu, Alan Michael Williams, Chris Tan, Suisui Wang, Ana Huang, Scott E. Myers, Lin Song, Di Wang, Jiling Duan, Lin Li, Wenxin Yan, Wen Liu, Ying-Chao Kao, Tyler Carson, Matt Galway, Mian Chen, Chenshu Zhou, and Mia Ma.

At the University of Toronto, I want to thank Alissa Trotz, Natalie Rothman, Connie Guberman, Li Chen, Michelle Murphy, Dana Seitler, Robert Diaz, Jordache Ellapen, Jed Kuhn, Naveen Minai, Cassandra Hartblay, Natalie Oswin, Jesook Song, Lisa Yoneyama, Yvon Wang, Ping-Chun Hsiung, Yue Meng, Yiching Wu, Jotaro Arimori, Yanfei Li, Diana Fu, Andre Schmid, Patrick Keilty, Atiqa Hachimi, Daniel Bender, Rick Halpern, Anup Grewal, William Nelson, Bhavani Raman, Nicole Charles, Chris Johnson, T. L. Cowan, Jas Rault, Greg de St. Maurice, Josh Arthurs, Matthew Mucha, and SJ Sindu for their camaraderie, mentorship, and collegiality. At the University of Minnesota, I thank Xiumei Pu, Hui Niu Wilcox, Kan Li, Mingwei Huang, Thorn Hongwei Chen, Mina Ahn, Angela Carter, Kong Pheng Pha, Ani Dutta, Rushaan Kumar, Sayan Bhattacharya, Guanda Wu, Kevin Murphy, David Valentine, Ann Waltner, Jackie Zita, Roderick Ferguson, Regina Kunzel, Kale Fajardo, Martin Manalansan IV, Karen White, Raquel Dantas, and Shereen Sabet for their guidance, inspiration, and friendship.

This project was generously supported by the following sources: the Interdisciplinary Center for the Study of Global Change Scholar Fellowship and the Doctoral Dissertation Fellowship at the University of Minnesota; Connaught New Researcher Award at the University of Toronto; Martha McCain Faculty

Research Fellowship at the Mark S. Bonham Centre for Sexual Diversity Studies; China and Inner Asia Council Research Travel Grant from the Association for Asian Studies; and multiple research and travel grants from the Department of Gender, Women and Sexuality Studies at the University of Minnesota, the Department of Historical and Cultural Studies at the University of Toronto Scarborough, the Women and Gender Studies Institute, and the Jackman Humanities Institute at the University of Toronto. These fellowships and grants provided financial support for me to conduct fieldwork, collect archival materials, attend conferences and workshops, hire professional editors, and sharpen my writing skills. The University of Michigan Press and the Department of Historical and Cultural Studies at the University of Toronto Scarborough also provided funding for making the book Open Access. I deeply appreciate the Press's and my department's efforts to deliver the work to the broadest possible audience and to promote scholarly equality, accessibility, and diversity.

Though substantially revised, sections of the book appeared in my previous publications. My discussions on sodomy and early-1990s gay identities were included in "Reparative Return to 'Queer Socialism': Agency, Desires and the Socialist Queer Space," in *Power and Pleasure: Writing the History of Sexuality in China*. Part of the chapters on Chinese feminism appeared in my article, "The Drama of Chinese Feminism: Post-socialist Trauma and Decolonization of Affect," *Feminist Studies*, and chapters on HIV/AIDS appeared in "'Paris' and 'Scar': Queer Social Reproduction, Homonormative Division of Labour and HIV/AIDS Economy in Postsocialist China," *Gender, Place & Culture: A Journal of Feminist Geography*. Sections of my introduction also can be seen in my chapter, "Queering Postsocialist Coloniality: Decolonizing Queer Fluidity through Postsocialist Condition," in *Postcolonial and Postsocialist Dialogues: Intersections, Opacities, Challenges in Feminist Theorizing and Practice*. I thank the University of Washington Press, the *Feminist Studies* journal, and the Taylor & Francis Publishing Group for granting permissions to reproduce the texts.

References

Abu-Lughod, Lila. *Do Muslim Women Need Saving?* Cambridge, MA: Harvard University Press, 2013.

Alexander, Jeffrey C. *Trauma: A Social Theory.* Cambridge, MA: Polity, 2012.

Altman, Dennis. "Global gaze/global gays." *GLQ: A Journal of Lesbian and Gay Studies* 3, no. 4 (1997) : 417–36. https://doi.org/10.1215/10642684-3-4-417

Amin, Kadji. *Disturbing Attachments: Genet, Modern Pederasty, and Queer History.* Durham: Duke University Press, 2017.

Andrucki, Max. "Queering Social Reproduction, Or, How Queers Save the City." *Society and Space,* October 31, 2017. https://societyandspace.org/2017/10/31/queering-soci al-reproduction-or-how-queers-save-the-city/

Arondeka, Anjali. "In the Absence of Reliable Ghosts: Sexuality, Historiography, South Asia." *Differences* 25, no. 3 (2014): 98–122. https://doi.org/10.1215/10407391-284 7964

Atanasoski, Neda. *Humanitarian Violence: The U.S. Deployment of Diversity.* Minneapolis: University of Minnesota Press, 2013.

Bao, Hongwei. Queer Comrades: *Gay Identity and* Tongzhi *Activism in Postsocialist China.* Copenhagen: Nordic Institute of Asian Studies, 2018.

Bao, Hongwei. *Queer China: Lesbian and Gay Literature and Visual Culture under Postsocialism.* London: Routledge, 2020.

Bao, Hongwei. "Screening Sexualities, Identities and Politics: Queer Cinema in Contemporary China." In *Routledge Handbook of Chinese Culture and Society,* edited by Kevin Latham, 361–75. London: Routledge, 2020.

Bao, Hongwei. "'We Are Here': The Politics of Memory in Narrating China's Queer Feminist History." *Continuum* 34, no. 4 (2020): 514–29. https://doi.org/10.1080/103043 12.2020.1785079

Barlow, Tani. "Green Blade in the Act of Being Grazed: Late Capital, Flexible Bodies, Critical Intelligibility." *Differences: A Journal of Feminist Cultural Studies* 10, no. 3 (1998): 119–58. https://doi.org/10.1215/10407391-10-3-119

Berlant, Lauren, and Michael Warner. "What Does Queer Theory Teach Us about X?"

PMLA: Publications of the Modern Language Association of America 110, no. 3 (1995): 343–49.

Berlant, Lauren. *Cruel Optimism*. Durham: Duke University Press, 2011.

Berry, Chris, Lü Xinyu, and Lisa Rofel. *The New Chinese Documentary Film Movement: For the Public Record*. Hong Kong: Hong Kong University Press, 2010.

Bersani, Leo. "Is the Rectum a Grave?" *October* 43 (1987): 197–222. https://doi.org/10.2307/3397574

Bersani, Leo. *The Culture of Redemption*. Cambridge, MA: Harvard University Press, 1990.

Bérubé, Allan. *My Desire for History: Essays in Gay, Community, and Labor History*. Chapel Hill: University of North Carolina Press, 2011.

Bhattacharya, Tithi. *Social Reproduction Theory: Remapping Class, Recentering Oppression*. London: Plato Press, 2017.

Boyd, Nan Alamilla, and Horacio N. Roque Ramírez, eds. *Bodies of Evidence: The Practice of Queer Oral History*. Oxford: Oxford University Press, 2012.

Bravmann, Scott. *Queer Fictions of the Past: History, Culture, and Difference*. New York: Cambridge University Press, 1997.

Breman, Jan. 2013. "A Bogus Concept. Review Article." *New Left Review*, no. 84 (2013): 130–38.

Breman, Jan, Kevan Harris, Ching Kwan Lee, and Marcel van der Linden. "The Social Question as the Struggle over Precarity: The Case of China." In *The Social Question in the Twenty-First Century*, 1st ed., 58–76. Los Angeles: University of California Press, 2019. https://doi.org/10.1515/9780520972483-007

Brown, Gavin. "Homonormativity: A Metropolitan Concept that Denigrates 'Ordinary' Gay Lives." *Journal of Homosexuality* 59, no. 7 (2012): 1065–72. https://doi.org/10.1080/00918369.2012.699851

Brown, Jeremy, and Matthew Johnson, eds. *Maoism at the Grassroots: Everyday Life in China's Era of High Socialism*. Cambridge, MA: Harvard University Press, 2015. https://doi.org/10.4159/9780674287211

Brown, Wendy. "Resisting Left Melancholy." *Boundary 2* 26, no. 3 (1999): 19–27.

Buelens, Gert, Sam Durrant, and Robert Eaglestone. *The Future of Trauma Theory: Contemporary Literary and Cultural Criticism*. New York: Routledge, 2014. https://doi.org/10.4324/9780203493106

Butler, Judith. *Gender Trouble: Feminism and the Subversion of Identity*. New York: Routledge, 1990.

Butler, Judith. "Critically Queer." *GLQ: A Journal of Lesbian and Gay Studies* 1, no.1 (1993): 17–32. https://doi.org/10.1215/10642684-1-1-17

Byrd, Jodi. *The Transit of Empire: Indigenous Critiques of Colonialism*. Minneapolis: University of Minnesota Press, 2011.

Byrnes, Corey. "Men at Work: Independent Documentary and Male Bodies." *Journal of Chinese Cinemas* 14, no. 3 (2020): 157–80. https://doi.org/10.1080/17508061.2020.1838417

Cacho, Lisa. *Social Death: Racialized Rightlessness and the Criminalization of the Unprotected*. Durham: Duke University Press, 2012.

Caruth, Cathy. *Unclaimed Experience: Trauma, Narrative, and History*. Baltimore: Johns Hopkins University Press, 1996.

Casper, Monica, and Eric Wertheimer, eds. *Critical Trauma Studies: Understanding Violence, Conflict and Memory in Everyday Life*. New York: New York University Press, 2016. https://doi.org/10.29173/cjs28223

Castiglia, Christopher, and Christopher Reed. *If Memory Serves: Gay Men, AIDS, and the Promise of the Queer Past*. Minneapolis: University of Minnesota Press, 2012.

Chakrabarty, Dipesh. *Provincializing Europe: Postcolonial Thought and Historical Difference*. Princeton: Princeton University Press, 2000.

Chan, Shelly. *Diaspora's Homeland: Modern China in the Age of Global Migration*. Durham: Duke University Press, 2018.

Chao, Shi-Yan. *Queer Representations in Chinese-language Film and the Cultural Landscape*. Amsterdam: Amsterdam University Press, 2020.

Chari, Sharad, and Katherine Verdery. "Thinking Between the Posts: Postcolonialism, Postsocialism, and Ethnography after the Cold War," *Comparative Studies in Society and History* 51, no. 1 (2009): 6–34. https://doi.org/10.1017/S0010417509000024

Chen, Kuan-Hsing. *Asia as Method: Toward Deimperialization*. Durham: Duke University Press, 2010.

Chen, Ya-chen. *The Many Dimensions of Chinese Feminism*. New York: Palgrave Macmillan, 2011.

Chen-Dedman, Adam. "*Tongzhi* Sovereignty: Taiwan's LGBT Rights Movement and the Misplaced Critique of Homonationalism." *International Journal of Taiwan Studies*, no. 2 (2023): 261–90. https://doi.org/10.1163/24688800-20221267

Chiang, Howard. *Transtopia in the Sinophone Pacific*. New York: Columbia University Press, 2021.

Chiang, Howard. *After Eunuchs: Science, Medicine, and the Transformation of Sex in Modern China*. New York: Columbia University Press, 2018.

Chiang, Howard. Review of *Queer Marxism in Two Chinas*, by Petrus Liu. *The China Quarterly* 227 (2016): 847–50.

Chiang, Howard. "(De)Provincializing China: Queer Historicism and Sinophone Postcolonial Critique." In *Queer Sinophone Cultures*, edited by Howard Chiang and Ari Larissa Heinrich, 39–71. New York: Routledge, 2014. https://doi.org/10.4324/9780203590928

Chiang, Howard, and Alvin Wong. "Queering the Transnational Turn: Regionalism and Queer Asias." *Gender, Place and Culture: A Journal of Feminist Geography* 23, no. 11 (2016): 1643–56. https://doi.org/10.1080/0966369X.2015.1136811

Chiang, Howard, and Alvin Wong. "Asia is Burning: Queer Asia as Critique." *Culture, Theory and Critique* 58, no. 2 (2017): 121–26. https://doi.org/10.1080/14735784.2017.1294839

Ching, Yau, ed. *As Normal as Possible: Negotiating Sexuality and Gender in Mainland China and Hong Kong*. Hong Kong: Hong Kong University Press, 2010.

Chou, Wah-shan. *Tongzhi: Politics of Same-sex Eroticism in Chinese Societies*. New York: Haworth Press, 2000.

Chow, Rey. *Primitive Passions: Visuality, Sexuality, Ethnography, and Contemporary Chinese Cinema*. New York: Columbia University Press, 1995.

Crary, Jonathan. *24/7: Late Capitalism and the Ends of Sleep*. Brooklyn: Verso, 2014.

Crimp, Douglas. *Melancholia and Moralism: Essays on AIDS and Queer Politics*. Cambridge, MA: MIT Press, 2002.

232 *References*

Cvetkovich, Ann. *An Archive of Feelings: Trauma, Sexuality, and Lesbian Public Cultures.* Durham: Duke University Press, 2003.

De Villiers, Nicholas. *Opacity and the Closet: Queer Tactics in Foucault, Barthes, and Warhol.* Minneapolis: University of Minnesota Press, 2012.

Debord, Guy. *The Society of the Spectacle.* Translated by Ken Knabb. Berkeley: Bureau of Public Secrets, 2014.

D'Emilio, John. "Capitalism and Gay identity." In *Powers of Desire: The Politics of Sexuality,* edited by Ann Snitow, Christine Stansell, and Sharon Thompson, 100–113. New York: Monthly Review Press, 1983.

Deng, Weiling. "The Limit of Critical Thinking? On the Contested Positionality of Diasporic Chinese Scholars in the Transitional/Translingual Practices of Feminism." Conference presentation at National Women's Studies Association, San Francisco, November 16, 2019.

Dinani, Husseina. "Gendered Migrant Labour: Marriage and the Political Economy of Wage Labour and Cash Crops in Late Colonial and Post-Independence Southern Tanzania." *Gender & History* 31, no. 3 (2019): 565–83. https://doi.org/10.1111/1468 -0424.12455

Dinshaw, Carolyn. *How Soon is Now? Medieval Texts, Amateur Readers, and the Queerness of Time.* Durham: Duke University Press, 2012.

Dittmer, Lowell. "The Structural Evolution of 'Criticism and Self-Criticism.'" *The China Quarterly* 56, no. 56 (1973): 708–29. https://doi.org/10.1017/S0305741000019561

Dollimore, Jonathan. *Sex, Literature and Censorship.* New York: Polity, 2001.

Dong, Limin 董丽敏, "Nüxingzhuyi: Bentuhua yu qi weidu" 女性主义：本土化及其维度 [Feminism: Indigenization and Its Dimensions], *Nankai Xuebao* 南开学报 [Nankai Journal] no. 2 (2005): 7–12, https://www.docin.com/p-1430365368.html

Drunker, Peter. *Warped: Gay Normality and Queer Anti-Capitalism.* New York: Historical Materialism, 2015.

Du Gay, Paul, and Stuart Hall. *Questions of Cultural Identity.* London: Sage, 1996.

Duggan, Lisa. *The Twilight of Equality?: Neoliberalism, Cultural Politics, and the Attack on Democracy.* Boston: Beacon Press, 2003.

Duggan, Lisa. "The New Homonormativity: The Sexual Politics of Neoliberalism." In *Materializing Democracy: Toward a Revitalized Cultural Politics,* edited by Russ Castronovo and Dana D. Nelson, 175–94. Durham: Duke University Press, 2002. https://doi.org/10.1515/9780822383901-008

Dutta, Aniruddha. "On Queerly Hidden Lives: Precarity and (In)visibility between Formal and Informal Economies in India." *QED: A Journal in GLBTQ Worldmaking* 5, no. 3 (2018): 61–75. https://doi.org/10.14321/qed.5.3.0061

Edelman, Lee. *No Future: Queer Theory and the Death Drive.* Durham: Duke University Press, 2007.

Eng, David. "The Queer Space of China: Expressive Desire in Stanley Kwan's *Lan Yu.*" *Positions: East Asia Cultures Critique* 18, no. 2 (2010): 459–87. https://doi.org/10.12 15/10679847-2010-010

Eng, David. *The Feeling of Kinship: Queer Liberalism and the Racialization of Intimacy.* Durham: Duke University Press, 2010.

Eng, David, Jack Halberstam, and José Muñoz. "What's Queer about Queer Studies

Now?" *Social Text* 23, no. 3–4 (2005): 1–17. https://doi.org/10.1215/01642472-23-3-4_84-85-1

Engebretsen, Elisabeth L. *Queer Women in Urban China: An Ethnography*. London: Routledge, 2013.

Engebretsen, Elisabeth L., William F. Schroeder, and Hongwei Bao. *Queer/Tongzhi China: New Perspectives on Research, Activism and Media Cultures*. Copenhagen: Nordic Institute of Asian Studies, 2015.

Escobar, Arturo. *Encountering Development: The Making and Unmaking of the Third World*. New Jersey: Princeton University Press, 1995.

Evans, Harriet. *Women and Sexuality in China: Female Sexuality and Gender Since 1949*. New York: Continuum, 1997.

Fan, Christopher. "Techno-Orientalism with Chinese Characteristics: Maureen F. McHugh's *China Mountain Zhang*." *Journal of Transnational American Studies* 6, no. 1 (2015): page not indicated in the original text. https://doi.org/10.5070/T861019585

Federici, Silvia. *Revolution at Point Zero: Housework, Reproduction, and Feminist Struggle*. Oakland: PM Press, 2012.

Fejes, Nárcisz, and Andrea Balogh. *Queer Visibility in Post-socialist Cultures*. Chicago: Intellect, 2013.

Ferguson, Niall, and Moritz Schularick. "'Chimerica' and the Global Asset Market Boom." *International Finance* 10, no. 3 (2007): 215–39. https://doi.org/10.1111/j.1468-2362.2007.00210.x

Fernandes, Leela. Transnational *Feminism in the United States*. New York: New York University Press, 2013.

Fincher, Leta Hong. *Leftover Women: The Resurgence of Gender Inequality in China*. London: Zed Books, 2014.

Florida, Richard L. *Cities and the Creative Class*. New York: Routledge, 2005.

Floyd, Kevin. *The Reification of Desire: Toward a Queer Marxism*. Minneapolis: University of Minnesota Press, 2009.

Forrester, Sibelan, Magdalena Zaborowska, and Elena Gapova, eds. *Over the Wall/After the Fall: Post-Communist Cultures Through an East-West Gaze*. Bloomington: Indiana University Press, 2004.

Foucault, Michel. *The History of Sexuality: An Introduction, Volume 1*. Translated by Robert Hurley. New York: Random House, 1978.

Fraser, Nancy. *Justice Interruptus: Critical Reflections on the "Postsocialist" Condition*. New York: Routledge, 1997.

Freeman, Elizabeth. *Time Binds: Queer Temporalities, Queer Histories*. Durham: Duke University Press, 2010.

Freeman, Jo. "The Tyranny of Structurelessness." *Women's Studies Quarterly* 41, no. 3–4 (2013): 231–46. https://doi.org/10.1353/wsq.2013.0072

Fournier, Lauren. *Autotheory as Feminist Practice in Art, Writing, and Criticism*. Boston: MIT Press, 2021.

Gapova, Elena. "Becoming Visible in the Digital Age: The Class and Media Dimensions of the Pussy Riot Affair." *Feminist Media Studies* 15, no. 1 (2015): 18–35. https://doi.org/10.1080/14680777.2015.988390

234 *References*

Ghodsee, Kristen. "Revisiting the United Nations Decade for Women: Brief Reflections on Feminism, Capitalism and Cold War Politics in the Early Years of the International Women's Movement." *Women's Studies International Forum* 33 (2010): 3–12. https://doi.org/10.1016/j.wsif.2009.11.008

Gibson-Graham, Julie-Katherine. *A Postcapitalist Politics*. Minneapolis: University of Minnesota Press, 2006.

Glenn, Evelyn Nakano. "From Servitude to Service Work: Historical Continuities in the Racial Division of Paid Reproductive Labor." *Signs* 18, no. 1 (1992): 1–43. https://doi.org/10.1086/494777

Gordon, Avery. *Ghostly Matters: Haunting and the Sociological Imagination*. Minneapolis: University of Minnesota Press, 2008.

Greenhalgh, Susan, and Xiying Wang. "China's Feminist Fight: #MeToo in the Middle Kingdom." *Foreign Affairs* 98, no. 4 (2019): 170–76.

Grewal, Inderpal, and Caren Kaplan. *Scattered Hegemonies: Postmodernity and Transnational Feminist Practices*. Minneapolis: University of Minnesota Press, 1994.

Halberstam, Jack. "The Anti-Social Turn in Queer Studies," *Graduate Journal of Social Science* 5, no. 2 (2008): 140–56. http://gjss.org/sites/default/files/issues/chapters/papers/Journal-05-02--07-Halberstam.pdf

Halberstam, Jack. *In a Queer Time and Place: Transgender Bodies, Subcultural Lives*. New York: New York University Press, 2005.

Halperin, David M. *How to Be Gay*. Cambridge: Belknap Press of Harvard University Press, 2012. https://doi.org/10.4159/harvard.9780674067516

Hartman, Saidiya. "Venus in Two Acts." *Small Axe: A Caribbean Journal of Criticism* 12, no. 2 (2008): 1–14. https://doi.org/10.1215/-12-2-1

Hartman, Saidiya. *Lose Your Mother: A Journey Along the Atlantic Slave Route*. New York: Farrar, Straus and Giroux, 2007.

Hartman, Saidiya. *Scenes of Subjection: Terror, Slavery, and Self-making in Nineteenth-century America*. New York: Oxford University Press, 1997.

Harvey, David. *A Brief History of Neoliberalism*. New York: Columbia University Press, 2009.

Harvey, David. *The New Imperialism*. Oxford: Oxford University, 2003.

Hawkesworth, Mary. *Globalization and Feminist Activism*. Lanham: Rowman & Littlefield, 2006.

Hegde, Radha Sarma, ed. *Circuits of Visibility: Gender and Transnational Media Cultures*. New York: New York University Press, 2011.

Heinrich, Ari Larissa. *Chinese Surplus: Biopolitical Aesthetics and the Medically Commodified Body*. Durham: Duke University Press, 2018.

Heinrich, Ari Larissa. "'A Volatile Alliance': Queer Sinophone Synergies Across Literature, Film, and Culture." In *Queer Sinophone Cultures*, edited by Howard Chiang and Ari Larissa Heinrich, 3–16. New York: Routledge, 2014. https://doi.org/10.4324/9780203590928-9

Henderson, Lisa. *Love and Money: Queers, Class, and Cultural Production*. New York: New York University Press, 2013.

Hennessy, Rosemary. "Queer Theory, Left Politics." *Rethinking Marxism: A Journal of Economics, Culture & Society* 7, no. 3 (1994): 85–111. https://doi.org/10.1080/08935699408658114

Hershatter, Gail. "State of the Field: Women in China's Long Twentieth Century." *Journal of Asian Studies* 63, no. 4 (2004): 991–1065. https://doi.org/10.1017/S00219118040 02396

Hershatter, Gail. *Dangerous Pleasures: Prostitution and Modernity in Twentieth-Century Shanghai*. Berkeley: University of California Press, 1997.

Hershatter, Gail, Emily Honig, and Lisa Rofel. "Reflections on the Fourth World Conference on Women, Beijing and Huairou, 1995." *Social Justice (San Francisco, Calif.)* 23, no. 1–2 (1996): 368–75.

Hildebrandt, Timothy. "Development and Division: The Effect of Transnational Linkages and Local Politics on LGBT Activism in China." *The Journal of Contemporary China* 21, no. 77 (2012): 845–62. https://doi.org/10.1080/10670564.2012.684967

Hobson, Emily. *Lavender and Red: Liberation and Solidarity in the Gay and Lesbian Left*. Oakland: University of California Press, 2016.

Hong, Grace Kyungwon. *Death Beyond Disavowal: The Impossible Politics of Difference*. Minneapolis: University of Minnesota Press, 2015.

Honig, Emily. "Socialist Sex: The Cultural Revolution Revisited." *Modern China* 29, no. 2 (2003): 143–75. https://doi.org/10.1177/0097700402250735

Honig, Emily. "Iron Girls Revisited: Gender and the Politics of Work in the Cultural Revolution, 1966–76." In *Re-Drawing Boundaries: Work, Households, and Gender in China*, edited by Barbara Entwisle and Gail Henderson, 97–110. Berkeley: University of California Press, 2000.

Huang, Xin. "*Funü* in the Gender Legacy of the Mao Era and Contemporary Feminist Struggle in China." In *Gender Dynamics, Feminist Activism and Social Transformation in China*, edited by Guoguang Wu, Yuan Feng, and Helen Lansdowne, 15–31. New York: Routledge, 2019. https://doi.org/10.4324/9780429492099-2

INCITE! *The Revolution Will not be Funded: Beyond the Non-profit Industrial Complex*. Cambridge, MA: South End Press, 2007.

Jameson, Fredric. *The Political Unconscious: Narrative as a Socially Symbolic Act*. Ithaca: Cornell University Press, 1981.

Jeffreys, Elaine, and Haiqing Yu. *Sex in China*. Cambridge, MA: Polity, 2015.

Kam, Lucetta Y. L. "Desiring T, Desiring Self: 'T-Style' Pop Singers and Lesbian Culture in China." *Journal of Lesbian Studies* 18, no. 3 (2014): 252–65. https://doi.org/10.10 80/10894160.2014.896613

Kam, Lucetta Y. L. *Shanghai Lalas: Female Tongzhi Communities and Politics in Urban China*. Hong Kong: Hong Kong University Press, 2013.

Kaneva, Nadia. "Mediating Post-Socialist Femininities: Contested Histories and Visibilities." *Feminist Media Studies* 15, no. 1 (2015): 1–17. https://doi.org/10.1080/146 80777.2015.988389

Kang, Wenqing. "Seeking Pleasure in Peril: Male Same-Sex Relations During the Cultural Revolution." *Positions: East Asia Cultures Critique* 30, no. 1 (2022): 61–84. https://doi.org/10.1215/10679847-9417955

Kang, Wenqing. "The Decriminalization and Depathologization of Homosexuality in China." In *China In and Beyond the Headlines*, edited by Timothy Weston and Lionel Jensen, 231–48. Lanham: Rowman & Littlefield Publishing Group, 2012.

Kang, Wenqing. *Obsession: Male Same-Sex Relations in China, 1900–1950*. Hong Kong: Hong Kong University Press, 2009.

Kao, Ying-Chao. "The Coloniality of Queer Theory: The Effects of 'Homonormativity' on Transnational Taiwan's Path to Equality." *Sexualities* October 11, 2021. https://doi.org/10.1177/13634607211047518

Kong, Travis S. K. "Transnational Queer Sociological Analysis of Sexual Identity and Civic-political Activism in Hong Kong, Taiwan and Mainland China." *The British Journal of Sociology* 70, no. 5 (2019): 1904–25. https://doi.org/10.1111/1468-4446.12697

Kong, Travis S. K. "Sex and Work on the Move: Money Boys in Post-Socialist China." *Urban Studies (Edinburgh, Scotland)* 54, no. 3 (2017): 678–94. https://doi.org/10.1177/0042098016658411

Kong, Travis S. K. "Transnational Queer Labor: The 'Circuits of Desire' of Money Boys in China." *English Language Notes* 49, no. 1 (2011): 139–44. https://doi.org/10.1215/00138282-49.1.139

Koobak, Redi, Madina Tlostanova, and Suruchi Thapar-Björkert. "Uneasy Affinities between the Postcolonial and the Postsocialist." In *Postcolonial and Postsocialist Dialogues: Intersections, Opacities, Challenges in Feminist Theorizing and Practice*, edited by Redi Koobak, Madina Tlostanova and Suruchi Thapar-Björkert, 1–10. London: Routledge, 2021.

Kristeva, Julia. *About Chinese Women*. London: Marion Boyars Publishers, 1977.

Lang, Sabine. *NGOs, Civil Society, and the Public Sphere*. New York: Cambridge University Press, 2012.

Lee, Ching Kwan. *The Spector of Global China: Politics, Labor, and Foreign Investment in Africa*. Chicago: University of Chicago Press, 2018.

Leung, Helen Hok-Sze. *Undercurrents: Queer Culture and Postcolonial Hong Kong*. Vancouver: UBC Press, 2008.

Levenstein, Lisa. "A Social Movement for a Global Age: U.S. Feminism and the Beijing Women's Conference of 1995." *Journal of American History* 105, no. 2 (2018): 336–65. https://doi.org/10.1093/jahist/jay147

Lewis, Nathaniel. "Queer Social Reproduction: Co-opted, Hollowed Out, and Resilient." *Society and Space*, October 31, 2017. http://societyandspace.org/2017/10/31/queer-social-reproduction-co-opted-hollowed-out-and-resilient/

Li, Sipan 李思磐, "Weibo Nvquan de Qianshi Jinsheng: Cong 'Zhengzhi Zhengque' dao 'Shangye Zhengque'" 微博女权的前世今生:从 '政治正确' 到 '商业正确' [The History and Future of WeChat Feminism: from 'Political Correctness' to 'Commercial Correctness'] *Pengpai* 澎湃 [the Paper], June 16, 2020, https://www.thepaper.cn/newsDetail_forward_7854160

Lionnet, Françoise. *Autobiographical Voices: Race, Gender, Self-Portraiture*. Ithaca: Cornell University Press, 1989.

Liu, Petrus. "Cold War as Method." *Prism* 16, no. 2 (2019): 408–31. https://doi.org/10.1215/25783491-7978547

Liu, Petrus. *Queer Marxism in Two Chinas*. Durham: Duke University Press, 2015.

Liu, Petrus. "Queer Human Rights in and Against China: Marxism and the Figuration of the Human." *Social Text* 30, no. 1 (2012): 71–89. https://doi.org/10.1215/01642472-1468326

Liu, Petrus. "Why Does Queer Theory Need China?" *Positions: East Asia Cultures Critique* 18, no. 2 (2010): 291–320. https://doi.org/10.1215/10679847-2010-002

Liu, Tingting. "The Empowerment of Rural Migrant Lalas: Contending Queerness and Heteronormativity in China." *China Information* 33, no. 2 (2019): 165–84. https://doi.org/10.1177/0920203X19825589

Liu, Wen, Ana Huang, and Jingchao Ma. "Young Activists, New Movements: Contemporary Chinese Queer Feminism and Transnational Genealogies." *Feminism & Psychology* 25, no. 1 (2015): 11–17. https://doi.org/10.1177/0959353514563091

Liu, Wen, and Charlie Yi Zhang. "Homonationalism as Site of Contestation and Transformation: On Queer Subjectivities and Homonationalism across Sinophone Studies." In *Homonationalism, Femonationalism and Ablenationalism: Critical Pedagogies Contextualised*, edited by Angeliki Sifaki, C. L. Quinan, and Katarina Lončarević, 31–47. London: Routledge, 2022.

Liu, Xiao. *Information Fantasies: Precarious Mediation in Postsocialist China*. Minneapolis: University of Minnesota Press, 2019.

Love, Heather. *Feeling Backward: Loss and the Politics of Queer History*. Cambridge, MA: Harvard University Press, 2007.

Lowe, Lisa. *The Intimacies of Four Continents*. Durham: Duke University Press, 2015.

Lugones, María. "The Coloniality of Gender." *Worlds and Knowledges Otherwise: The Latin American Modernity/Coloniality Research Program*, Spring 2008. https://globalstudies.trinity.duke.edu/sites/globalstudies.trinity.duke.edu/files/file-attachments/v2d2_Lugones.pdf

Manalansan IV, Martin. "Queering the Chain of Care Paradigm." *The Scholar and Feminist Online* 6, no. 3 (2008). http://sfonline.barnard.edu/immigration/print_manalansan.htm

Mann, Susan. *Gender and Sexuality in Modern Chinese History*. New York: Cambridge University Press, 2011.

Marling, Raili. "Opacity as a Feminist Strategy: Postcolonial and Postsocialist Entanglements with Neoliberalism." In *Postcolonial and Postsocialist Dialogues: Intersections, Opacities, Challenges in Feminist Theorizing and Practice*, edited by Redi Koobak, Madina Tlostanova and Suruchi Thapar-Björkert, 94–108. London: Routledge, 2021.

Marshall, Daniel, Kevin Murphy, and Zeb Tortorici. "Queering Archives: Historical Unravelings." *Radical History Review* 14, no. 3 (2014): 1–11.

Martin, Fran. *Dreams of Flight: The Lives of Chinese Women Students in the West*. Durham: Duke University Press, 2022.

Martin, Fran, John Nguyet Erni, and Audrey Yue. "(Im)mobile Precarity in the Asia-Pacific." *Cultural Studies (London, England)* 33, no. 6 (2019): 895–914. https://doi.org/10.1080/09502386.2019.1660690

Massad, Joseph A. *Desiring Arabs*. Chicago: University of Chicago Press, 2007.

Massad, Joseph. "Re-Orienting Desire: The Gay International and the Arab World." *Public Culture* 14, no. 2 (2002): 361–86. https://doi.org/10.1215/08992363-14-2-361

McGrath, Jason. *Postsocialist Modernity: Chinese Cinema, Literature, and Criticism in the Market Age*. Stanford: Stanford University Press, 2008.

Meinhof, Marius, Junchen Yan, and Lili Zhu. "China and Postcolonialism: Some Introductory Remarks." *InterDisciplines* 1 (2017): 1–25.

Melamed, Jodi. *Represent and Destroy: Rationalizing Violence in the New Racial Capitalism*. Minneapolis: University of Minnesota Press, 2011.

238 *References*

Melamed, Jodi. "W. E. B. Du Bois's UnAmerican End." *African American Review* 40, no. 3 (2006): 533–50.

Meng, Yue. "Female Images and National Myth." In *Gender Politics in Modern China, Writing and Feminism*, edited by Tani Barlow, 118–36. Durham: Duke University Press, 1993.

Mignolo, Walter D. "Geopolitics of Sensing and Knowing: On (de)coloniality, Border Thinking and Epistemic Disobedience." *Postcolonial Studies* 14, no. 3 (2011): 273–83. https://doi.org/10.1080/13688790.2011.613105

Mignolo, Walter D., and Madina V. Tlostanova. *Learning to Unlearn: Decolonial Reflection from Eurasia and the Americas*. Columbus: Ohio State University Press, 2012.

Mignolo, Walter D., and Madina V. Tlostanova. "Theorizing from the Borders: Shifting to Geo- and Body-Politics of Knowledge." *European Journal of Social Theory* 9, no. 2 (2006): 205–21. https://doi.org/10.1177/1368431006063333

Miller, Casey James. 2016. "Dying for Money: The Effects of Global Health Initiatives on NGOs Working with Gay Men and HIV/AIDS in Northwest China." *Medical Anthropology Quarterly* 30, no. 3 (2016): 414–30. https://doi.org/10.1111/maq.12300

Mohanty, Chandra Talpade. "'Under Western Eyes' Revisited: Feminist Solidarity through Anticapitalist Struggles." *Signs: Journal of Women in Culture and Society* 28, no. 2 (2003): 499–535. https://doi.org/10.1086/342914

Mohanty, Chandra. "Under Western Eyes: Feminist Scholarship and Colonial Discourses." *Feminist Review* 30, no. 1 (1988): 61–88. https://doi.org/10.1057/fr.1988.42

Mungello, David Emil. *Western Queers in China: Flight to the Land of Oz*. Lanham: Rowman & Littlefield, 2012.

Muñoz, José Esteban. *Cruising Utopia: The Then and There of Queer Futurity*. New York: New York University Press, 2009.

Murphy, Michelle. *The Economization of Life*. Durham: Duke University Press, 2017.

Nagar, Richa. *Hungry Translations: Relearning the World through Radical Vulnerability*. Urbana: University of Illinois Press, 2019.

Nagar, Richa. *Muddying the Waters: Coauthoring Feminisms across Scholarship and Activism*. Chicago: University of Illinois Press, 2014.

Nyong'o, Tavia. 2018. *Afro-Fabulations: The Queer Drama of Black Life*. New York: New York University Press, 2018.

Ong, Aihwa. *Fungible Life: Experiment in the Asian City of Life*. Durham: Duke University Press, 2016.

Ong, Aihwa. *Flexible Citizenship: The Cultural Logics of Transnationality*. Durham: Duke University Press, 1999.

Ong, Aihwa, and Donald Nonini, eds. *Ungrounded Empires: The Cultural Politics of Modern Chinese Transnationalism*. New York: Routledge, 1997.

Ong, Aihwa, and Li Zhang, eds. *Privatizing China, Socialism from Afar*. Ithaca: Cornell University Press, 2008.

Pan, Suiming. *Zhongguo Xinggeming Zonglun* 中国性革命纵论 *(Sex Revolution in China: Its Origin, Expressions and Evolution)*. Kaohsiung: Wanyou Press, 2006.

Plaenkers, Tomas. *Landscapes of the Chinese Soul: The Enduring Presence of the Cultural Revolution*. London: Karnac, 2010.

Popa, Bogdan. *De-centering Queer Theory: Communist Sexuality in the Flow during and after the Cold War*. Manchester: Manchester University Press, 2021.

Prashad, Vijay. *The Darker Nations: A People's History of the Third World*. New York: New Press, 2007.

Preciado, Paul. *Testo Junkie: Sex, Drugs, and Biopolitics in the Pharmacopornographic Era*. New York: The Feminist Press, 2013.

Puar, Jasbir. *Terrorist Assemblages: Homonationalism in Queer Times*. Durham: Duke University Press, 2007.

Pun, Ngai. *Made in China: Women Factory Workers in a Global Workplace*. Durham: Duke University Press, 2006.

Quijano, Aníbal. "Coloniality of Power and Eurocentrism in Latin America." *International Sociology* 15, no. 2 (2000): 215–32. https://doi.org/10.1177/0268580900015 002005

Rao, Rahul. "Global Homocapitalism." *Radical Philosophy*, no. 194 (2015): 38–49. https://www.radicalphilosophy.com/article/global-homocapitalism

Reddy, Chandan. *Freedom with Violence: Race, Sexuality, and the US State*. Durham: Duke University Press, 2011.

Repo, Jemima. *The Biopolitics of Gender*. Oxford: Oxford University Press, 2015.

Rofel, Lisa. "The Traffic in Money Boys." *Positions: East Asia Cultures Critique* 18, no. 2 (2010): 425–58. https://doi.org/10.1215/10679847-2010-009

Rofel, Lisa. *Desiring China: Experiments in Neoliberalism, Sexuality, and Public Culture*. Durham: Duke University Press, 2007.

Sang Tze-lan D. *The Emerging Lesbian: Female Same-Sex Desire in Modern China*. Chicago: University of Chicago Press, 2003.

Schierup, Carl-Ulrik, and Martin Bak Jørgensen, eds. *Politics of Precarity, Migrant Conditions, Struggles and Experiences*. Leiden: Koninklijke Brill, 2017.

Scully, Ben. "Precarity North and South: A Southern Critique of Guy Standing." *Global Labour Journal* 7, no. 2 (2016): 60–173. https://doi.org/10.15173/glj.v7i2.2521

Sears, Alan. "Body Politics: The Social Reproduction of Sexualities." In *Social Reproduction Theory: Remapping Class, Recentering Oppression*, edited by Tithi Bhattacharya, 171–91. London: Pluto Press, 2017.

Sears, Alan. "The Social Reproduction of Sexuality: An Interview." *Viewpoint Magazine*, October 31, 2015. https://www.viewpointmag.com/2015/10/31/the-social-reproduc tion-of-sexuality-an-interview-with-alan-sears/

Sedgwick, Eve Kosofsky. *Touching Feeling: Affect, Pedagogy, Performativity*. Durham: Duke University Press, 2003.

Sedgwick, Eve Kosofsky. *The Epistemology of the Closet*. Los Angeles: University of California Press, 1990.

Seidman, Steven. "Identity and Politics in a 'Postmodern' Gay Culture." In *Difference Troubles*, Queering Social Theory and Sexual Politics, 109–38. Cambridge: Cambridge University Press, 1997. https://doi.org/10.1017/CBO9780511557910.008

Shah, Svati. "Sexuality and 'The Left': Thoughts on Intersections and Visceral Others." *The Scholar and Feminist Online* 7, no. 3 (2009): Summer. https://sfonline.barnard .edu/sexuality-and-the-left-thoughts-on-intersections-and-visceral-others/

Shih, Shu-mei. "Is the *Post* in Postsocialism the *Post* in Posthumanism?" *Social Text* 30, no. 1 (2012): 27–50. https://doi.org/10.1215/01642472-1468308

Shih, Shu-mei. "Toward an Ethics of Transnational Encounters, or, 'When' Does a 'Chinese' Woman Become a 'Feminist'?" In *Minor Transnationalism*, edited by Françoise Lionnet and Shu-mei Shih, 73–108. Durham: Duke University Press, 2005.

240 *References*

Shih, Shu-mei, Chien-hsin Tsai, and Brian Bernards, eds. *Sinophone Studies: A Critical Reader*. Cambridge: Columbia University Press, 2013.

Snorton, C. Riley. *Black on Both Sides: A Racial History of Trans Identity*. Minneapolis: University of Minnesota Press, 2017.

Song, Lin. 2021. *Queering Chinese Kinship: Queer Public Culture in Globalizing China*. Hong Kong: Hong Kong University Press, 2021.

Song Shaopeng 宋少鹏. "Lizu Wenti, Wuguan Zhong Xi: zai Lishi de Neizai Mailuo zhong Jiangou de Xueke: dui Zhongguo 'Funü/Xingbie Yanjiu' de Sixiangshi Kaocha" 立足问题, 无关中西: 在历史的内在脉络中建构的学科—对中国 '妇女 /性别研究'的思想史考察 [Questions of Positionality: The Genealogy of Chinese Women's Studies in the History of Disciplinary Development], *Funü Yanjue Luncong* 妇女研究论丛 [Collections of Women's Studies] 5 (2018): 33–51.

Song Shaopeng 宋少鹏. "Zibenzhuyi, Shehuizhuyi, he Funü: Weishenme Zhongguo Xuyao Chongjian Makesizhuyi Nüquan Pipan" 资本主义、社会主义和妇女—为什么中国需要重建马克思主义女权主义批判 [Capitalism, Socialism and Women: Why Should China Reconstruct Its Marxists Feminist Criticism], *Open Times* 12 (2012): 98–112. http://www.opentimes.cn/bencandy.php?fid=341&aid=1693

Song Shaopeng 宋少鹏. "Shehuizhuyi Funüjuefang yu Xifang Nüquanzhuyi de Qübie: Lilun yu Shijian" 社会主义妇女解放与西方女权主义的区别: 理论与实践 [Differences between Chinese Socialist Women's Liberation and Western Feminism: Theory and Practice], *Shanxi Shida Xuebao* 山西师大学报 [Journal of Shanxi Normal University] 38, no. 4 (2011): 143–49. https://www.docin.com/p-1449500826.html

Spade, Dean. *Normal Life: Administrative Violence, Critical Trans Politics, and the Limits of Law*. Durham: Duke University Press, 2015.

Spakowski, Nicola. "Socialist Feminism in Postsocialist China." *Positions: East Asia Cultures Critique* 26, no. 4 (2018): 561–92. https://doi.org/10.1215/10679847-7050478

Spakowski, Nicola. "'Gender' Trouble: Feminism in China under the Impact of Western Theory and the Spatialization of Identity." *Positions: East Asia Cultures Critique* 19, no. 1 (2011): 31–54. https://doi.org/10.1215/10679847-2010-023

Spillers, Hortense. *Black, White and In Color: Essays on American Literature and Culture*. Chicago: University of Chicago Press, 2003.

Spillers, Hortense. "Mama's Baby, Papa's Maybe: An American Grammar Book." *Diacritics* 17, no. 2 (1987): 65–81.

Spivak, Gayatri Chakravorty. "Can the Subaltern Speak?" In *Marxism and the Interpretation of Culture*, edited by Cary Nelson and Lawrence Grossberg, 271–313. Basingstoke: Macmillan, 1988.

Stacey, Judith. *Patriarchy and Socialist Revolution in China*. Oakland: University of California Press, 1984.

Standing, Guy. *The Precariat: The New Dangerous Class*. London: Bloomsbury Academic, 2011.

Stella, Francesca. *Lesbian Lives in Soviet and Post-Soviet Russia: Post/socialism and Gendered Sexualities*. New York: Palgrave Macmillan, 2015.

Strauss, Kendra. "Labour Geography II: Being, Knowledge and Agency." *Progress in Human Geography* 44, no. 1 (2020): 150–59. https://doi.org/10.1177/0309132518803420

Suchland, Jennifer. *Economies of Violence: Transnational Feminism, Postsocialism, and the Politics of Sex Trafficking*. Durham: Duke University Press, 2015.

Suchland, Jennifer. "Is there a Postsocialist Critique?" *Russian Journal* 3, no. 65–66 (2012): 97–114.

Suchland, Jennifer. "Is Postsocialism Transnational?" *Signs: Journal of Women in Culture and Society* 36, no. 4 (2011): 837–62. https://doi.org/10.1086/658899

Sullivan, Nikki. *A Critical Introduction to Queer Theory*. New York: New York University Press, 2003.

Swarr, Amanda Lock, and Richa Nagar, eds. *Critical Transnational Feminist Praxis*. Albany: State Univerity of New York Press, 2010.

Tadiar, Neferti X. M. "Life-Times in Fate Playing." *South Atlantic Quarterly* 111, no. 4 (2012): 783–802. https://doi.org/10.1215/00382876-1724183

Tadiar, Neferti X. M. "Remaindered Life of Citizen-Man, Medium of Democracy." *Japanese Journal of Southeast Asian Studies* 49, no. 3 (2011): 464–95. https://doi.org/10.20495/tak.49.3_464

Tadiar, Neferti X. M. *Fantasy-Production: Sexual Economies and Other Philippine Consequences for the New World Order*. Hong Kong: Hong Kong University Press, 2004.

Tan, Jia. *Digital Masquerade: Feminist Rights and Queer Media in China*. New York: New York University Press, 2023.

Teng, Jinhua Emma. "The Construction of the 'Traditional Chinese Woman' in the Western Academy: A Critical Review." *Signs: Journal of Women in Culture and Society* 22, no. 1 (1996): 115–51. https://doi.org/10.1086/495138

Thomas, Lynn M. "Historicising Agency." *Gender & History* 28, no. 2 (2016): 324–39. https://doi.org/10.1111/1468-0424.12210

Thoreson, Ryan. *Transnational LGBT Activism: Working for Sexual Rights Worldwide*. Minneapolis: University of Minnesota Press, 2014.

Thoreson, Ryan Richard. "The Queer Paradox of LGBTI Human Rights." *InterAlia: A Journal of Queer Studies* 6 (2011): 1–27.

Tian, Ian Liujia. "On Rescuable and Expendable Life: Bioavailability, Surplus Time, and Queer Politics of Reproduction." *Journal of Canadian Studies* 54, no. 2 (2020): 483–507. https://doi.org/10.3138/JCS-2020-0015

Tinsley, Omise'eke Natasha. "Black Atlantic, Queer Atlantic: Queer Imaginings of the Middle Passage." *GLQ* 14, no. 2–3 (2008): 191–215. https://doi.org/10.1215/10642684-2007-030

Tlostanova, Madina. "Can the Post-Soviet Think?: On Coloniality of Knowledge, External Imperial and Double Colonial Difference." *Intersections* 1, no. 2 (2015): 38–58. https://doi.org/10.17356/ieejsp.v1i2.38

Tlostanova, Madina. "Postsocialist ≠ Postcolonial? On Post-Soviet Imaginary and Global Coloniality." *Journal of Postcolonial Writing* 48, no. 2 (2012): 130–42. https://doi.org/10.1080/17449855.2012.658244

Uncertain Commons. *Speculate This!* Durham: Duke University Press, 2013.

Verdery, Katherine. *The Political Lives of Dead Bodies: Reburial and Postsocialist Change*. New York: Columbia University Press, 1999.

Von Kleist, Heinrich. "On the Gradual Construction of Thoughts during Speech." Translated by Michael Hamburger." *German Life and Letters* 5, no. 1 (1951): 42–46. https://doi.org/10.1111/j.1468-0483.1951.tb01029.x

242 *References*

Vukovich. Daniel. "China and Postcolonialism: Re-Orienting All the Fields." *InterDisciplines* 1 (2017):145–64.

Wang, Hui. *China's New Order: Society, Politics, and Economy in Transition*. Cambridge, MA: Harvard University Press, 2003.

Wang, Lingzhen 王玲珍, and Xiao Hua 肖画. "Zhongguo Shehuizhuyi Nüquan Shijian Zaisikao: Jianlun Meiguo Lengzhansichao, Ziyou/benzhu Nüquanzhuyi dui Shehuizhuyi Funüyanjiu de Chixuyingxiang" 中国社会主义女性主义实践再思考–兼论美国冷战思潮、自由/本质女性主义对社会主义妇女研究的持续影响 [Chinese Socialist Feminist Practice Reconsidered: A Critical Review of the Persistent Influence of Cold War Ideology and Liberal/Radical Feminism on Socialist Women Studies], *Funü Yanjue Luncong* 妇女研究论丛 [Collection of Women's Studies] no. 3 (2015): 5–19, https:/doi.org/10.3969/j.issn.1004-2563.2015.03.001

Wang, Zheng. *Finding Women in the State: A Socialist Feminist Revolution in the People's Republic of China*. Berkeley: University of California Press, 2016.

Wang, Zheng. "Maoism, Feminism, and the UN Conference on Women: Women's Studies Research in Contemporary China." *Journal of Women's History* 8, no. 4 (1997): 126–52. https://doi.org/10.1353/jowh.2010.0239

Wei, John. *Queer Chinese Cultures and Mobilities: Kinship, Migration, and Middle Classes*. Hong Kong: Hong Kong University Press, 2020.

Wei, Wei. "Queer Organizing and HIV/AIDS Activism: An Ethnographic Study of a Local Tongzhi Organization in Chengdu." In *Queer/Tongzhi China: New Perspectives on Research, Activism and Media Cultures*, edited by Elisabeth Engebretsen, William Schroeder, and Hongwei Bao, 192–216. Copenhagen: Nordic Institute of Asian Studies, 2013.

Welland, Sasha Su-Ling. "What Women Will Have Been: Reassessing Feminist Cultural Production in China: A Review Essay." *Signs: Journal of Women in Culture and Society* 31, no. 4 (2006): 941–66. https://doi.org/10.1086/500602

White, Melissa Autumn. "Archives of Intimacy and Trauma: Queer Migration Documents as Technologies of Affect." *Radical History Review* 2014, no. 120 (2014): 75–93. https://doi.org/10.1215/01636545-2703733

Wiegman, Robyn, and Elizabeth A. Wilson. "Introduction: Antinormativity's Queer Conventions." *Differences* 26, no. 1 (2015): 1–25. https://doi.org/10.1215/10407391-2880582

Wilson, Ara. "Lesbian Visibility and Sexual Rights at Beijing." *Signs: Journal of Women in Culture and Society* 22, no. 1 (1996): 214–18. https://doi.org/10.1086/495146

Winnubst, Shannon. "The Many Lives of Fungibility: Anti-Blackness in Neoliberal Times." *Journal of Gender Studies* 29, no. 1 (2020): 102–12. https://doi.org/10.1080/09589236.2019.1692193

Winnubst, Shannon. *Way Too Cool: Selling Out Race and Ethics*. New York: Columbia University Press, 2015.

Wong, Alvy K. "Queering the Quality of Desire: Perverse Use-Values in Transnational Chinese Cultures." *Culture, Theory and Critique* 58, no. 2 (2017): 209–25. https://doi.org/10.1080/14735784.2017.1288581

Xu, Feng. *Looking for Work in Post-Socialist China: Governance, Active Job Seekers and the New Chinese Labor Market*. London: Routledge, 2012.

Xu, Feng. "Chinese Feminisms Encounter International Feminisms: Identity, Power and Knowledge Production." *International Feminist Journal of Politics* 11, no. 2 (2009): 196–215. https://doi.org/10.1080/14616740902789567

Yang, Fan. *Disorienting Politics: Chimerican Media and Transpacific Entanglements*. Ann Arbor: University of Michigan Press, 2024.

Yang, Mayfair. *Spaces of Their Own: Women's Public Sphere in Transnational China*. Minneapolis: University of Minnesota Press, 1999.

Yapp, Hentyle. *Minor China: Method, Materialisms, and the Aesthetic*. Durham: Duke University Press, 2021.

Ye, Shana. "*Word of Honor* and Brand Homonationalism with 'Chinese Characteristics': The *Dangai* Industry, Queer Masculinity and the 'Opacity' of the State." *Feminist Media Studies* 23, no. 4 (2023): 1593–1609. https://doi.org/10.1080/14680777.2022.2037007

Yuxin, Pei, Sik-ying Ho Petula, and Ng Man Lun. "Studies on Women's Sexuality in China Since 1980: A Critical Review." *The Journal of Sex Research* 44, no. 2 (2007): 202–12. https://doi.org/10.1080/00224490701263868

Zhan, Mei. "Human Oriented? Angels and Monsters in China's Health Care Reform." In *Health Care Reform and Globalisation: The US, China and Europe in Comparative Perspective*, edited by Peggy Watson, 71–92. London: Routledge, 2013. https://doi.org/10.4324/9780203106785-10

Zhang, Charlie Yi. *Dreadful Desires: The Uses of Love in Neoliberal China*. Durham: Duke University Press, 2022.

Zhang, Charlie Yi, Wen Liu, and Casey Lee. "Ethno-Racial Paranoia and Affective Cold Warism: Remapping Rival US-PRC Imperial Formations." *American Quarterly* 74, no. 3 (2022): 499–521. https://doi.org/10.1353/aq.2022.0032

Zhang, Everett. *The Impotence Epidemic*. Durham: Duke University Press, 2015.

Zhao, Jamie J., and Alvin K. Wong. "Introduction: Making a Queer Turn in Contemporary Chinese-Language Media Studies." *Continuum (Mount Lawley, W.A.)* 34, no. 4 (2020): 475–83. https://doi.org/10.1080/10304312.2020.1785076

Zheng, Tiantian. *Tongzhi Living: Men Attracted to Men in Postsocialist China*. Minneapolis: University of Minnesota Press, 2015.

Zhu, Ping. "From Patricide to Patrilineality: Adapting *The Wandering Earth* for the Big Screen." *Arts* 9, no. 3, 94 (2020): 1–12. https://doi.org/10.3390/arts9030094

Index

A&W restaurant, 109, 129, 209, 212, 213
Abbey Road (Beatles), 143
ACT-UP, 195
activism, x, xii, 26, 91, 93, 141, 165, 180, 192, 202; advocacy-oriented, 161; cyberspace, 154; gay/lesbian, 138; human rights, 19, 140; *lala,* 137, 155, 179; pocket, 17, 21; professionalization of, 95; queer, 14, 60, 216; social, 51; social-media, 21. *See also* feminist activism; lesbian activism, LGBT activism
advocacy, 89, 163, 166, 178; feminist, 139, 219; LGBT, 18, 59, 160, 161; Western, 161, 162
agency, xiv, 13, 19, 154; desire and, 74; feminist, 144; political, 58, 81; violence and, 74
agenda, 6, 147–48, 190; anti-capitalist, 148; feminist, 150; imperialist, 150; LGBT, 20n41, 154; peace, 147; political, 150, 203
Aibai, 88, 178–79, 180
AIDS, 18, 87, 92, 93, 95, 169, 193, 195–96; community, 160; education about, 194; fear of, 4; gay sex and, 164; history of, 90; preventing, 98; stigmatization of, 91; trivia, 97
"AIDS and Homosexuality," 69 (fig.)

AIDS epidemic, 4, 85–86, 154; gay culture and, 70
Aizhi Jianbao (*Love Knowledge Newsletter*), 77
Aizhixing, 169
Alexander the Great, 47
All-China Women's Federation, 145–46, 153
American Factory (Bognar and Reichert), 15
anal sex, 67, 101, 109
Anatomy of the Male Human Body, 62
anticolonialism, 10, 151
anticommunism, 147, 151
antinormativity, 14, 26, 80, 130, 179
anus, 34, 97, 100–101, 186
arts: non-*zhuxuanlü,* 112; performance, 143; politics and, xv; queer, 179
Asian Games, 5, 151
assimilation, 12, 13, 56, 171
Association of Chinese Sexologists, 64
autoethnography, xiv, xv, 60
Autotheory as Feminist Practice in Art, Writing, and Criticism (Fournier), xiv

Babaoshan Cemetery, 170Bankok, *ketoy* in, 215
Barry & Martin's Trust, 85
BBC, 40n4

246 Index

BBS. *See* Bulletin Board System
BDSM, 116, 164
Beatles, 143
Beeatles, 30
Beet Yourself Up, 30
Beets, 31, 37, 40, 42, 57, 58, 60, 64, 134, 135–36, 214; distribution of, 38; donors, 30, 61; observation in, 71; production, 30; queer experiences and, 39; stealing/trading, 130, 133; stolen, 29, 30, 106, 159
Beets Mafia, 38
Beginning of Human (Renzhichu), 67
behavior, 7, 48, 88, 98, 130, 155; criminal, 34; hooligan, 33, 34; promiscuous, 164; same-sex, 35, 76, 86, 94, 103, 111
Beijing, 25, 48, 52, 85, 91, 92, 109, 131, 136, 137, 139, 140
Beijing Aizhi Action Project, 169n2
Beijing *Aizhixing* Institute, 169n2
Beijing Comrades (Myers), 18, 107n1
Beijing Declaration and Platform for Action, 1
Beijing Dome, 28, 29, 30, 40, 42, 58, 134, 155, 210, 211, 212, 214, 216; building, 81; infrastructure of, 38
Beijing Foreign Affairs University, 4748
Beijing Gushi (Beijing Story), 107, 110, 114, 121, 122
Beijing Hotel, 48
*Beijing moshi (*Beijing Model), 138
Beijing Olympic Games, 19, 185
Beijing Platform for Action, 1n1
Beijing Railway Station, 85
Belt and Road Initiatives, 21, 124
Bersani, Leo, 4
Bingfei "Liumang" (Not a "Hooligan"), 68
biodata, 30, 31, 57, 136
biological determinism, 146, 171, 173, 178, 179; queer theory versus, 177
biopower, 67, 146
black body, 8, 217
blackness, 8, 10
blockchain, creation of, 210
Blue Sun, 31, 61

Blue Sun Nano Pod, 27, 42
Bognar, Steven, 15
Boss Jiang, 107, 108, 119, 120, 129, 212–13
Boys Don't Cry (film), 108
Brainer, Amy, 114
Brave New World (Huxley), 50
Brown, Gavin, 13
Bulletin Board System (BBS), 107, 108n2
Butler, Judith, 172

cancer, 195–96, 197
capital, 38, 151; culture and, 117; logic of, 118; metrics of, 8; moving, 163; queer and, 118
capital accumulation, 5, 8, 15, 121
capitalism, 4, 14, 31, 111, 117, 147, 171; advanced, 132; alternatives to, 216; digital, 154; emergence of, 49; free labor and, 21; global, 10, 19; homosexuality and, 12, 50; labor and, 16; media, 21; postwar, 146, 150, 153; racial, xii, 10, 146; surveillance, 7, 21, 144
Centers for Disease Control (CDCs), 88, 92, 167; transnational monies and, 89–90
Chakrabarty, Dipesh, xiv, xivn15
Chameleon, The, 47n1
Chen Bingzhong, 85
Chen Handong, 107, 108, 110, 120; Lan Yu and, 121, 122, 123, 124
Chen Kaige, 111, 115
Chen, Mian, 66, 66n12
Chi Ta-wei, 179
Chiang, Howard, 11
Chiang Kai-shek, 103, 114
Chimera Purple, 27, 132
China Global Fund AIDS Program, 88, 89
China-Gates Foundation HIV Prevention Program, 88, 92
"China in Africa," 21
China-UK HIV/AIDS Prevention and Care Project, 88

Chinese Association of STD and AIDS Prevention and Control, 88
Chinese New Year, 116, 136
Chinese Preventive Medicine Association, 88
Chinese Society for Sexual Minorities (CSSM), 108n2
Chinese Society for Women's Studies (CSWS), 146
Chineseness, 10; queerness and, 114
Chongwenmen subway station, 142
Chou Wah-shan, 77
Chow, Rey, 112n10
cinema: art, 116, 117, 118; banned/underground, 117; LGBTQ, 114; queer, 111, 113, 179
citizenship, rights and, 149
civil rights, 16, 166
civil society, 8, 21, 39, 60, 153, 220
civilization, 56, 56n3, 65, 76, 160
class: creative, 3, 3n9, 117; formation, 13; gender and, 149; intellectual, 18; struggle, 31, 121
Clinton, Hillary, 1, 141, 148
Cold War, xii, 4, 10, 114, 147, 151, 154
colonialism, 10, 154, 192; British, 114; European, 150; legacy of, 12
"Come Out" (Grasshopper band), 77, 81, 106
communism, 2, 35, 149, 151, 154; collapse of, 148; disillusionment with, 150; international, 147
Communist Party, 26, 45, 52, 153; gay story and, 8687; ideology of, 47; leadership of, 31
Communist Revolution, 41, 47
community, 75; building, 177; materials of, 165; Sinophone, 80, 178; targeted, 163
comrades, 36, 80, 105, 170, 176, 219, 223; *tongzhi* and, ixn1
condoms, 67, 87, 95, 97, 98, 199; using, 96, 167
Confederation Celebration, 29
confessions, 31–32, 32n2, 38

consciousness-raising, 98, 144, 177, 180
conservatism, 6, 12
Cool, Uncool and, 7–8, 9, 10
Cool Child, x, xn2, xi, xiii, 19, 20, 200, 205, 214
cool kid, x, xn2, 21, 26, 179
corruption, 45, 89, 92, 194; capitalist, 2, 36, 150; financial, 107
cosmopolitanism, 5, 71, 80
counterculture, 143, 176
Crary, Jonathan, 58n5
creative class, 3, 3n9, 117
critical race studies, 8
cruising, 35, 51, 75, 81, 85, 163, 170, 200
cruising parks, 35–36, 50, 90, 91, 98, 160, 164, 168, 197, 209
Crystal Boys (Pai), 217
csssm.org, 107–8
Cuban Five, 144
Cui Zi'en, 77, 113, 179
cult of the icon, 73
cultural fever, 59, 112, 122
Cultural Revolution (1966–1976), 5, 33, 35, 36n2, 47, 50, 65, 73, 74, 76, 79, 94, 101, 121, 151n15, 190; correcting mistakes of, 59
Cultural Revolution of the LGBT, 216
culture, xii, 12, 65, 77, 173; capital and, 117; Chinese, xn2; consumer, 19, 72; dynamics of, 117; high, 179; homosexual, 70; indigenous minority, 117; LGBT, x, 70, 80, 92–93; mainstream, 113n14; mass, xiii; material changes in, 74; political, 15; Sinophone, 118; Weberian thesis of, 73; Western, 116. *See also* queer culture
cyberspace, 143, 154, 183

dark matter, xiii, 22
Dazhong Yixue (Popular Medicine), 62
"Death of a Lesbian, The," 68–69, 68 (fig.)
Decade for Women, The (UN), 147
decolonization, xv, 14, 17
D'Emilio, John, 16

248 Index

democracy, 39; corporatized, 203; Western, 149, 160
Deng, Weiling, 41n7, 201n1
Deng Xiaoping, 51, 59, 66, 109, 121; reform mantra of, 65; social inequalities and, 122; state-planned economy and, 5
depression, 40n5, 42, 59
Derrida, Jacques, 138, 179
desire, 76, 187, 212; agency and, 74; diverse, 160; queer, 123; same-sex, 66; sexual, 170
development, 162, 177; economic, 151, 168, 173; military, 73; national, 6; postsocialist, 112
Dinani, Husseina, 16n40
discrimination: class-based, 70; education, 139
diversity, xiii, 10, 18, 26, 137; sexual, 79, 154
"DNA Gone Wrong" (Lai Ming), 77
documentary film movement, 113
Dong Limin, on gender, 152–53
Dongdan People's Park, 50, 91, 166, 170, 190, 193, 199; cruising at, 85
Douglas, Lord Alfred, 47n1
Douyin, 140
Du Jie, 153
Duggan, Lisa, 13
Dunye, Cheryl, xiv

East Palace, West Palace (film), 110, 111, 187
Eastern Bloc, 148, 151
economic change, 13, 122
economic growth, 21, 125
Economic Special Zones, 109
economy: Cold War, 146; flexibilization of, 5; global, 65, 93, 116, 144, 147; HIV/AIDS, 93; labor migration-oriented, 167; national, 21; neoliberalization of, 5; new media, 139; pink, 7; political, xii, 10–11, 148; queer, 9, 20; socialist planned, 5, 124
Edeman, Lee, 26

education, 75, 194; exam-oriented, 26; feminist, 139; HIV/AIDS, 86; sexual, 67, 91, 95
"Eighth Route Army Song," 110
empty chair method, 135, 136–41, 142–45, 155, 216
Eng, David, 114
Enlightenment, 122
equality, 6, 26; gender, 2, 146, 203
Er Yan, 108n2
Essentials of Journalist Literature, 68
Eurydice, 42, 132
Everything Everywhere All at Once (Yeoh), 217
experience: density of, 58; LGBT, 178; queer, 11, 30, 38, 39, 57–58, 115; women's, 152
exploitation, 10, 133, 145; capital/labor, 12

Facebook, gender expression and, 18
Fan, Christopher, 15n36
Fan Popo, 113
Fang Gang, 77, 85
Farewell My Concubine (film), 110, 111
FEMEN, 144
femininity, 145; commodification of, 152; male, 20
feminism, 139, 203; allegiance to, 204; attacking, 155; Chinese, 80, 145, 146, 150, 151, 152, 202, 205, 221; cyber queer, 21; global, 153–54; grassroots, 139, 219, 220; intersectional, 178; *lala,* 180, 217; liberal, 149, 201; popular, 130; queerness and, 203; socialist, 147, 150, 151, 152n16, 153, 203; state, 21, 154; transnational, 218; Western, 6, 147, 148, 149. *See also* gender feminism
feminist activism, 1, 2, 17, 154; grassroots, 139140; NGOization of, 111
Feminist Five Incident, 60, 142, 154, 184, 201
feminist movement, 153, 180, 184, 201, 221

Feminist Studies, xv, 7, 60
feminist theory, 20n41, 201
Ferguson, Niall, 7
fetishization, 39, 124
Fifth Gens, 111, 115
filter model, 88, 90
Florida, Richard, 3n9, 117
Floyd, Kevin, 15
Ford Foundation, 85
Fordism, 58n4, 73
Forster, E. M., 47
Foucault, Michel, xn2, 4, 56n2, 172, 179; String Theory and, 108
"Four Frees and One Care" policy, 92, 194
Fournier, Lauren, xiv
Freeman, Jo, 180, 181
#FreeTheFive, 143 (fig.), 144
Freud, Sigmund, 25, 64, 187
fuck buddies, 85, 138
fungibility, 8n19; black, 10; concept of, 216–17; postcolonial, 10; postsocialist, 10; queer, 7–10
funü, 5, 80, 202
Fuyao, 15

GAD. *See* gender and development
Garner, Karen, 147
Gates Fund, 90
gay, term, 46–47
Gay China, 19
gay life, depicting, 118
gay men, 96, 98, 113n14, 165; reputation of, 51
gay organizations, 138, 178
gaydar, 20, 63
gays, 3, 78, 79, 162
gender, xi, xiv, 8, 15, 39, 80, 116, 202; biopolitical apparatus of, 5, 146; class and, 149; concept of, 5, 146, 152; difference, 145; discourse of, 146; feminism and, 152; formation of, 146, 148; geopolitical apparatus of, 147; globalization of, 152, 153; history of, 147, 153; nation building and, 8; nonbinary, 179; performativity of, 26, 176; produc-

tion and, 18; queer, 6; social/sexual engineering and, 146; translation of, 152; women's issues and, 147
gender and development (GAD), 148, 149, 151
gender feminism, 144, 152n16; transitional history of, 145–54
gender fluidity, 130, 179, 215
gender mainstreaming, 1, 1n1, 147, 149
gender roles, 152; changing, 72; Westernized model of, 149
gender studies, 60, 130, 173, 201
gender variances, x, 65, 70; pathologization/stigmatization of, 66
geopolitics, xii, 119, 182, 216; biopolitical management of, 22; Cold War, 73, 144; complexity of, 204; postwar, 147; power and, 21
Ghodsee, Kristen, 147
global expansion, 21, 211
Global Fund, 90, 91–92
Global Queer Asia Studies, 10, 14, 217
Global War on Terror, xii, 21, 125
globalization, 76, 79, 113, 167; China and, 57n4, 124; neoliberal, 57n4, 71
Globe and Mail, 45
Golden Triangle, 50
Gordon, Avery, xv
government-organized NGOs (GONGOs), 88
Grasshopper band, 77, 106
Guang Hui, 62, 64–65, 72, 75, 76–77, 79, 80, 85, 93, 94, 132, 168–69, 176, 182, 192, 194–95, 205, 214; CDC and, 194; conversations with, 74; dialogue with, 81; HIV/AIDS intervention and, 77, 86, 87, 90–91, 194; homosexuality and, 63, 67; ID card of, 193–94; *kuaihuo shan* and, 86; Lao Zhang and, 166; on lesbianism, 68–69; letter from, 165, 173–74; letter to, 161, 165, 171–72, 174, 190, 191; meeting, 160; Q&A with, 74; quarrel for, 91; queerness of, 193; Xiao Yao and, 95; Yang and, 92, 93, 99

250 Index

"Guang Hui's Box," 72 (fig.)
Guangzhou, 51, 77, 139, 140, 172
Guangzhou Bodybuilding Competition, 64
Guevara, Che, 27

Halberstam, Jack, 56n2
Hamburger, Michael, 40n4
Hao Jia, 77
Happy Valley Park, 192
Hartman, Saidiya, xiv, 8, 217
Harvest (Shuohou), 67
Haynes, Todd, xiv
He Xiaopei, 113
hegemony, 3, 10, 117, 118, 180; heteronormative, 80; neoliberal, 148
Henan, plasma trade in, 86
Hero (film), 117
heteronormativity, 66, 80, 129
heteropatriarchy, 55, 130
heterosexuality, 16, 67, 73, 172
history, ix, 17, 42, 58–59, 65, 210, 211; deleting, 184; individual/collective praxis and, 37n1; memory and, xv; pain of, 27; performativity of, xiv; personal, 75; queer, xiv, 55, 65, 79, 81; social, 22; trauma and, 60
Hite Report, The, 187
HIV, 95, 215; antiviral medicine for, 90; preventing, 87, 88; testing for, 92, 167, 177
HIV/AIDS, 7, 18, 51, 65, 85, 116; epidemic, xi, 63, 178; preventing, 87, 89
HIV/AIDS intervention, 8, 9, 26, 66, 77, 78, 85, 87, 88–89, 90, 92, 96, 160, 168; beginning of, 88, 177; volunteers for, 86
HIV/AIDS movement, professionalization of, 166
HIV/AIDS work, 86, 160, 166, 171
Hollywood, 116, 188
Homeland Security, 176
homocapitalism, xi, 9, 12–13
homonationalism, xi, xii, 2–3, 12, 13, 56n3

homonormativity, xi, 9, 12–13, 80
homophobia, 8, 115, 115n22, 168; internalized, 66, 93; state-sanctioned, 6
homopostsocialism, xii, 7, 10, 12, 13
homosexuality, 18, 26, 78, 79, 116, 164, 178, 179, 187; approaching, 73, 171; biopolitical management of, 66; capitalism and, 12, 50; criminalization of, 63, 74; decriminalization of, 71; denouncing, 125; depathologization of, 63, 108n2; erasing, 6; identity politics and, 72; legalization of, 173; naturalness of, 178; pathologization of, 74; promoting, 70, 71, 76; psychiatry and, 66; romanticization of, 70; stigma surrounding, 86; strangeness of, 79; wonder of, 69
"Homosexuality: An Unsolved Mystery," 63
homosexuals, 26, 27, 66, 69, 108, 112, 162, 200; campaigns against, 11; constructing, 164;
correspondence with, 75; justice for, 64; life of, 71; loving/harmless, 64; opposition to, 76; situations of, 72; treatment for, 73
Hong, Grace, 12
Hong Kong, 51, 78, 80, 109, 110n5, 178
Hong Ling, 179
honorary whites, 149, 216
Hooker, Evelyn, 64
hooligans, 34, 35, 51, 75, 88
"hooligan's Confession, The," 32 (fig.)
"Hope," 78 (fig.)
Hope, 77, 79, 80, 81
Hu Jintao, 116
Hua Jinma, 63, 64, 69
Huang Pin-Yuan, 110
human rights, 6, 26, 125, 137, 161; women's rights and, 1
humanism, 73; Christian, 150; democratic, 122; liberal, 56n2, 112; Western, 112, 122
Huxley, Aldous, 50
hyper-visibility/hypo-visibility, 22

"I Lived in Darkness, and There is No Way to Look for Hope" (Wong), 55, 58

identity, ix, xiv, 8, 81, 113, 187; cultural, 80; deconstruction of, 176; formation, 18, 58, 113; gay, 56, 170; homosexual, 112; lesbian, 6, 56; LGBT, x, 6, 13, 113, 163, 170; liberal, 38, 133; measurements of, 7; personal, 98; political, 4, 17, 72, 193; queer, 58, 80; self-consciousness of, 40; single-lens, 79–80

ideology, 12; democratic, 10; liberal, 148; Maoist, 5, 65

Immersive Synchronization, ix, 135, 216

imperialism, 3, 10, 203; American, 31, 147; disrupting, 150; gay, 6; patriarchy and, 152; racial, 146

Inception (movie), 106

inequality, 18, 133; economic, 79; gender, 5, 139, 152; material, 13; resource, 21; social, 89, 122

infanticide, female, 220

intellectual class, economic/sexual labor of, 18

interconnectedness, 123, 124

interdependence, 10, 12, 17

International Lesbian and Gay Human Right Commission (ILGHRC), 1

International Women's Day, 60, 140, 202, 219

intersex children, 146

Interview with the Vampire (film), 110

intimacy, xiii, 138; queer, 113, 123

invisibility: politics of, xii; queer, 113, 117

Islamophobia, 21

Jameson, Frederic, 25

JD.com, 202

Ji'ande (Gender and Health Research Center), 78

Jiang Zemin, 116

job security, 146, 161

Journal of Health, The (JianKang Bao), 67

Journalist Literature (Jishi Wenxue), 67

justice, 52, 56, 64, 123, 152

Kentucky Fried Chicken, 47

Kinsey, Alfred, 64

Kinsey Reports, 187

kinship, 113, 217, 221

Kleist, Heinrich von, 40n4

knowledge, 75; advanced, 171; dry, 97; HIV/AIDS-related, 96; improper/premature, 81; LGBT, 18; public, 180; queer, 17

Kolkata, *hijra* in, 215

Kristeva, Julia, 150

Kuaishou, 199

ku'er lilun (queer theory), xn2, 179, 180, 182

Kwan, Stanley, 108, 118

labor, xii, 13; capitalism and, 16, 21; cheap, 7; economic, 18; feminization of, 152; flexibilization of, 17; forced, 125; free, 16, 21, 75; invisible, 171; restructuring, 168; sexual, 18; sexuality and, 20n41; social reproductive, 6

labor camps, 34, 124

Lai Ming, Leon, 77

lala, 26, 141, 179

Lam, Edward, 80

Lan Yu, 107, 108, 110, 116n25, 120; agitation by, 123; death of, 107, 120n31; demise of, 126; Handong and, 121, 122, 123, 124; intellectualism of, 122; make-up sex and, 129; thesis on, 175; understanding, 119

Lan Yu (film), 18, 108, 110, 114, 115, 116; anti-Chinese essentialism and, 118; Chineseness of, 118; commentaries on, 119

Land of Oz, 51

Lao Zhang, 93, 99, 168–69, 190, 191; mutual aid and, 171; as queer encyclopedia, 94; scopophilia and, 170; work of, 166, 167; Xiao Yao and, 98

Last Truck: Closing of a GM Plant, The (Reichart and Bognar), 15

Lawrence v. Texas, 56

252 Index

Lenin, Vladimir, 27, 40, 50
Lenkov, Andrei, 29, 30, 31, 37, 40, 41, 42,
    55, 56, 57, 58, 60, 71, 81, 106, 130, 132,
    175, 209, 210, 210 (fig.), 211, 212, 216;
    Beets and, 135–36, 184; empty chair
    with, 136–41, 142–45; gaze of, 155;
    insults by, 131; letters to, 135; Na and,
    156; rebuttals from, 133; smile of, 38
Leonardo da Vinci, 63
lesbian activism, 1, 2, 6; gay activism and,
    138
lesbian organizations, 138, 177, 178, 180
lesbian rights, sexual rights and, 1
lesbianism, 2, 68–69
lesbians, 51, 78, 79, 162, 180; erasing, 6
LGBT, ix, x, 26, 78, 210
LGBT activism, x, 4, 5, 17, 18, 19, 79, 95,
    140, 154, 161, 163, 177, 199; Chinese,
    192; NGOization of, 111
LGBT community, 4, 18, 79, 88, 162
LGBT Internationalism, 19
LGBT movement, 85, 165, 177, 184;
    professionalization of, 166
LGBT organizations, x, 7, 113, 160
LGBT people: erasing, 7; marriage/job
    security and, 161
LGBT rights, xii, 3, 6, 9, 12
LGBTQ, 3, 27, 38, 114, 194–95
Li Xiaojiang, 145
Li Yinhe, 26, 77, 180, 187
Li Yuchun, 19
Liang Xiaowen, 202, 203, 204
liberalism: multicultural, 203; racial, 148
liberation, 47, 53; agenda of, 6; LGBT,
    138, 139; movement, 164; queer, x, xv;
    state-sponsored, 145. See also sexual
    liberation; women's liberation
Liberation Army, 46
Life Beets, 27, 29, 30, 216
Little Wang, 34
Liu, Petrus, 11
Liu Changshan, 19, 20, 20n41
Liu Qiangdong, 202
Liu Xiaohui, 19, 20n41
Liu Ye, 116n25

Liu Zhu, 20
Lu, Damien, 178, 179–80
Lu Longguang, 66, 102
Lushan Lian (Love on Mount Lu), 64

Majuqiao, 197
male privilege, gay, 179
Mama (film), 111n7
Mankind Unity of Chimerica, 7, 27
Mao Zedong, xn2, 29, 49, 66, 103, 105,
    141, 168; death of, 5; mistakes and, 32;
    quotations of, 31–32; thanking, 52;
    Third Front and, 102
Maoism, 39, 73, 167
marginalization, xiii, 10, 117, 153, 212
marketization, 72, 79, 122
marriage: job security and, 161; same-
    sex, 160
Marx, Karl, 4, 163
Marxism, 5, 40, 72, 108, 201, 203; rheto-
    ric of, 11; socialism and, 11. *See also*
    queer Marxism
masculinity: Fordist, 15; lesbian, 183;
    trans, 20; working-class, 3, 3n8
Massad, Joseph H., 19
materialism, 133, 173, 179, 213
Maybelline, 222
MB (money boys), 97
McCarthyism, 151
McGrath, Jason, 115
#Me Too movement, 204
media: economy, xi; international, 154;
    LGBT, 114; platforms, 140; print, 74,
    180; queer, 114; sexual mass, 65; West-
    ern, 2. *See also* social media
medical care, 89, 161, 167
meishanonü, 178, 179, 180
Meishanonü Zhanshi Lala Incident,
    177–82
memory, 38, 48, 213; collective, 187; cre-
    ativity of, xiii; history and, xv; murki-
    ness of, 48; painful, 58; sharing, 57
men who have sex with men (MSM), xi,
    85, 86, 91, 95
#MeToo movement, 160

Index 253

militarism: gay story and, 86–87; socialist, 35
military-industrial complex, xii, 3
Minh-ha, Trinh T., xiv
Minhaj, Hasan, 202, 204
misogyny, 70, 130, 178
Miss Butterfly, 175, 213
Mitchell, W. J. T., 132n3
model minorities, 4, 203
modernity, 56n2, 57n4; discrepant, 114; proper, 57; socialist, 52, 72, 73, 74, 173; Western, 56
Mohanty, Chandra, 149
Money, John, 146
Moscow Games, 185
Mountain City, 102
MSM. *See* Men Who Have Sex with Men
Murphy, Michelle, xiiin10
Muslims, as sexual-racial other, 56, 56n3
Myers, Scott, 107n1

Na Na, 131, 133, 134, 135, 138, 141, 143, 197, 198, 199, 200, 210–11, 212, 214; activists and, 137; Beets and, 130; betrayal by, 155; on doing feminism, 153–54; field notes of, 159, 175, 184; humility of, 144–45; letter from, 165, 171–72, 174, 182–83, 190, 191; letter to, 165, 191–92; meeting with, 142; notebook of, 209, 211; queer theory and, 137; restoring, 156; transporters and, 132
Nagar, Richa, 174n3
Nanjing Medical University, 66
Nano Pod, 55, 129, 130, 155, 212
narcissism, 109, 131, 135, 217
nation building, gender/sexuality and, 8
National College Entrance Examination, 121
National Department of Foreign Affairs, 45
National People's Congress, 140
National Security, 140, 141
nationalism, 3, 10; anti-colonial, 173; Chinese, 59, 117; Han-centric, 21; Marxist, 153

neoliberalism, 5, 6, 20, 80, 89, 114, 120, 124, 144, 146, 150, 167; authoritarian/democratic, xii–xiii, 21, 125; Chinese LGBT, 7; global, 10, 18, 39; postwar, 153; queer subjects and, 71; social problems and, 12
networks, 151; diasporic/Sinophone, 122; NGO, 60; queer, 75; transnational, 122
New Culture Movement, xn2, 76
NGOization, xii, 7, 92, 144, 150
NGOs. *See* nongovernmental organizations
Niezi (Crystal Boys) (Pai), 77
1984 (Orwell), 50
nongovernmental organizations (NGOs), 2, 9, 87, 99, 140, 149, 161, 177, 184, 201, 219; development, 116; feminist queer, 179; gender, 1; HIV/AIDS funds and, 90; industry, xi, 19, 162, 168; LGBT, 88, 160; networks, 60; transnational, 153; women's, 8, 9, 140; work, 19, 95, 152, 160, 182
North American Feminist WeChat group, 204

Occupy Men's Toilet, 139
Occupy Wall Street, 139
"On the Gradual Construction of Thoughts during Speech" (Kleist), 40n4
One Child policy, 63, 73, 89–90, 201
One is Not Enough, 100
organizing, *lala,* 137, 138, 182
Orpheus, 132
Orwell, George, 50
other, 4, 180; racialized, xi, 15, 146; symbolic, xii
othering, 11, 145, 150, 154

Pai Hsien-yung, 77, 217
Pan Suiming, 65, 77, 85
Parents and Friends of Lesbians and Gays (PFLAG), 171, 173
Parking Lot, 97
Parsons, Talcott, 73

254   Index

patriarchy, 29, 74, 151, 179, 205, 219; Confucian, 150; dismantling, 154; heterosexist, 27; imperialism and, 125; opposition to, 147; subordination of, 146

Patriot Act, 202, 203

Peking Opera, 95, 96

Peking Union Medical College, 85

Pengyou Tongxin (Correspondences of Friends), 77

People's University of China, 153

personhood, xi, xv

PFLAG. *See* Parents and Friends of Lesbians and Gays

pharmaceutical industry, 92

"Phenomenon of Homosexuality in *Red Chamber Dream*, The," 62

plasma trade, 86

Plato, 47, 63

Playboys, 69

political actions, 21, 120

political issues, 3, 151

political movements, 59

politics, x, 6, 21, 46, 76, 77, 81, 170; arts and, xv; authoritarian, 202; Chinese, 218; feminist, 10, 154; gender, 149; identity, 4, 17, 72, 193; labor, 4, 15; leftist, 4, 202; LGBT, 19, 164; material changes in, 74; patriarchal, 202; queer, 10, 13, 15, 17, 215; sexual, 13; Sinophone, 118; socialist, 76; trauma and, 60

Pony Garden, 200

Popular Medical, 67

pornography, 49, 62, 116, 154

postcolonialism, 4, 14, 153

postsocialism, xii, 6, 13, 26, 58, 65; mortality/immortality and, 39; socialist oppression and, 66; as vampires/zombies, 39, 39n2

poststructuralism, 163, 215

power, 74; disciplinary, 66, 173; geopolitics and, 21; global, 201; purchasing, 9; relations/asymmetrical, 203

Power, Samantha, 141

precarity, xiii, 10, 132

Preciado, Paul B., xiv

prison industrial complex, 3, 21

production, 115; cultural, 112, 117–18; economic, 122; gender and, 18; mass, 3; sexuality and, 18; Sinophone, 110, 116

progressiveness, 117, 130

Prometheus, 129

prosperity, 3, 10, 19, 20, 31, 52, 122, 201

psychology, 59, 65, 66, 71

Puar, Jasbir, 56n3

public health, 65, 74

Pussy Riot, 144

Qianmen, 48, 50, 137, 138, 168

Qianmen Pedestrian Street, 136

Qingdao Medical University, 66

queer, ix, 39, 78, 80, 193, 218; being, xiv, 118; capital and, 118; conceptualization of, xii; Mandarin translation of, 26; subjugation and, 118; transforming meaning of, xiii; translation of, 179

queer Africa, 215

Queer China, 38, 40, 131

queer communities, 3, 16, 18, 19

queer culture, 80, 116, 192; Chinese, 176; emergence of, 74; hegemonic, 13

queer feminists, 4–5, 21, 139, 177, 181; gay male domination of, 180; organizing by, 181; surveillance of, 180

queer fluidity, xiii, 18, 173

queer future, xiv, 10, 27

queer India, 215

queer individuals, 120, 131; agency of, 19

queer intervention, 113, 120

queer Iran, 215

queer life, xiii, 3, 8, 168; Chinese, x; economization of, 9, 19; fungibility of, 9; shared, 22

queer Marxism, xiii, 7, 10–11, 12, 216

queer studies, xii, xiii, 7, 10, 56, 60, 115, 171, 193, 199, 201, 215; (im)proper subjects of, 14–17; institutionalization

of, 111; Sinophone, 114, 119; subject matter of, 14
queer subjects, 17, 75; neoliberalism and, 71; rural, 20n41
queer theory, ix, xn2, 3, 12, 26, 77, 79, 137, 163, 176, 178, 182, 187, 200, 215; biological determinism versus, 177; Butlerian, 4; Chinese, 20n41; embracing, 130; Foucauldian, 4, 173; reintroduction of, 179–80; sense of belonging and, 175; Taiwanese, x
Queer Theory: Western Thoughts on Sexuality in the 1990s, 26
queer world, ix, xv, 78, 200
QueerFi, 210
queerness, xii, 22, 30, 188, 193; black, 8n19; capitalizing on, 9; Chinese, 57, 111, 114; East Asian, 217; feminism and, 203; neoliberal/authoritarian rules of, 9; Sinophone, 116n25; theorization of, 15–16; transnational economy of, 6
queers, 27, 56, 79, 109; anti-neoliberal, 190; Chinese, 187; lagging, 56, 58n4; as outcasts, 217; postcolonial, 14; postsocialist, 14; urban cosmopolitan, 120
quick funs, 85

racial tensions, 125, 188
racialization, 12, 80, 188
racism, xv, 3, 203
radicality, 131, 133, 202
Rankin, John, 217
realism, 112, 117
Red Army, 47
red capital, financialization/risk management of, 9
"Red Father, Pink Son," 53 (fig.), 54, 55
Red Guard, 36
Red Sorghum (film), 115
redistribution, politics of, 4, 60, 121
Reichart, Julia, 15
Reification of Desire, The (Floyd), 15
Repo, Jemima, 146

representation, xiv; politics of, xiii; queer, 113
reproduction, 75; feminist, xiii; human sexuality and, 63
resources, 60; distribution of, 177; intellectual, 173; limitation of, 181; queer, 133
rice bunny, 204
"Rictus of 'War of Words', A," 155
Rimbaud, Arthur, 109
Rofel, Lisa, 57n4
Ruan Fangfu, 64, 65, 69, 72–73

Said, Edward, 4
Scenes of Subjection (Hartman), 217
Scheman, Naomi, 40n5
Schularick, Moritz, 7
science, 73, 173, 178; popularization of, 75
scopophilia, 170
security: job, 146, 161; national, 8, 72, 152, 154, 168; social, 8, 72, 152, 168; state, 140, 181, 219
self-consciousness, 40, 145
sex: gay, 93, 95, 98; nonreproductive, 72; promiscuous, 154
sex workers, 86, 88, 98, 139, 154, 182, 197
sexual harassment, 182
sexual liberation, 75–76, 160
sexual minorities, 79, 112n10
sexual norms, 6, 168
sexual orientation, 80, 178
sexual rights, 79; lesbian rights and, 1
sexual variances, x, 65, 66, 70
sexuality, xii, 4, 15, 26, 49, 80, 85, 192; investment in, 65; labor and, 20n41; medicalization of, 74; nation building and, 8; perverse, 50; production and, 18; queer, 6, 112n11, 113; scientific knowledge of, 75; sociology of, 65; speaking truth of, 76; studies, 64, 65, 173, 187; translating, 172; transnational, 176
sexually transmitted diseases, 65, 74

256   Index

Shanghai Public Health Education Institute, 85
Shenzhen, 51, 136, 139
Shi Tou, 2, 113
Shih, Shuh-mei, 145
"shrimp dumpling" incident, 29, 37, 38, 159
Sin City, 133, 214
Sina Weibo, 140, 155, 178, 182
Sinophobia, 116
Sinophone, xii, 14, 114, 118
Sinophone studies, 10, 16, 114–15, 216
Sixth Gens, 111, 112n8, 113, 116
slave trade, 8
Slut Walk, 139
snow bunny, 204
social acceptance, 71, 79
social capital, 132, 176
social change, 21, 122
social media, x, xiii, 60, 139, 141, 143, 144, 180, 181
social movements, 12, 165, 180, 217; leftist, 3; queer, 11; rights-based, 13
social norms, 8, 14, 112
social order, 27, 64
social problems, 12, 39, 79
social psyche, 116–17
social relations, ix, xii, 58
social reproduction, xii, xiii, 16, 167
social security, 8, 72, 152, 168
socialism, 57, 117, 149; building, 102; Chinese, 57n4; defending, 11; disillusionment with, 150; legacy/monuments/museums of, 131; Maoist, 122; Marxism and, 11; queer, 11n27; state, 5, 12, 20n41, 40; viability of, 150
socialist realism, 112
socialist state studio system, 111, 111n7
"Socialist Women's Liberation and Western Feminism" workshop, 153
sociality, xi, 170
Sodom and Gomorrah, 132, 214
solidarity: building, 144; international, 6; undermining, 205
Song Shaopeng, 153

Soviet Union, 147, 148
space: leaderless, 180; Sinophone, 14, 119; urban, 16
Spears, Britney, 21
Spillers, Hortense, 8
spiritual health, 70
Spring Festival, 102
Stacey, Judith, 150
State Administration of Radio, Film, and Television, 110n5
stereotypes, 118, 183, 217; cultural/political, 117; gay, 96
Stories Club (Gushi Hui), 67
String Theory, 108
struggle sessions, 36
stuckness, xi, xii, 118
Subculture of Homosexuality, The (Li), 187
subjectivity, 18; bodies and, xv; female, 5, 8, 80, 145, 152; independent, 122; poststructuralist/postmodernist, 81, 173; queer, 13
Suchland, Jennifer, 12
Surname Viet Given Name Nam (Minh-ha), xiv
surveillance, 2, 116, 178, 180; authoritarian, 28; capitalist, 7, 21, 144; cultural, 117–18; governmental, 139–40; political, 173; state, 117–18, 144, 219; technology of, 125; transnational, xii, 153
Synchronization, ix, 29, 57, 60, 68, 81, 130, 131, 135, 216, 217

Tadiar, Neferti X. M., x, 58n5
Taijichang, 50
Taiwan, 51, 78, 178
Tamen de Shijie (Their World) (Li and Wang), 77
Tan Tang Mo, 179
Tang Wenli, 48
Taose Zuichun (Pink Lips) (Cui Zi'en), 77
Taylorism, 73
technology, 38, 140, 173, 217; dehumanizing, xv; modern, 58n5; recording, 3
Testo Junkie (Preciato), xiv

Thatcher, Margaret, 49
theory, 193; hegemonic, 163; practice
    and, xiii. *See also* queer theory
Third Front, 102
Third World, 2, 4, 154
Third World Conference on Women, 1n1
Thompson, Eric Lee, 48, 49, 50
Thought Liberation, 5, 121
Three Essays on the Theory of Sexuality
    (Freud), 187
Tian'anmen Square, 50, 53, 55, 94, 136,
    168
Tian'anmen upheaval, 5, 12, 39, 107, 122,
    123, 151
Titanic, 26, 48
TOEFL, 45, 109, 124
Tong Ge, 36n2
Tongxingai (Same-Sex Love) (Zhang), 77
*Tongxinglian zai Zhongguo (Homosexual-
    ity in China)* (Fang), 77
tongzhi (homosexual), ix, ixn1, xn2,
    18, 26, 85, 86, 94, 95, 96, 119, 162,
    167; anti-normative anomaly of, 80;
    articulation of, 80; meaning of, 171;
    subjective formation of, 170; term, 79;
    volunteers, 91, 93; wedding, 137
Tongzhou District, 197
Total Eclipse (film), 110
transgender rights, 16
transnationalism, 14, 114, 168
trauma, 17, 58, 59; creativity of, xiii;
    history/politics and, 60; inter-/trans-
    generational, 217
Trump, Donald, 202
"Two Bombs and One Satellite," 103
"Two Loves" (Douglas), 47n1

UNAIDS, 85
Uncool, xi, xiii, 20, 217; Cool and, 7–8,
    9, 10
"Under Western Eyes" (Mohanty), 149
United Kingdom Department of Interna-
    tional Development, 88
United Nations, 93, 147, 148, 219
United Nations Decade, 151, 151n15

United Nations Fourth World Conference
    on Women, 1, 3, 5, 6, 7, 9, 10, 145,
    147, 151, 177
Unity, 29, 38, 40, 131
unremembering, 38, 59, 59n6, 212, 217
Uyghur, 124, 125

Valentine's Day, 136, 139
Velvet Goldmine (film), xiv, 110
Verlaine, Paul, 109, 109n3
violence, xv, 56, 59; agency and, 74;
    domestic, 139, 220; gender, 12, 60,
    139, 182; greater good and, 183; racial,
    12; sexual, 60; state, 75, 154
visibility, 21, 22, 58, 65, 112, 117, 120,
    133, 139, 176, 180, 204, 215; LGBT,
    130; politics of, xii, xiii, 58; queer, xii,
    3, 9, 113, 140
Volunteer Army, 101

Wan Yanhai, 85, 169n2
Wang Xiaobo, 50, 77, 180, 187
Wang Zheng, 141, 146
Warhol, Andy, 143
Watermelon Woman, The (Dunye), xiv
We Are Here (Zhao and Shi), 2
"We are in this together," 41 (fig.)
Weber, Max, 72
WeChat, 140, 141, 204
Wei Jiangang, 113
Weibo, 182
Wenchuan, earthquake in, 185
"What is Queer Theory and How Does
    It Relate to the Gay Movement" (Lu),
    178
whiteness, 6, 17, 49, 124, 149, 156
WID. *See* women in development
Wilde, Oscar, 47, 47n1
Wish You Good Health, 63, 67
women in development (WID), 148, 149,
    151
women's issues, 6, 150, 220; agenda for,
    147–48; gender and, 147
women's liberation, 145, 151, 152, 152n16
Women's March, 202

258 Index

women's movement, 148, 153
women's rights, 2, 5–6, 139, 140, 177, 221; human rights and, 1
"Women's Rights are Human Rights" (Clinton), 148
women's studies, 1, 5, 60, 145, 152
Work for LGBT, 88
World Asian Pacific Women's Conference, 153

Xi Jinping, 116, 202
xiahai (jumping into the sea), 75, 121, 186
Xiao Hai, 170, 171, 197, 198–99
Xiao Yao, 94, 95, 98–99
Xidan, 50
Xili, 198, 199
Xingzhishi Shouce (A Handbook of Sexual Knowledge), 64
Xinjiang Internment Camp, 21
Xu Zhilian, 91

Yalu River, 101, 103, 104
Yanda yundong, 75, 94, 190
Yang Tao, 45–46, 51, 54, 55, 61, 87, 90, 91, 94, 95, 97, 98, 132, 185, 188, 189, 214, 217; coming out and, 47; education of, 48; gay and, 46–47, 55; Guang and, 92, 93, 99; phallus and, 49–50; pornography and, 49; Thompson and, 50; youth of, 47, 48

Yang Xiaofei, 29, 71, 101, 107, 108, 109, 118–19, 131, 174, 175, 176, 179, 204, 205, 212, 215, 217; as domestic violence abuser, 177; fallout with, 125; individuality of, 120; *Lan Yu* and, 110; letter from, 219–22; seven sins of, 182; VCDs and, 120
Yang Zhongguo, 100, 101, 102, 103, 217; death of, 189; male-male indecency and, 104; Party cadre and, 34; Zhang and, 104–5
Yanwang (Lord of Death), 104
Ye Guangwei, 77
Ye Shana, 156, 161, 162–64
Yellow Earth (film), 115
Yeoh, Michelle, 217
Yizhuang Development District, 197

Zhang Beichuan, 66, 77, 85
Zhang Shanping, 37–38, 100, 101, 103, 132, 214; confession of, 31–32, 33–34; criminal behavior of, 34; cruising sites and, 35–36; hooligan behaviors and, 34; reeducation and, 35; sexual incident and, 34; treatment for, 102; Yang and, 104–5
Zhang Yimou, 111, 112n10, 115, 117
Zhang Yuan, 50, 111
Zhao Jing, 2